T0345045

A Beginner's Guide to Amazon Web Services

Amazon Web Services (AWS) provides on-demand cloud computing platforms and application programming interfaces (APIs) to individuals, companies, and governments, along with distributed computing processing capacity and software tools via AWS server farms. This text presents a hands-on approach for beginners to get started with Amazon Web Services (AWS) in a simple way.

Key Features

- It discusses topics such as Amazon Elastic Compute Cloud, Elastic Load Balancing, Auto Scaling Groups, and Amazon Simple Storage Service.
- It showcases Amazon Web Services' identity, access management resources, and attribute-based access control.
- It covers serverless computing services, Virtual Private Cloud, Amazon Aurora, and Amazon Comprehend.
- It explains Amazon Web Services Free Tier, Amazon Web Services Marketplace, and Amazon Elastic Container Service.
- It includes security in Amazon Web Services, the shared responsibility model, and high-performance computing on Amazon Web Services.

The text is primarily written for graduate students, professionals, and academic researchers working in the fields of computer science, engineering, and information technology.

Parul Dubey is currently working as an Assistant professor in the Department of Artificial Intelligence at G H Raisoni College of Engineering, Nagpur, India. She has filed for 15 Indian patents. She is responsible for about 10 publications in conference proceedings, Scopus, and journals. She has contributed book chapters in an edited book published by CRC Press and other reputed publishers. She is also an AWS Certified Cloud Practitioner.

Rohit Raja is working as an associate professor and head in the Department of Information Technology at Guru Ghasidas Vishwavidyalaya, Bilaspur, India. His research interests include facial recognition, signal processing, networking, and data mining. He has published 100 research papers in various international and national journals (including publications by the IEEE, Springer, etc.) and proceedings of reputed international and national conferences (again including publications by Springer and the IEEE).

A Beginner's Guide to Amazon Web Services

Parul Dubey

Rohit Raja

CRC Press
Taylor & Francis Group
Boca Raton London New York

CRC Press is an imprint of the
Taylor & Francis Group, an **informa** business
A CHAPMAN & HALL BOOK

First edition published 2024
by CRC Press
2385 NW Executive Center Drive, Suite 320, Boca Raton, FL 33431

and by CRC Press
4 Park Square, Milton Park, Abingdon, Oxon, OX14 4RN

CRC Press is an imprint of Taylor & Francis Group, LLC

© 2024 Parul Dubey and Rohit Raja

ISBN: 9781032521565 (hbk)
ISBN: 9781032521558 (pbk)
ISBN: 9781003406136 (ebk)
ISBN: 9781032523248 (eBook+)

DOI: 10.1201/9781003406136

Typeset in Times
by Deanta Global Publishing Services, Chennai, India

Contents

Preface

Welcome to *A Beginner's Guide to Amazon Web Services*. In today's digital landscape, cloud computing has revolutionized the way businesses operate and individuals leverage technology. Among the leading cloud service providers, Amazon Web Services (AWS) has emerged as a dominant force, offering a vast array of services and tools to meet the diverse needs of users around the world.

This book is your companion on the journey to understanding and navigating AWS, whether you're a developer, a system administrator, an IT professional, or simply someone curious about cloud computing. Our aim is to provide a comprehensive and accessible guide that empowers beginners to confidently explore and utilize the power of AWS.

In the pages that follow, we have structured the content in a logical and progressive manner, ensuring that you build a solid foundation before diving into more advanced topics. We explain the fundamental concepts of cloud computing and introduce you to the core services offered by AWS. From there, we guide you through setting up your AWS account, configuring tools, and gaining access to the AWS Management Console.

It's important to note that AWS is a dynamic platform, constantly evolving to meet the needs of its users. While we have made every effort to provide the most up-to-date information at the time of writing, we encourage you to refer to the official AWS documentation for the latest updates.

We hope that this book serves as a valuable resource on your journey to mastering AWS. Whether you're starting a new project, migrating existing systems to the cloud, or expanding your skill set, AWS offers endless possibilities. By understanding the core concepts and leveraging the services provided by AWS, you'll be well equipped to innovate, streamline operations, and accelerate growth.

Thank you for choosing *A Beginner's Guide to Amazon Web Services*. We wish you the best of luck and success as you explore the vast capabilities of AWS.

Happy learning!

Parul Dubey

1 Introduction to Cloud Computing Platforms

1.1 INTRODUCTION

The term "cloud computing" refers to a wide range of distinct practices, all of which are centered on the delivery of hosted services via the use of the internet. There are three primary components that make up a cloud computing service: the infrastructure, the platform, and the software as a service (SaaS).

There are two distinct categories of clouds: public and private. Customers have the ability to make purchases of services from a public cloud provider over the internet. A private cloud is a network or data center that only offers hosted services to a select set of users. These users are subject to stringent regulations on who has access to the network as well as the activities that they are permitted to do with the network's resources. Computing in the cloud, whether it's done on a public or private network, has the goal of making computer resources and information technology services more readily available and scalable.

It is important to have both the appropriate software and hardware components in order to start a cloud computing paradigm. The concepts of "utility computing" and "on-demand computing" are often used synonymously when referring to "cloud computing."

The term "cloud computing" was coined as a play on the cloud symbol, which is frequently used in flowcharts and designs to symbolize the internet.

1.2 WORKING PRINCIPLE

1.2.1 CLOUD ARCHITECTURE

In the architecture of cloud computing software systems, for instance, a message queue is a typical example of a loose coupling strategy that links many different cloud components. [16] In order to properly use tight or loose coupling in the context of approaches such as these and others, one has to have a solid grasp of elastic provision (Figure 1.1).

The concept of cloud computing centers on client devices' capacity to access data and cloud applications stored on faraway physical servers, databases, and computers over the internet. Client devices may connect to the data and cloud applications stored in these faraway places. An internet network connection connects the front end (the accessing client gadget, website, internet, and web software applications) to the back end (data warehouses, administrators, and processors). This connection is made possible by the fact that the front end is connected to the back end. The data is kept in a repository on the back end, which is accessed and used by the front end, which is responsible for retrieving and using the data.

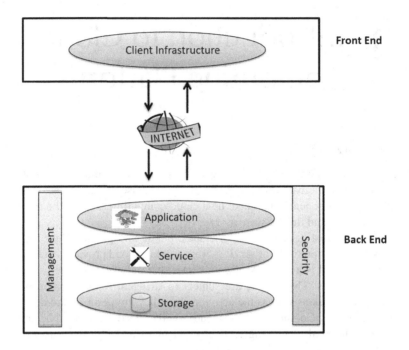

FIGURE 1.1   Architecture for cloud computation.

The communications between the front end and the back end are managed by a central server, which is accountable for the responsibility. The use of protocols by the central server makes the procedure of data transmission much more straightforward. Through the use of software as well as middleware, the central server is responsible for managing the communication that occurs between a variety of client devices and cloud servers. The majority of the time, a specialized server that is solely committed to a certain workload or application is used.

The use of technologies such as virtualization and automation is essential to the functioning of cloud computing. The simplicity with which users may abstract and supply underlying cloud services and systems enables users to make requests for and make use of logical entities that may be generated through virtualization. Users are able to supply resources, connect services, and deploy workloads without the direct participation of the IT personnel of the cloud provider. This is made possible by the high level of self-service that is offered. Automation and the capabilities associated with it make this a reality, along with the ability to orchestrate related processes.

1.2.2   CLOUD ENGINEERING

"Cloud engineering" refers to the practice of applying the many engineering disciplines that are involved in cloud computing. Methodical solutions are proposed for high-level problems in cloud computing systems, such as commercialization, standardization, and governance. Within this multidisciplinary approach, there are contributions from a broad variety of fields, including risk and quality engineering, web performance engineering, information technology engineering, and systems and software engineering.

1.3 DIFFERENT KINDS OF CLOUD COMPUTING SERVICES

It is possible to divide cloud computing services into three broad types of cloud computing. Figure 1.2 describes these types of cloud services at a glance.

1.3.1 INFRASTRUCTURE AS A SERVICE (IaaS)

IaaS vendors such as Amazon Web Services (AWS) provide their clients with a virtual server instance and storage space, in addition to application programming interfaces (APIs) that facilitate the migration of their workloads to a virtual machine (VM). The VM and the storage may be launched, terminated, visited, and customized in any manner that the user sees fit. Cloud computing service providers offer a choice of sized and optimized instances for various workloads, as well as the option to tailor an instance depending on individual needs. In terms of cloud computing, the IaaS idea is the closest thing to a remote data center for organizations.

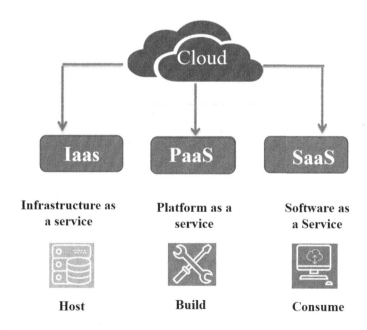

FIGURE 1.2 Types of cloud services.

1.3.2 PLATFORM AS A SERVICE (PAAS)

In the platform as a service model, cloud providers make their infrastructures available to host application development tools. These technologies are accessed by users through the internet by means of APIs, web portals, or gateway software. PaaS is used in the process of general software development, and the majority of PaaS providers host the program after it has been created. Salesforce's Lightning Platform, Amazon Web Services' Elastic Beanstalk, and Google's App Engine are examples of common PaaS systems.

1.3.3 SOFTWARE AS A SERVICE (SAAS)

SaaS is a delivery model that is used for web services. Web services are software applications that are distributed through the internet. No matter where the user is located, they are always able to access their SaaS applications and services from any computer or mobile device that has an internet connection. Using the software as a service model, application software as well as databases may be accessed. An example of an SaaS program is Microsoft 365, which offers productivity and email capabilities.

Through the use of the SaaS paradigm, users are granted access to database software and application software (SaaS). Cloud service providers are responsible for managing the infrastructure and platforms that run applications. Some individuals refer to SaaS as "on-demand software," and a charge is levied whenever the service is called into use. [17] Cloud service providers are in charge of hosting application software, which may then be accessed by consumers through a web browser running on a cloud-based client. Customers who run their apps in the cloud do not have any influence or control over the underlying platform or infrastructure. Users of the cloud don't need to set up the application or run it on their own computers, and thus it is much simpler to maintain and give technical assistance to these users. Cloud applications are more flexible than conventional kinds of software because they have the ability to clone tasks onto a large number of virtual computers while they are running. Through the use of load balancers, the work is dispersed among all of the virtual machines. This method is understandable to cloud users since they are only presented with a single access point. It is possible for cloud applications to support many tenants in order to accommodate a large number of cloud users. This allows several cloud-user organizations to share the resources of a single machine.

Since SaaS programs often charge a flat fee per user on a monthly or yearly basis, adding or removing users at any time will not have an effect on the overall cost [19] and may even be free. [18] It is the contention of proponents of SaaS that organizations who use the service may be able to reduce their expenditures on information technology operations by contracting out the management, upkeep, and support of their infrastructure and software to a cloud service provider. This enables the corporation to redirect its spending on information technology operations away from the expense of purchasing hardware and software and toward the achievement of other business goals. When applications are hosted centrally, users do not need to install new software or get updates. The disadvantage of using SaaS is that users' data must be kept on the cloud provider's server. Because of this, there is the potential for unauthorized access to data. [18] Two examples of SaaS programs that may be used for both gaming and productivity are Google Docs and Microsoft Word Online. It's possible that one will have the option to integrate various SaaS applications if one is already utilizing a cloud storage provider such as Google Drive or OneDrive.

1.4 MODELS FOR CLOUD COMPUTING DEPLOYMENT

Cloud computing deployment can be implemented in various modes: private, public, or hybrid. Figure 1.3 shows various cloud deployment models.

1.4.1 PRIVATE CLOUD

The data center of an organization is leveraged to provide its workers with private cloud services. When we use a private cloud, we have the flexibility to build and run our very own cloud infrastructure, which is just one of the many benefits of utilizing a private cloud. This design is good for scalability because it blends cloud computing with the management and security of local data centers. As a result, this architecture is optimal. Internal users may or may not be billed via the use of IT chargeback. VMware and Open Stack are two of the most widely used technologies and providers of private clouds.

1.4.2 PUBLIC CLOUD

In this instance, the cloud service is supplied by a cloud service provider (CSP) that is not affiliated with the organization. The vast majority of public cloud services can be used on a pay-as-you-go basis, with packages beginning at only a few cents per minute or hour. Customers are solely responsible for paying for the resources that

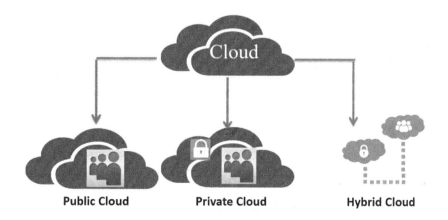

FIGURE 1.3 Cloud deployment models.

they actually use, regardless of how much memory, storage space, or bandwidth they use. Public cloud service providers such as IBM, Oracle, and Tencent are among the most prominent in the industry.

1.4.3   HYBRID CLOUD

One of the benefits of using hybrid cloud environments is the fact that they incorporate the benefits associated with both public and private cloud settings. [8, 9] Because of this, businesses are able to reap the benefits of a diverse selection of deployment techniques, such as private clouds and resources located on their premises. The capability of linking collocation, managed, and/or dedicated services to cloud resources may alternatively be referred to as a "hybrid cloud," which is another use of the phrase. [10] When discussing cloud computing, Gartner defines a hybrid model as one in which a number of different cloud service providers mix their private, public, and community cloud capabilities. This model is referred to as a multi-cloud environment. [11] One of the three main classifications of cloud computing—public, private, or community—does not adequately describe a hybrid cloud service's characteristics. It is possible to expand the capacity or functionality of a cloud service by aggregating cloud resources from several cloud providers, integrating cloud resources from multiple cloud providers, or customizing cloud resources.

There are several applications for hybrid cloud composition that may be employed. A corporation may, for instance, use a private cloud application to store sensitive customer data but then connect that application to a business intelligence tool that is housed in a public cloud. This is just one example of how this might work. [7] One example of hybrid cloud use is when a corporation increases its ability to supply a certain kind of commercial service by using cloud services that are accessible to the general public. The implementation of a hybrid cloud approach is determined by a number of factors, such as the requirements for data security and compliance, the level of control that is needed over the data, and the applications that are used by an organization. [12]

The use of public cloud computing resources by information technology organizations may also be an example of hybrid cloud computing. These companies use these resources to meet short-term capacity needs that their own private clouds are unable to meet.

It is now possible for hybrid clouds to take advantage of cloud bursting in order to scale up to many clouds. [10] This is a method for the deployment of applications in which an application first runs on a private cloud or data center and then "bursts" into a public cloud when the need for more processing capacity arises. For instance, in a cloud bursting or hybrid cloud architecture, a company will only pay for additional computer resources when those resources are really needed by the business. [13] During times of heavy processing demand, an internal IT infrastructure that can manage ordinary workloads may have its capabilities augmented with additional resources sourced from either public or private clouds. [14] A customized hybrid cloud concept that is built on several kinds of hardware is known as a "cross-platform hybrid cloud." Behind the scenes of a cross-platform hybrid cloud, there are a variety of unique CPU architectures. Users are not aware of the wide range of hardware that the cloud provides, which makes it simple for them to deploy and grow applications. This kind of cloud was made possible as a consequence of the development of advanced RISC machine-based systems-on-chip for use in server-class computing.

Private cloud networking's inherent limitations of various access relays may be circumvented by the use of hybrid cloud architecture. The increased runtime flexibility and adaptive memory processing offered by virtualized interface models are two of the advantages of using these models. [15]

Businesses may use the private cloud to run workloads and applications that are vital to the operation of the company and sensitive in nature, while the public cloud may be used to handle spikes in demand or bursts in strain. Building a unified, automated, and scalable environment while retaining control over mission-critical data is a goal that can be accomplished via the use of a hybrid cloud.

Enterprises are increasingly adopting a multi-cloud strategy, which refers to the practice of using a variety of IaaS providers. This technology enables the transfer of applications across many clouds as well as the simultaneous operation of clouds.

Many businesses make the decision to make use of several cloud providers for a number of reasons. They might do so either because there is a chance that their cloud service will be interrupted or because they want to take advantage of the more competitive price offered by a certain supplier. Because different cloud providers provide different services and application programming interfaces, multi-cloud deployment and application development may be challenging to do.

However, the installation process for many clouds ought to become less complicated as service providers' APIs and services converge and become more standardized as a result of industry-wide initiatives such as the Open Cloud Computing Interface.

There is a distinct community that may reap the advantages of a corporate cloud that is shared by several companies, including a common goal, the requirements of policy and security, and compliance difficulties. A community cloud may be hosted either on or off a company's premises, and it may be administered either by an on-premises community cloud or by a third-party provider.

1.5 CLOUD COMPUTING'S CHARACTERISTICS AND BENEFITS

When it comes to cloud computing, businesses of any size have the potential to benefit from the vast variety of benefits that have been demonstrated by the architecture of cloud computing in use today. Figure 1.4 explains the benefits of cloud computing. It has a variety of different benefits, including the following:

Provisioning at one's leisure: An end user has the ability to rapidly develop computational resources to do almost any task. End users have the option of self-provisioning computing capabilities such as server time and network storage rather than depending on IT professionals to manage the computing resources at their disposal.

Elasticity: The need for significant investments in regional infrastructure, which may or may not be operational at any given point in time, is mitigated as a result of

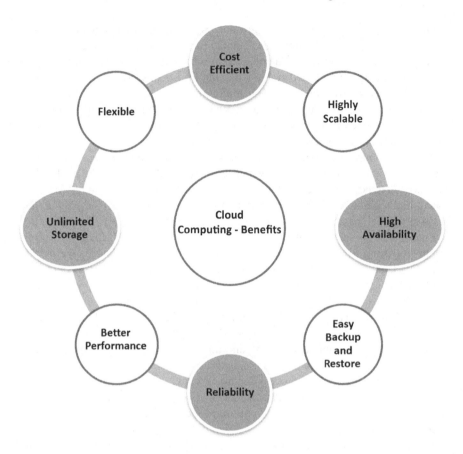

FIGURE 1.4   Benefits of cloud computation.

the fact that businesses are able to easily scale up or down in response to fluctuating demands for their computer systems. For example, if a company needs to scale up to meet rising demand, it can easily do so.

Pay per use: As a result of computing resources being quantified down to the finest granule, users are only required to pay for the resources and workloads that they actually use.

Resilience of the workload: It is not unusual for communications service providers (CSPs) to make use of redundant resources in order to offer dependable storage and to keep essential workloads running for their clients located all over the globe.

The capacity to change locations with relative ease: Through the use of cloud computing, organizations are able to shift specific workloads to or from numerous cloud platforms on a whim, therefore saving money and gaining access to the most recent technological advancements.

The capacity to establish connections with a wide variety of different networks: Any computing device that has access to the internet may be used to access or upload data to a cloud storage service.

Shared use of resources and several tenants: Through the use of multi-tenancy, different customers may utilize the same physical infrastructures or applications while preserving their own level of privacy and security. With resource pooling, cloud service providers are able to deliver services to a large number of customers while using the same set of physical resources. The cloud service providers' resource pools should be large enough and versatile enough to accommodate the requirements of several customers, all at the same time.

A wide range of advantages for a contemporary company may be attributed to these traits, such as the following:

Cost control: When businesses employ cloud infrastructure, they don't have to spend as much money on the initial purchase of equipment or on its ongoing maintenance. This can potentially assist in reducing total capital expenditures. They don't have to make as large an investment in pricey hardware, infrastructure, and utilities, and they don't have to build as many enormous data centers to support their growing businesses, which means that their capital expenditures are lower. In addition, businesses can rely on the know-how of the teams working for their cloud providers to manage the operations of cloud data centers without having to hire a large number of IT workers. The costs associated with downtime are cut significantly thanks to cloud computing. Owing to the infrequency of downtime, businesses don't have to invest time or money in finding a solution to issues related to it. Cloud computing makes this possible.

Mobility of data and work: Information saved in the cloud is accessible to users from any device that has an active internet connection. Users who want to access data do not need any USB devices, external hard drives, or multiple CDs. Smartphones and other mobile devices make it possible for professionals to continue working from home while still maintaining contact with their coworkers and customers. End users have easy access to resources that can be processed, saved, retrieved, and recovered while using the cloud computing service. The fact that the cloud provider handles all of the upgrades and updates is another way in which time and effort are saved.

Business continuity and disaster recovery (BCDR): Every company should be very concerned about the possibility of data loss. Even if a user's computer or mobile device (such as a smartphone or laptop) is damaged, they will still be able to access their data saved on the cloud. Using cloud-based services, businesses are able to quickly recover their data in the event that they have a power outage or a natural disaster. Benefiting BCDR is the fact that data and workloads may still be accessible in this way, even in the event that an organization suffers damage or disruption.

1.6 NEGATIVE ASPECTS OF CLOUD COMPUTING

In spite of the obvious advantages of depending on cloud services, IT professionals face a number of difficulties while using this technology.

Security in the cloud: When discussing cloud computing, one of the most common concerns that is brought up is that of data security. When relying on the cloud, we run the risk of having our data compromised, of having our interfaces hacked, of having our credentials leaked, and of having authentication problems. Another issue arises if the cloud service provider does not offer sufficient details on the manner in which it stores the private data that it is given and its location. In order to guarantee data safety, cloud configurations as well as business procedures and regulations need to be thoroughly analyzed.

Cost variability: When adopting pay-as-you-go subscription plans for cloud computing and scaling resources to meet variable workload demands, it may be difficult to define and anticipate eventual expenditures. This is because of the nature of these plans. One cloud service may make use of a large number of other cloud services, and the monthly fee for using all of these services will remain the same. Cloud costs are often reliant on one another as well. Because of this, there is the possibility of unforeseen expenditure.

The absence of skill and knowledge: Enterprises are finding it more challenging to keep up with the growing need for the tools and employees that are essential to plan, deploy, and manage cloud-hosted workloads and data as the demand for these resources continues to grow.

Governance of information technology: IT governance may become difficult owing to the lack of control that cloud computing imposes on do-it-yourselfers over the provisioning, deprovisioning, and management of infrastructure operations. This lack of control is caused by cloud computing. It might be challenging from a risk and security perspective, as well as from an IT compliance and data quality management one.

Observance of industrial regulations: When it comes to coping with industry rules via a third-party service provider, the movement of data from local storage to the cloud might create some difficulties. It is necessary to host both data and workloads in a manner that guarantees compliance with applicable legislation and promotes sound corporate governance.

Managing various cloud providers: Owing to the fact that every cloud is different, multi-cloud deployments may result in disconnected efforts to tackle more general problems associated with cloud computing.

Efficiency when using the cloud: An organization that enters into a contract with a cloud service provider does not have a significant amount of control over the performance of the cloud services it purchases, such as latency. Failures of a network or a service provider might potentially create problems with productivity and interfere with the operations of a corporation if no emergency preparations have been made.

Getting a personal cloud: When trying to build, develop, and operate private clouds, whether for an independent purpose or as a component of a hybrid cloud strategy, IT departments and staff confront a significant problem.

The transition to the cloud: Migration to the cloud is notoriously difficult, and so this is nothing unusual. It is not at all unusual for migration projects to go over their intended budget and take far longer than anticipated to complete. The process of data repatriation, which involves moving workload and data from the cloud to a local data center, is often ignored until it results in unanticipated expenses or performance problems.

"Locking in" a vendor: Changing cloud providers often results in complications. Incompatibilities in terms of technology, limits imposed by legal and regulatory authorities, and the significant costs involved with transferring massive amounts of data are all components of this issue.

1.7 THE EVOLUTION OF CLOUD COMPUTING

It is possible to trace the origins of cloud computing all the way back to the 1950s and 1960s. In the 1950s, businesses started using enormous mainframe computers, but it was too expensive to buy one for each individual worker. A system known as time-sharing was developed in the 1950s and 1960s in response to the need for more efficient use of the expensive mainframe processor time that was available then.

Through time-sharing, customers were able to have access to many computing mainframes at the same time, which helped to maximize processing capacity and minimize downtime. This strategy, which made use of shared computer resources for the very first time, was crucial in laying the framework for the cloud computing of today.

In 1969, Licklider was one of the people who contributed to the construction of the Advanced Research Projects Agency Network, now known as ARPANet. This network served as a predecessor to the internet. He envisioned connecting computers all over the globe so that users could access information and programs regardless of where they were physically located.

Users have had the ability to run several operating systems on the same physical computer ever since the introduction of virtual machines in the 1970s. The capabilities of VMs led to the development of virtualization, which in turn had a major influence on the creation of cloud computing.

When cloud technologies were developed in the 1970s and 1980s by companies such as Microsoft, Apple, and IBM, these companies made significant improvements to the cloud environment and made it simpler to use and host cloud servers. In 1999, Salesforce pioneered the delivery of business software through the internet, becoming the first company to do so.

Computing and storage in the cloud are both services that Amazon Web Services, which was founded in 2006, provides. A number of companies, including Microsoft and Google, have built their own cloud services in order to compete with AWS.

1.8 EMERGING TECHNOLOGIES AND CLOUD COMPUTING

According to the "RightScale 2019 State of the Cloud Report," more than 30 percent of enterprise IT decision-makers identified the public cloud as their top priority for 2019. Mission-critical software, in particular, will need some time before the public cloud is completely embraced by corporations.

Public cloud computing is becoming increasingly popular as a solution for organizations to migrate mission-critical workloads to the cloud. One reason for this transition is that business executives are turning to the public cloud to make sure their organizations can compete in the new era of digital transformation.

For the flexibility and modernization of internal computer systems, as well as the empowerment of their DevOps teams to take advantage of the cloud's agility, corporate leaders are fast shifting to the public cloud.

Furthermore, cloud providers such as IBM and VMware are concentrating on satisfying corporate IT expectations, in part by reducing the impediments to public cloud adoption that previously drove IT decision-makers to resist completely embracing the public cloud.

It's usual for firms to concentrate on producing cloud-native apps when contemplating cloud adoption, which involves designing and implementing cloud-optimized applications. They have been unable to migrate their most crucial apps to the cloud. Cloud computing is ready for companies, but only if they choose the correct cloud platforms, which are those that have a track record of serving the demands of enterprises.

Cloud providers are immersed in an ongoing struggle for cloud market share, and thus the public cloud continues to innovate, expand, and increase the diversity of its services. Since then, IaaS providers have extended their capabilities considerably beyond basic processing and storage resources.

Cloud computing services that execute specialized activities such as image processing and database updates may be found in serverless computing. Traditional cloud deployments require users to establish a compute instance and load code into that instance. Then, the user selects how long to run—and pay for—that instance.

This implies that cloud providers don't have to worry about maintaining servers or instances, and so clients can concentrate on creating their apps without having to worry about the technical parts of their cloud deployment. Users are solely responsible for paying a charge for each individual transaction the service completes. Examples of serverless computing include Google Cloud Functions, Microsoft Azure Functions, and Amazon's Lambda.

Processing large volumes of data requires just brief periods of access to massive amounts of computer power, which makes public cloud computing the most logical option. Cloud firms have reacted to the need for large-scale data storage and processing by developing big data services. Examples of these services are Google BigQuery and Microsoft Azure Data Lake Analytics.

The concepts of artificial intelligence (AI) and machine learning (ML) are at the center of the latest generation of cloud-based technology and applications. These technologies make a wide range of AI and ML capabilities available through the cloud. The Google Cloud Speech API and the Google Cloud Machine Learning Engine are two examples of the services that fall under this category.

1.9 CONTRASTING TRADITIONAL WEB HOSTING WITH CLOUD COMPUTING

Because there is such a wide variety of public cloud services and capabilities, there has been a great deal of misunderstanding about the relationship between cloud computing and fundamental applications such as web hosting. The public cloud and web hosting are two fundamentally different services, despite the fact that the public cloud is often used for the latter. There are some important distinctions to be made between conventional web hosting and cloud hosting.

End users of cloud-based approaches have access on demand to massive amounts of computing power. Transmissions on an hourly basis or even minute by minute are not unheard of.

TABLE 1.1

Comparison between Traditional and Cloud-Based Approaches

Dimension	Cloud-based approach	Traditional approach
Capacity	No limit on capacity	Limited capacity available
Containers	Rented storage at low cost	Local storage that is costlier
Availability	Over internet, 24/7	Limited
Synergy	Real-time in nature	Not real-time in nature
Expenditure	Less—pay per use	More—upfront cost and maintenance
Scalability	No limits on scaling	Limited to available resources
Accessibility	Anywhere, anytime	Limited

Customers are able to use as much or as little of a certain service as they choose at any given time, and the service should be flexible enough to accommodate their needs. Table 1.1 details the differences between the two different approaches—cloud-based and traditional.

To make use of the service, all that is required of the customer is a working computer and connection to the internet; the provider retains full control over all other aspects of the offering. The rise in availability of high-speed internet access, in addition to significant advancements in virtualization and distributed computing, is one theory that attempts to account for the craze around cloud computing's meteoric rise in popularity.

1.10 CLOUD SERVICE PROVIDERS

There is no shortage of companies offering cloud computing services in the market today. The following are the three most significant public CSPs that have become standard-bearers in their respective industries: AWS, GCP, and Azure—a Microsoft product.

When searching for a cloud service provider, it is important to take into consideration a number of different variables. As a business client, we have the responsibility of selecting a service provider that has the competencies necessary to meet the requirements of the use case we plan to implement, such as artificial intelligence or big data analytics.

In spite of the fact that cloud services typically operate on a pay-as-you-go model, different providers may have significantly different pricing structures. Additionally, if the data that is stored in the cloud is sensitive, it is important to take into consideration the physical location of the servers that the cloud provider uses.

Obviously, dependability and safety are two very important factors to take into account. In a service-level agreement, the degree of service uptime that is acceptable to the client's business needs should be specified. When evaluating different cloud service providers, it is essential to have a solid understanding of the security protocols that are used to secure vital information.

1.11   SECURITY IN CLOUD COMPUTING

Organizations continue to face significant difficulties with cloud adoption, especially when it comes to the deployment of public cloud services. The public cloud is a multi-tenant environment; hence, public CSPs share their underlying hardware infrastructure with a significant number of customers. Because of the nature of this scenario, a high level of logical computing resource separation is required. To get access to public cloud storage and computing services, one will need to have login credentials for an existing account.

As a result of their adherence to tight legal regulations and governance norms, many businesses are still hesitant to store data or workloads in the public cloud out of fear that they may experience failures, loss, or theft as a result of their compliance. This resistance is losing ground since logical isolation has been demonstrated to be reliable and data encryption and multiple identity and access control systems have strengthened cloud computing security, and there are a growing number of these systems.

If the user is an enterprise user who is tasked with the creation and upkeep of a secure cloud environment, then it is ultimately responsible for the construction and application of the security features that are provided by the cloud provider.

When data is stored in the cloud, the supplier of the service may access it at any time. This creates issues with privacy. It is possible for unintended or intentional changes to be made to the data; it can also be destroyed. [1] There are a lot of cloud service providers out there, and many of them have the power to share information with third parties, even without a warrant, if it is necessary for maintaining law and order. Users of cloud services are required to acknowledge and agree to the providers' privacy rules before they can use the services. The ability of end users to exercise control over the storage of their data is a critical component of any solution to the problem of data privacy. [1] Users may choose to encrypt data that is processed or stored in the cloud in order to prevent unauthorized access to such data. [1, 2] Using identity management systems as a means to solve cloud computing's privacy issues is one possibility. These systems decide who is permitted access to the data and how much of it is made accessible to them, which in turn determines who has access to the data. [3] In order for the systems to perform their functions, identities must be created and characterized, activities must be logged, and unused identities must be removed as they accumulate.

According to the Cloud Security Alliance, the three primary concerns about cloud security are unprotected application programming interfaces, data loss and leakage, and hardware failure. These issues are responsible for 29 percent, 25 percent, and 10 percent, respectively, of all outages that occur with cloud security. These security flaws are only a symptom of a much larger and more widespread problem in the information technology industry. If a cloud provider has a large number of customers using its platform, it is possible that the data from all of those customers will be stored on the same data server. According to Eugene Schultz, the chief technology officer of Emagined Security, fraudsters are making significant efforts focused on gaining access to cloud storage. Cloud computing infrastructure suffers from a variety of major vulnerabilities that make it possible for malicious actors to get access. The act of hacking into large cloud servers that hold the data of tens, hundreds, or even thousands of companies is known as hyperjacking. Because of this, the hacker is able to get access to a significant quantity of data. To name just a few examples, there was a security breach in Dropbox in 2014, as well as a data breach involving iCloud. [4] In October of 2014, hackers gained access to over seven million Dropbox accounts in an effort to mine Bitcoins (BTC), using those accounts to generate revenue from the service. As a consequence of getting these credentials, which provide them authorization to do so, they are able to access and search any confidential information (making the information public). [4] With regard to legal ownership of the data, is it possible for a cloud provider to profit from the data of a user if it is kept in the cloud? In many cases, the question of ownership is not addressed within the terms and conditions. [5] Instead of keeping computer equipment off-site and under the control of a third party, it is preferable to maintain it on-site in the form of a private cloud. This offers a higher level of protection and safety (compared with a public cloud). As a direct consequence of this, public cloud computing service providers have a powerful incentive to place a primary emphasis on the creation and upkeep of secure services. [6] There are some kinds of small businesses that don't have a lot of expertise in dealing with information technology security, and it's possible that using a public cloud may provide them with a better degree of protection. End users run the risk of being unaware of the dangers associated with using cloud services if they are not well prepared (persons sometimes do not read the numerous pages of the terms of service agreement and simply click "Accept"). Because cloud computing is utilized in such a wide variety of contexts, it is vital to have a cloud-hosted personal assistant (such as Apple's Siri or Google Assistant). The user of a public cloud is viewed to have greater freedom and spend less time and money overall, despite the fact that the owner of a private cloud has increased degrees of security and control over their system.

1.12 CONCLUSION

We'll sum up by noting that cloud computing is a relatively recent concept with massive worldwide consequences. It provides a broad variety of benefits to both its customers and its providers. For example, organizations may save money on maintenance and software upgrades while concentrating more on their core capabilities owing to this technology. However, cloud computing has extra challenges. In this chapter, we have discussed cloud computing in detail. Different deployment modes and services available in cloud computing have also been discussed here. Many individuals are worried about the safety and privacy of their personal information. Cloud computing delivers data without conventions or regulations around the world. Users are also worried about who has access to and management of their personal information. Cloud computing, on the other hand, will reshape the world once there are global standards and rules in place.

2 An Overview of Amazon Web Services

2.1 INTRODUCTION

There are a number of cloud-based services provided by Amazon Web Services (AWS), ranging from data storage and processing to databases and analytics to networking and portable devices to Internet of Things (IoT) and governance to corporate applications. Everything we need is at our fingertips in the blink of an eye, and we only pay for what we use. Over 200 AWS services are supplied, including data storage, technology and processing, directories, and content delivery. As a consequence, new services may be delivered without incurring any upfront fees. Businesses, new enterprises, small and medium-sized organizations, and customers in the public sector may all profit from this.

AWS is credited with coining the phrase "cloud computing" in 2006. This was the year that AWS first began delivering web-based access to IT infrastructure services for businesses. One of the key benefits of cloud computing is the opportunity to replace upfront expenditures on capital infrastructure with low variable expenses that may expand with your organization. This is one of the most significant advantages of cloud computing. Because of the availability of the cloud, businesses no longer need to plan and acquire servers and other IT equipment weeks or months in advance. Instead, they can just utilize the cloud, and hundreds or even thousands of servers might be brought up instantly or within a matter of minutes, resulting in a more rapid distribution of the results.

AWS is currently the cloud infrastructure platform of choice for hundreds of thousands of businesses located in 190 countries around the world. It is known for its high reliability, scalability, and competitive pricing.

2.2 EVOLUTION OF AWS

AWS is very popular in the present era. But this was not an overnight achievement; rather it began early in the year 2000. Different phases in which the development took place are listed below. Figure 2.1 explains the same in a pictorial way.

2.2.1 THE FORMATIVE YEARS (2000–2005)

AWS was established not long after the turn of the century. Because Amazon's e-commerce platform enables third-party merchants to build their own web stores, the company came to the conclusion that adopting service-oriented architecture (SOA) was the most effective method to expand its technological operations. [20–24]

DOI: 10.1201/9781003406136-2

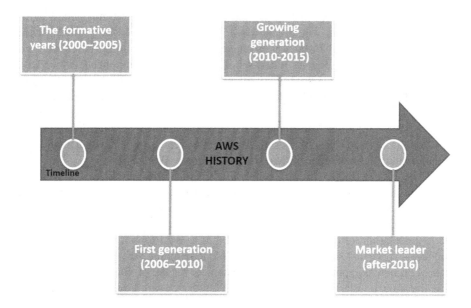

FIGURE 2.1   Evolution of AWS.

Following the suggestions that Matt Round made at the time about how to accelerate Amazon's software engineering, the business implemented a number of improvements, including increased autonomy for teams, the use of representational state transfer, and the standardizing of infrastructure. Additionally, gatekeeping decision-makers and other forms of bureaucracy were eliminated, and continuous deployment was implemented. In addition to this, Round argued for increasing the amount of time that is spent on software development in lieu of doing other things. [28] Because the majority of Amazon's engineering teams were focusing on "undifferentiated heavy-lifting," such as IT and infrastructure problems, the business decided to build "a common IT platform" to free up their time so they could focus on customer-facing innovation instead. [29] In addition, Amazon's infrastructure team, which was led by Tom Killalea, [30] Amazon's first chief information security officer (CISO) [31], had already been operating its data centers and related services in a manner that was "quick, dependable, and affordable" in order to accommodate unforeseen patterns of peak traffic, particularly during the holiday season. [30]

When Colin Bryar took over as CEO of Amazon.com Web Services in July 2002, [31] the business published its first set of web services, opening up the Amazon platform to all programmers.

[32] It had been used to create over a hundred distinct applications by 2004. [33] Amazon was taken aback by this unanticipated developer involvement and convinced that developers were "eager for more." Despite this, Amazon was nonetheless surprised. [27]

As part of the "Internet Operating System," it put out a set of fundamental infrastructure primitives that would enable software applications to be deployed more rapidly. [20–22, 24–26] Databases, storage space, and computing power were all early components of Amazon's initial set of infrastructure components, which date back to the fall of 2003. [20, 22, 24, 29] AWS was formed from Amazon's aim to "create, develop, reinvent, rebuild, begin again, and do it again" as soon as possible, and this drive led to "2 teams" and distributed systems, which led to the establishment of AWS. [35] After Amazon purchased Alexa Internet in 1999, Brewster Kahle said that his start-up's design assisted Amazon in overcoming huge data challenges and ultimately defined the technologies that underpin AWS. [36]

At the end of 2003, Amazon presented a paper to its employees in which it described an Amazon retail computing infrastructure that was fully standardized and automated, relied heavily on web services for services such as storage, and drew upon internal work that was already in progress. In the end, this article would serve as the foundation for the establishment of EC2. A few lines in, it proposed renting out access to virtual servers as a means of monetizing the business's recent expenditures on new equipment by charging customers for the privilege. [37] Following that, the Amazon Elastic Compute Cloud (EC2) service was developed by a group in Cape Town, South Africa. [38]

Shortly after introducing its initial public infrastructure service in November 2004, Amazon Web Services came out with its Simple Queue Service (SQS).

2.2.2 FIRST GENERATION (2006–2010)

Cloud storage service Amazon S3 [39], offered by AWS, was first made available on March 14, 2006, followed by EC2 in August of the same year. [40] Back in 2006, the vice president of AWS stated that Amazon S3

> facilitates programmers to focus on developing rather than worrying about where data should be stored, whether or not it will be safe and secure, whether or not it will be available when they need it, the associated costs with routine maintenance, or whether or not they have enough storage capacity. Rather than storing data, Amazon S3 allows its users to innovate with the data.

Pi Corporation went on to become the first company outside of Amazon to utilize EC2's beta version. [24] Microsoft was also one of EC2's first commercial customers. [41] SmugMug, an early client of Amazon Web Services, claimed that using S3 had helped them save around US$400,000 in costs related to storage by the end of the year. [42] According to Vogels, the first version of S3 was released in 2006 with eight components, but, by 2022, it had more than 300 microservices.

[43] When AWS first began hosting its annual Start-Up Challenge in September 2007, the company offered a total of US$100,000 in prizes to American business owners and software developers who had used AWS services such as S3 and EC2 to get their companies off the ground.

2.2.3 GROWING GENERATION (2010–2015)

AWS was believed to have become the new home for all of Amazon.com's retail sites by November 2010. [44] Before 2012, when it was determined that Amazon Web Services was no longer considered an independent organization, the company's financial statements did not differentiate the income earned by AWS from that earned by Amazon.com. The projections made by market analysts for Amazon Web Services' revenue in that year exceeded US$1.5 billion for the first time. [44]

On April 30, 2013, Amazon Web Services began offering a certification program for computer engineers as part of its efforts to spread cloud computing skills across the industry. [45] In October of the same year, the Activate program for start-ups was launched. This program gives start-ups the opportunity to make free use of AWS credits, third-party integrations, and access to AWS professionals in order to assist them in expanding their enterprises on a worldwide scale. [46]

AWS launched its partner network, known as APN (AWS Partner Network), in 2014 with the intention of assisting businesses that run on AWS to grow and scale their commercial success via the use of tight collaboration and industry best practices. [47, 48]

Amazon said that AWS was profitable for the first time in April 2015, citing sales of US$1.57 billion for the first quarter of 2015 and operating earnings of US$265 million for that period. "Astonishingly profitable in comparison to what was anticipated": Jeff Bezos characterized it as a rapidly expanding US$5-billion business venture. [49] In its quarterly results report for the third quarter, which was released in October, Amazon.com disclosed that the operational income of AWS was US$521 million, and that its operating margins were 25 percent. The amount of money that was created by AWS in the third quarter of 2015 was US$2.1 billion, which is a 78 percent increase over the amount of revenue that was generated in the third quarter of 2014, which was US$1.17 billion. [50] AWS sector revenues increased by 69.5 percent year over year to US$2.4 billion for the fourth quarter of 2015, which resulted in an operating profit of 28.5 percent and a US$9.6-billion annual run rate. According to Gartner, customers of AWS were adopting the cloud computing platform at a rate that was ten times higher than the adoption of the next 14 providers combined in 2015. [50]

2.2.4 MARKET LEADER (AFTER 2016)

An expansion of 64 percent in revenue and net profit in the first quarter of 2016 led to AWS becoming more profitable than Amazon's retail business in North America for the first time. [51] Additionally, Amazon saw its stock price grow by 42 percent as a result of improved profitability, with AWS accounting for 56 percent of the company's net income during this time period. [52]

In 2017, AWS generated sales of US$17.46 billion. [52] As of 2020, it has hit US$46 billion in revenue. [53] Amazon unveiled its AWS Auto Scaling service in January of that year. [54, 55] Customized ARM cores for AWS servers were introduced in November 2018. [56] AWS was also hard at work on ground stations that would, come November 2018, be able to communicate with client satellites. [57]

In 2019, Amazon Web Services had annual growth of 37 percent, accounting for 12 percent of the company's overall revenue (up from 11 percent in 2018). [58] According to numbers that were made public in April 2021, Amazon Web Services accounted for 32 percent of the cloud computing industry's revenue of US$41.8 billion during the first quarter of 2021.

2.3 GLOBAL INFRASTRUCTURE OF AWS

Amazon Elastic Compute Cloud is hosted from a variety of locations all around the world. AWS Outposts, Local Zones, Availability Zones, Wavelength Zones, and Regions are the components that make up these locations. From a geographical point of view, every territory has its own Region. Each Region is split into Availability Zones, and each zone has a scattering of small settlements.

With the aid of Local Zones, it is possible to organize resources such as computation and storage in a number of places that are closer to the end clients. These sites may be spread out across a wider geographic area.

AWS Outposts is a service that brings AWS's infrastructure and services to on-premises, co-location, or data center facilities, allowing such facilities to reap the benefits of using AWS Outposts.

Ultra-low-latency applications that are designed using Wavelength Zones will be beneficial to both 5G devices and end users. On the periphery of 5G networks, computing and storage services compliant with AWS standards are being deployed by Wavelength on behalf of telecom companies.

The data centers that AWS maintains are state of the art and have a high degree of redundancy. Failures that have an effect on the availability of instances in the same Region are very rare, although they do occur on occasion. If the instances were hosted in a single place and that location had a failure, then all the instances would become inaccessible. In Figure 2.2, we can relate the architecture of Region, Availability Zone, and data center.

2.3.1 REGIONS

It is expected that each of the Amazon EC2 Regions will be entirely isolated from the others. Because of this, the maximum possible degree of fault tolerance and stability is achieved.

When one looks at the resources, one will only see those that are connected to the Region that we have chosen to focus on. This is because resources are not automatically duplicated between areas, and Regions are not connected to one another. In addition, each Region has its own unique environment.

When starting an instance, users are required to utilize an Amazon Machine Image (AMI) created in the same Region. Users may relocate an AMI from one Region to another by duplicating it and using that copy in the new Region. A charge will be assessed for any data transfer that takes place between different Regions.

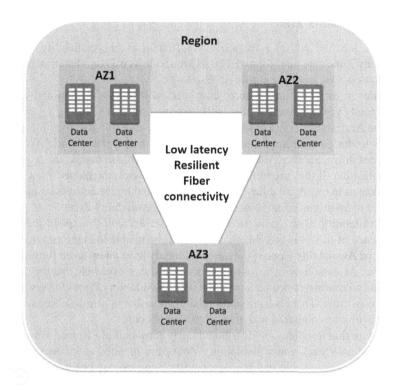

FIGURE 2.2   AWS Region, Availability Zone, and data center.

2.3.2   AVAILABLE REGIONS

The multiple Regions that come standard with an AWS account make it possible to start Amazon EC2 instances in a wide range of geographic locations. Establishing a base of operations in Europe might be beneficial to a business on a number of fronts, including providing superior support to customers based in Europe and ensuring full compliance with applicable regulations.

A user is required to have an account in the AWS GovCloud (US-East) Region in order to access the AWS GovCloud (US-West) Region. With an Amazon AWS (China) account, users may use the cloud computing services of just the Beijing and Ningxia Regions.

2.3.3   REGIONS AND ENDPOINTS

When working with an instance using the command line interface or API operations, users must specify its Regional endpoint.

Users may get this information by using either the command line interface or the Amazon EC2 console, and they are able to learn about their Regions by using the console.

2.3.4 AVAILABILITY ZONE

A specific location within a Region is referred to as an Availability Zone. An Availability Zone may be recognized by its area code as well as a letter identification that follows it. One example of this is US-east-1a.

In order to establish an instance, customers will need a Region and a virtual private cloud (VPC). After that, they will have the option of selecting a subnet from one of the Availability Zones or letting Amazon take care of it for them. It is possible for users to design their application in such a way that, if one of their Availability Zones goes down, another Availability Zone will be able to handle the requests for their application. If they are utilizing Elastic IP addresses, the failure of an instance that is located in one Availability Zone can be masked by the address being quickly remapped to an instance that is located in another Availability Zone.

As Availability Zones grow in size, it is more difficult to expand them. As a consequence of this, it is possible that users will be unable to launch an instance in a restricted Availability Zone if they do not already have an instance running in the same zone. At some time in the not-too-distant future, it's possible that the restricted Availability Zone might be taken from the list of Availability Zones for new customers to choose from. There is a possibility that the number of available Regions on the account is unique compared with that of another account.

To ensure that resources are distributed fairly across all of a Region's Availability Zones, each AWS account's Availability Zones are mapped to its own unique set of codes. It is conceivable that the Availability Zone us-east-1a associated with an AWS account is not at the same physical location as the Availability Zone us-east-1a associated with another AWS account.

When coordinating Availability Zones across different accounts, users need to make use of the AZ ID, which is an identity that is both unique to an Availability Zone and reliable. For instance, use1-az1 is an AZ ID that may be found in any AWS account. This particular example applies to the us-east-1 Region. There is the option of seeing the AZ IDs associated with the account to have a better idea of where its resources stand with respect to those of other accounts. A subnet in the Availability Zone that has the AZ ID use1-az2, for instance, is accessible to any account in the Availability Zone that has the AZ ID use1-az2.

2.3.5 LOCAL ZONES

In the location of the users, an AWS Local Zone acts as an extension of the regional infrastructure. As resources created in a Local Zone may serve local users with reduced communications, Local Zones have their own internet connections and allow AWS Direct Connect.

To identify a Local Zone, the Region code is attached to the name of the area it serves. In Los Angeles, for example, it is us-west-2-lax-1.

Local Zones must be enabled before they may be utilized. Such applications should be placed locally to the clients by deploying resources such as instances in the Local Zone subnet.

2.3.6 WAVELENGTH ZONES

AWS Wavelength gives programmers the ability to design applications that provide very low latency to mobile devices and the people who use them. Wavelength brings the standard computing and storage capabilities offered by Amazon Web Services to the edge of 5G networks used by telecommunications providers. Developers have the ability to extend a VPC to one or more Wavelength Zones. They may then use AWS resources, such as Amazon EC2 instances, to run applications that need very low latency and a connection to AWS services located in the Region.

A Wavelength Zone is a section of the carrier area that is separated from the rest of the Region and is the location where the Wavelength infrastructure is built. A Region is associated with a number of Wavelength Zones. A Wavelength Zone is a logical extension of a Region, and the control plane of the Region is the entity that is responsible for administering Wavelength Zones.

A Wavelength Zone's code is its Region code followed by an identifier that indicates the actual location.

2.3.7 AWS OUTPOSTS

AWS Outposts is a fully managed solution that brings the infrastructure, services, application programming interfaces, and tools of AWS to the locations of individual clients. It is feasible to develop and run programs on-premises using the same programming APIs as in AWS Regions, while making use of the low-latency computational power and storage that AWS Outposts provides.

An AWS Outpost is a cluster of computing and storage resources that is established at a customer location and provided by AWS. AWS is responsible for the upkeep, monitoring, and operation of this capacity since it is part of an AWS Region. Subnets can be made use of in the Outpost and added as resources in Amazon Web Services. Instances located in Outpost subnets have the ability to communicate with other instances located in AWS Regions using private IP addresses.

2.4 AWS SHARED RESPONSIBILITY MODEL

Security and compliance are mutual obligations between AWS and the customer. This shared method may help lighten the customer's operational burden as AWS operates, maintains, and manages the components from the host system and virtualization layer down to the physical security of the premises in which the service operates. The client acknowledges ownership and management of the guest operating system (including updates and security patches) and other associated application software as well as the setup of the AWS-provided security group firewall. Customers should carefully analyze the services they choose, as their duties vary according to the services used, the integration of those services into their IT infrastructure, and applicable laws and regulations. The nature of this shared responsibility also affords the flexibility and customer control that simplifies the deployment. As shown in Figure 2.3, this split of duties is commonly referred to as Security "of" the Cloud versus Security "in" the Cloud.

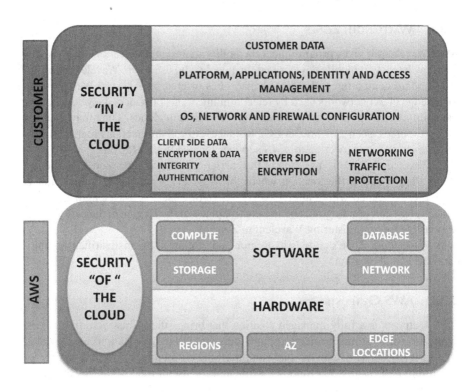

FIGURE 2.3   Share responsibility model in AWS.

2.4.1   AWS's Responsibility—"Security of the Cloud"

AWS is the entity in charge of ensuring the safety of the underlying infrastructure in the AWS Cloud, which is responsible for providing power to all of the services. The AWS Cloud services are run on this infrastructure, which comprises the facilities, as well as the hardware, software, and networking components. Physical and environmental controls are the responsibility of AWS.

2.4.2   Customer's Responsibility—"Security in the Cloud"

The amount of responsibility a customer has is determined by the AWS Cloud services it uses. This determines the level of effort that the customer is required to put in as part of its responsibilities regarding security. IaaS stands for "infrastructure as a service." One example of a service that comes into this category is Amazon EC2, which requires the customer to take care of all security settings and administrative responsibilities on its own. Any customer-installed software or utilities, as well as the configuration of the AWS-provided firewall (which is referred to as a security group), must be kept up-to-date and patched on Amazon EC2 instances. Customers are accountable for fulfilling these responsibilities. Users are responsible for accessing the service endpoints in order to save and retrieve data for AWS-abstracted services such as Amazon S3 and Amazon DynamoDB. Customers are responsible for the upkeep of their data (including the selection of an encryption method), the categorization of their assets, and the use of Identity and Access Management (IAM) technologies in order to allocate the appropriate access privileges. Customers are entirely responsible for ensuring that AWS services are running in accordance with their application's requirements.

Customers and AWS both share duties under this arrangement, with the former including additional IT controls. In the same way as AWS and its customers are jointly responsible for the operation of the IT environment, they are also jointly responsible for the management, operation, and verification of the IT controls. It is possible for Amazon Web Services to lighten the load of operating controls that customers are responsible for by taking over the controls that are associated with the physical infrastructure that is installed in Amazon Web Services. These controls may have formerly been controlled by the customers themselves. For the convenience of its customers, AWS offers a dispersed control environment in which the company handles some information technology controls on customers' behalf. The AWS control and compliance documentation may then be used to carry out customer control evaluation and verification procedures. The following are some instances of controls that can be managed by AWS, by AWS customers, or by both AWS and AWS customers working together.

There are controls that may be imposed at both the infrastructure and the consumer level, but they must be seen from fundamentally distinct perspectives in order to be effective. A shared control arrangement is one in which AWS is responsible for providing the necessary infrastructure, but the customer is in charge of implementing its own control mechanisms inside the AWS services that it makes use of.

2.5   ACCEPTABLE USE POLICY

The following acceptable use policy (the "policy") governs user behavior while using the services provided by Amazon Web Services, Inc. and its affiliates, as well as its website(s). Users are not permitted to use any of the AWS services or the AWS site for activities including, but not limited to, the following:

- any form of dishonesty or illegal behavior.
- violating the legal rights of another individual.
- advocating or actively encouraging acts of violence or terrorism, or making threats of acts of violence or terrorism which are violations of the law.
- anything that promotes the commercial exploitation of minors or abuse of children for the sake of monetary gain.
- putting at risk the accessibility, authenticity, or privacy of any connection or system belonging to a user.
- sending or distributing unsolicited mass emails (also known as "spam") or other messages, promotions, advertising, or solicitations (such as, for example, "chain letters") in any form, including electronically.

2.6   FOUNDATIONAL CAPABILITIES OF AWS

Transformation domains are made possible by the key capabilities that are depicted in Figure 2.4. The competency of an organization is the ability to utilize processes to organize its resources in order to achieve a certain objective successfully. With the support of the AWS Cloud Adoption Framework, it is possible to improve company cloud preparedness. The AWS Capability Adoption Framework is built on six distinct pillars, which are business, people, governance, platform, security, and operations. There is a group of stakeholders in the cloud journey that are functionally connected and correspond to each perspective. These stakeholders either own or manage the associated set of capabilities in the cloud journey. When it comes to deploying, running, and regulating business workloads in the cloud, Amazon Web Services recommends that they have a fundamental set of abilities. All these capabilities are listed in Figure 2.4.

A competence is a set of skills that may be used to develop and operate a cloud-based system. These skills may include definition, use cases, opinionated counsel, and supporting automation. In order to successfully develop, create, and run a cloud environment, it is necessary to take into account the individuals, techniques, and technology involved. In order to perform their intended functions, capabilities need to have the ability to communicate with the rest of the IT system.

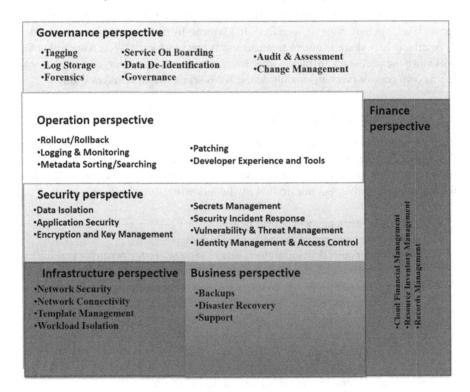

FIGURE 2.4   Foundational capabilities of AWS.

In addition to the technical implementation recommendations, each capability also contains the operational guidance that is necessary to set up and manage it.

A list of 30 capabilities that may be grouped into six different categories has been compiled by AWS as a place to begin.

2.6.1 GOVERNANCE PERSPECTIVE

Organizations may utilize GRC (governance, risk management, and compliance) to offer a basis for attaining policies and privacy compliance objectives, as well as to describe the general rules with which the cloud architecture must comply. Defining what needs to happen, identifying the tolerance for risk, and harmonizing internal regulations are all facilitated by the abilities in this area.

Viewpoint on governance includes the following checkpoints:

- Tagging: Users are able to organize groups of cloud resources by marking them with metadata, which can then be allocated to those cloud resources. An attribute-based access system may serve several functions, including reporting on costs, automating processes, and providing access control. Tagging may also be used to establish new resource structures for visibility and control, which can be done in a variety of ways (such as grouping together resources that make up a microservice, application, or workload). Tagging is necessary in order to provide visibility and control at the corporate level.
- Log storage: Log management makes it possible to store environment logs in a way that prevents tampering, which increases their level of safety. This capability is made available by AWS so that the usage, tracking, and reporting of AWS services and events can be investigated later.
- Forensics: In forensics, an examination of log files and photos of potentially compromised resources is used to determine whether or not a security breach really occurred (and if so, how). Investigations conducted for forensic purposes often provide findings from root cause analyses, which are then used to develop and drive the adoption of preventative measures.
- Onboarding: When using service onboarding, it is feasible to investigate and authorize the use of AWS services based on internal, regulatory, and compliance issues. This may be done in a timely manner. This competence encompasses a wide range of responsibilities, including risk assessment, documentation, patterns of implementation, and the communication of change.
- Anonymization: Anonymization is the capability to lower the sensitivity of certain kinds of information (for example, national ID numbers or trade data) while maintaining the underlying data structure when it is important to do so. In addition, part of this feature is the ability to tokenize sensitive data, such as credit card information, physical addresses, and medical records.

- Governance: Governance refers to the capability to establish executive board rules that the AWS Cloud environment must adhere to. Over time, a component of this ability will be integrated into all of the other capabilities, making it possible to guarantee compliance with governance requirements.
- Audit and assessment: The cloud infrastructure and its operations may be assessed through comparison with predetermined criteria by collecting and organizing the relevant documents (including information about who accessed what, when, and from where, and what changes happened).
- Change management: Change management allows for the reconfiguration of any and all adjustable objects within the outlined scope, such as production and test environments. If a resource configuration change has been given the green light, it indicates that the threat posed to the existing IT infrastructure has been reduced and is now being seen as acceptable.

2.6.2 OPERATION PERSPECTIVE

The aim is to maintain a constant state of adaptability while guaranteeing the continued high quality of application and infrastructure improvements. With the help of these tools and capabilities, it will be simple for users to generate, deploy, and operate the workloads they want to run on the cloud. In terms of how things work, this involves the following:

- Rollback: Using the rollout/rollback approach, changes to an application or configuration may either be put into effect or undone. Application and configuration adjustments include things such as updated permissions, new rules, a new or updated network configuration, a new version of the program, or updated software development kits. Other examples of these kinds of changes include new versions of the program. As a possible additional aspect of these configuration alterations, modifications might be made to the orchestration framework.
- Log and monitor: The capability to gather and aggregate information about design and advanced activity in real time is a crucial aspect of a log and monitor solution. This enables anomalies, signs of compromise, technical difficulties, and configuration changes to be rapidly discovered.
- Metadata: Metadata sorting/searching is the process of searching for and filtering results using metadata that has been applied to tagged resources inside your environment.
- Patching: It is possible to apply patches to workloads and infrastructure in order to update, rectify, or enhance the performance and security of such components. Fixing bugs and addressing security concerns are inextricably linked throughout all of this. The term "patching" refers to the process of repairing vulnerabilities in operating systems, services, and any other essential software systems.

- Developer experience and tools: The term "developer experience and tools" refers to the processes, tools, and strategies that are used in the creation and deployment of workloads that are hosted on the cloud. The storage of code, the creation of processes, and the transfer of workloads from a test environment to a production environment are all covered by this functionality.

2.6.3 SECURITY PERSPECTIVE

A cloud infrastructure that is safe, dependable, and effective has to be constructed from the ground up. One may use the capabilities in this area to develop and execute security rules and controls at different levels of the stack in order to protect the resources from vulnerabilities and threats that originate from both outside and inside the organization. They protect the information and make it easily accessible, while at the same time detecting issues and providing recommendations on how these issues might be resolved. This encompasses the following in terms of safety:

- Teams will have the ability to swiftly and simply establish new users and centrally govern their access to the cloud platform environment when they utilize identity management and access control. Users are free to make use of this feature to develop a model of access with the lowest possible level of privilege for the organization, its accounts, and its surroundings.
- If data isolation is used, users will be able to control who may access data regardless of whether it is moving through the network or sitting at its destination. This feature also includes the ability to recognize inappropriate use of data as well as unauthorized access, data leakage, and data theft.
- This encompasses the protection of application software in addition to the detection of anomalous behavior in the context of how applications interact with customers. It is necessary to deal with a broad variety of risks, some of which include unauthorized access, the escalation of privileges, and other application-level concerns.
- The term "key management" refers to the ability to encrypt data both while it is at rest and while it is in transit, as well as the capability to centrally manage encryption keys for a variety of applications. Keys to decryption are dispersed among users in a manner that is consistent with the concept of least privilege, and any unexpected behavior is logged and reported. Altering rotation patterns in order to fulfill the requirements of an application is another possibility.
- Under the umbrella phrase "secrets management," several forms of secrets, such as passwords, access keys, other API keys, X.509 certificates, and Secure Shell private keys, are all examples of the kinds of secrets that may be managed. This aspect of the secret management system includes storage, access restriction, access monitoring, revocation, and rotation among its many capabilities.

- A break in the security response is what gives the ability to respond to a security event as it occurs. The response comprises providing a description of the circumstance and making modifications in line with the policy options (which may involve activities including restoration of operational status, identification and remediation of root cause, and gathering evidence pursuant to civil or criminal prosecution).
- Vulnerability and threat management is a tool that may be used to look for environmental weak spots (availability, performance, or security). Using this feature, vulnerabilities and threats may be evaluated in terms of their impact and scope (such as the radius of their explosion), respectively.

2.6.4 Business Perspective

The capacity to persevere in the face of adversity has a direct bearing on the quality of service that is provided to consumers. In this industry, only a few of the features, such as disaster recovery, backups, and support, provide the ability to keep operations running smoothly even in the midst of inefficiency or an emergency situation. These precautions might help avoid unscheduled downtime in the case of power failures or other unforeseen occurrences. The following are components of a business operation:

- Backups are the capability to create a trustworthy duplicate of data in a trustworthy way, with the intention of retrieving that copy when necessary to meet both business and security needs. All of the following must be backed up: the data and settings from the orchestration framework, the data from the application, the logs, and the data from the customers.
- In the event that the physical environment in which the transactions were being processed when they were first being handled becomes suddenly unavailable, disaster recovery includes the utilization of automated procedures to continue the processing of transactions hosted in one physical environment in another physical environment.
- Support is described as the capability to troubleshoot an environment, ask questions, submit tickets, integrate into existing ticketing systems, and escalate issues to an appropriate organization for a speedy response, depending on the criticality and support level of the issue. The provision of access to essential resources in order to carry out troubleshooting and corrective measures is another aspect of support that may be included.

2.6.5 Finance Perspective

The elements included in this section aid in developing and enhancing the existing monetary procedures so that they are compatible with cloud computing. This makes it possible for businesses to begin and continue operations with cost transparency, control, planning, and optimization and to maintain compliance with the various compliance and regulatory standards while managing corporate records and resource inventories. The following is a list of competences related to finance:

- Businesses can keep track of the variable expenses associated with the cloud, and Cloud Financial Management can help a business lower those expenditures. This capability assists in decision-making by giving visibility and expense and utilization evaluations in almost real time. Using this capability, businesses will be able to have a defined cost-optimized architecture for particular workloads, determine the appropriate pricing model for the resources, and distribute the cost of resources in line with the requirements of the company. With the help of these technologies, they will be able to monitor the environment and resources, as well as take steps that will reduce expenses. The information on the costs is centralized and used, and access to the appropriate stakeholders may be given in order to achieve targeted visibility.
- Utilizing Resource Inventory Management enables the management of cloud-based resources that are components of an IT service or job. This is achievable because of the nature of cloud computing.
- Records Management gives the ability to select which data should be kept and for how long in accordance with the internal standards and regulatory requirements of the organization. It also shows customers how to transfer data to an archive before it is deleted permanently. Keeping this information might include storing financial records and transaction logs, audit logs, corporate records, and other types of information that are governed by certain regulations.

2.6.6 INFRASTRUCTURE PERSPECTIVE

With the aid of the skills provided in this section, businesses will be able to plan, construct, and manage a cloud infrastructure that is both secure and fault-tolerant. They could find it easier to create and put into practice security rules and controls at different levels of the networking stack with the assistance of practices such as network security and load-balancing. If an organization is moving apps from on-premises to the cloud or building them entirely in the cloud from the ground up, it needs a cloud infrastructure that is trustworthy and secure. The following are some of the capabilities offered by the infrastructure:

- Network security assists users in the creation and execution of security rules and controls at different levels of the networking stack. This function, which monitors data flow into and out of the network, helps prevent, identify, and stop anomalous network activity by keeping track of data coming into and going out of the network.
- Because of network connectivity, it is now feasible to have a cloud design for a network that is both safe and highly available. With these best practices and resources, it is much simpler to automate the process of creating new network infrastructure, setting it up, and expanding it.
- Template management is essential in order to swiftly and effectively deploy, maintain, and upgrade infrastructure, formats, and services across an entire environment. This feature includes not only the creation of templates but

also their testing, updating, and validation. A template such as this one is a pre-approved implementation of an AWS service that multiple teams may use based on the requirements that they have.

- With a workload isolation boundary, you can easily create and maintain isolated environments for newly migrated or existing workloads. This strategy minimizes the blast radius of vulnerabilities and threats while also simplifying compliance. It does this by enabling techniques to isolate access to resources.

2.7 CONCLUSION

In this chapter, we have completely reviewed AWS and its development since the year 2000. We concentrated on global infrastructure, such as Regions, Availability Zones, data centers, and so on. All of these will help the user grasp how AWS works. The AWS shared responsibility model is also described in depth in this chapter, allowing the user to understand their role as well as what AWS is liable for. Finally, we concentrated on the core competences, which are divided into six categories. This will enable the user to make greater use of AWS's services.

3 Identity and Access Management in AWS

3.1 INTRODUCTION

Amazon Web Services (AWS) Identity and Access Management (IAM) is a web service that helps ensure that access to AWS services is regulated in a secure manner. Admins will be able to set up and administer authentication services for any users with the assistance of this tool, as well as limit access to the AWS resources for certain users.

When AWS and IAM were not available, passwords were often disseminated in an unsecured manner via alternative channels, such as phone calls or emails sent among employees inside the office. In many instances, there was only one admin password, and it was stored in a single location that had been chosen in advance; alternatively, only one person could change the password, and doing so required making a phone call. This was not at all secure since anybody walking by might potentially listen in, figure out the password, and then have access to the whole system along with all of its data.

Users may host their applications in an environment that is dependable and secure using the AWS cloud. The security offered by AWS provides better data protection at a cost that is lower than the cost of an on-premises infrastructure. Identity and Access Management is one of the most common security solutions available today. There is the ability to limit user access to critical resources and services inside AWS if businesses make use of the AWS Identity and Access Management platform. IAM is the system that AWS uses to create and manage users and groups, as well as to give or revoke access to different AWS services, depending on the roles and permissions assigned to individual users.

3.2 AWS SECURITY

The safety and security of customer data stored in the cloud is Amazon Web Services' highest priority. The environment will be kept in a data center or network architecture that has been specifically created to meet the requirements of the most security-conscious companies, giving businesses the peace of mind that comes with having data hosted in the cloud. Additionally, this high level of protection may be obtained on a pay-as-you-go basis. [92] This means that there is essentially no upfront investment, and the continuous cost of using the service is far less expensive than it would be in an on-premises environment.

A few examples of the many security services that AWS makes use of include the IAM Key Management System (KMS), Cognito, and Web Access Firewall (WAF).

DOI: 10.1201/9781003406136-3

The topics of IAM will be covered in this outline. Businesses have the ability to securely govern who has access to what across the enormous network of services and resources offered by AWS by using IAM. It gives them the ability to pick which persons or groups are authorized to access particular servers and which are not authorized to do so for any given server.

3.3   IAM AND HOW IT WORKS

The following is a rundown of each of the six elements of the IAM process [89]:

- Principal: A person or group that has access to a certain AWS resource is referred to as a principal. The term "principal" may refer to either an individual (a user) or an entity (application).
- Authentication: This refers to the process by which the identity of a principal is checked in order to provide that principal with access to an AWS product. This check is required before a principal can be granted access. The principal is the one who is responsible for handing out credentials or authentication keys to the appropriate parties.
- Request: The beginning of an operation is marked by the submission of a request to AWS, which includes information about the operation as well as the resource that should carry it out.
- Permissions: When it comes to permissions, nothing is permitted by default. Default permissions do not allow anything. IAM won't comply with a request unless each of its constituent parts is in line with the matching policy and meets all of its requirements. After determining that the request has been made in good faith, AWS will then offer its approval for the operation to proceed.
- Action: Several operations, including viewing, creating, editing, and removing resources, are all possible with resources.
- Resource: An AWS resource is a group of actions or tasks that may be completed using the account.

3.3.1   CONSTITUENTS OF THE IAM

IAM also consists of a number of other fundamental parts. The user is the starting point; a collection of users is a group. The engines that determine whether a connection is authorized or denied are called policies. [90] A user may quickly get access to an instance by assuming a role.

Users: An identity that has credentials and access levels given to them is called an Identity and Access Management user. There is a chance that this user is a real person; however, there is also a chance that it is an application. A business will have complete control over who in the workforce may access which AWS services if it provides each employee with their own individual IAM username. Any given IAM user is restricted to using a single AWS account at a time. A new AWS user starts off with no permissions and is unable to do any actions unless they are given the appropriate rights. Granular user permissions, which are allowed by one-to-one user specification, provide a number of benefits, one of which is the capacity to personalize the access levels of each individual user.

Group: A group in the IAM system is essentially a collection of IAM users. IAM groups provide the ability to set permissions for a group of users, and those permissions will then be inherited by each individual user who is a part of that group. The management of a group is not difficult at all. The provision of rights to the group as a whole will be passed down to each individual member of the group. When a new user is added to a group, they will instantly be subject to all of the rules and permissions that have been defined for that group. [92] This is because the rules and permissions are specific to the group. As a direct consequence of this, less work will be required. Figure 3.1 shows the difference between users and groups.

Policies: IAM policies are what are used to govern who may access which AWS services. JavaScript Object Notation (JSON) files are used by AWS to store the policies. The permissions specify who is allowed to use the resources and what they are allowed to do with those resources. For example, a policy may provide an IAM user with authorization to access a certain Amazon S3 bucket. This would be done via the policy. There are two primary types of policies, which are referred to as managed policies and inline policies. Figure 3.2 shows the JSON document for the policies.

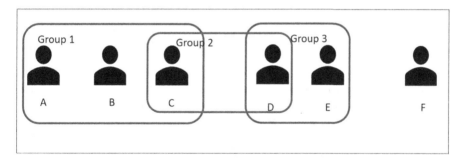

FIGURE 3.1   Users and group.

```
1▾ {
2      "version": "2012-10-17",
3▾     "statement": [
4▾         {
5              "Effect": "Allow",
6▾             "Action": [
7                  "sts:AssumeRole"
8              ],
9▾             "Principal": {
10▾                "Service": [
11                     "ec2.amazonaws.com"
12                 ]
13             }
14         }
15     ]
16 }
```

FIGURE 3.2   JSON sample for policy.

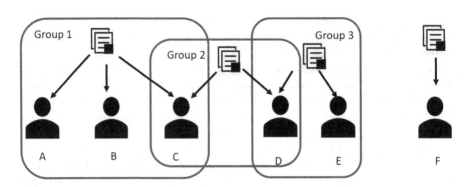

FIGURE 3.3   Policies—managed and inline.

A managed policy makes it possible to give the same default policy to a number of different AWS users, groups, and roles. Policies that are maintained by AWS and policies that are managed by customers are all identity-based policies that are independent of one another and may be allocated to a large number of users or groups.

When we construct an inline policy, we put it directly into the object that it applies to (user, group, or role). Figure 3.3 depicts managed and inline policies. The policy followed by user F is inline.

Role: An IAM role is a permissions hierarchy that specifies what a user or group of users can and cannot do inside the AWS management portal. It functions similarly to a user in that any entity may get access to it (an individual or AWS service). Permissions assigned to roles are just like a passcode.

For instance, one may wish to provide a mobile app with access to AWS resources without allowing the app to store any kind of access information. On the other hand, one may wish to provide access to a user who already has an identity specified elsewhere (say, using Google or Facebook authentication) than in AWS. One may also use roles to provide access to the account's resources while providing a service to another user. One may also wish to provide a consultant or an auditor with temporary access to the account.

3.3.2   SPECIFICATIONS OF IAM

- Access to the AWS account may be shared with another user. IAM primarily offers users the ability to generate one-of-a-kind login credentials for each user or piece of infrastructure. This makes it possible to more quickly grant access to certain groups of individuals.
- Capabilities can be split into more manageable parts and pieces. Any request may be subject to limitations if one is forced to do so by particular circumstances. Using the rules, one may give users permission to download data while also limiting their ability to alter it.
- Verification of credentials utilizing a variety of methods: The implementation of multi-factor authentication (MFA) by IAM requires users to provide

not only their login details, but also a one-time password (OTP) that was generated on their mobile device.

- It is possible to set the IAM system to recognize pre-existing user authentication (such as that obtained from a social network or a cloud service) as being enough for the purpose of providing access. Users will then be able to log in to both their on-premises and cloud-based accounts using the same password.
- It does not cost anything to use. IAM security may be used without incurring any costs whatsoever. There is no additional charge incurred when creating more users, groups, or policies.
- The Payment Card Industry Data Security Standard is a collection of recommendations for organizations that deal with credit cards that are issued by the major card schemes. These organizations are expected to conform to the standard in order to maintain a high level of data security. IAM operates in a manner that is consistent with this standard.
- Guidelines for the generation and use of passwords: When using the password policy of the IAM, changing or resetting a password is a piece of cake. The method by which users should choose their passwords as well as the maximum number of erroneous attempts before being locked out may be governed by rules that may be created.

3.4   ABAC FOR AWS

An authorization technique known as attribute-based access control, or ABAC, is where permissions are specified. Within AWS, these features are characterized by the use of tags. Tags may be used to mark IAM resources such as users and roles, as well as AWS resources such as anything else users choose to label. It is possible that one or more ABAC policies will be produced for the IAM principals. In order for the ABAC policy to relax its restrictions and enable the operation to continue, the principal's tag and the resource's tag have to be the same. ABAC is helpful in situations and settings when it is difficult to administer policies, such as when the environment is rapidly growing.

Using the access-project key, for example, one has the ability to generate three distinct roles. The tag value for the first role ought to be Heart, the tag value for the second role ought to be Sun, and the tag value for the third role ought to be Lightning. If both the role and the resource are tagged with the same value for the access-project property, then we may use a single policy to provide access to both the role and the resource.

3.4.1   ABAC vs THE STANDARD RBAC PARADIGM

The authorization method that is often used for IAM is referred to as role-based access control (RBAC). A person's job function outside of AWS is used to determine what permissions they have in RBAC. These permissions are established according to a person's role. When discussing AWS, the word "role" is almost always used to refer to an individual's potential identity inside the AWS Identity and Access Management system. In a model based on RBAC, IAM consists of regulated rules for various job activities, and these rules provide the required rights for various roles.

Developing policies that are role-specific is required in order to implement RBAC in IAM. After that, the user IDs are connected with the corresponding policies (IAM users, groups of users, or IAM roles). The best course of action is to provide users with just the access they need to carry out their responsibilities. This is something that ought to take place according to the concept of least privilege. A list should be made of all the different kinds of equipment and materials that a particular job function can call for. One of the problems with the typical RBAC design is that it requires adjustments to be made to policies in order to make room for resources newly provided by staff.

Let's assume that a firm is now working on three separate projects: Heart, Sun, and Lightning. Every project has its own one-of-a-kind IAM role, which we will need to build. We are able to designate which resources the holders of a certain IAM role are permitted to utilize by attaching rules to each IAM role. When a company employee transfers to a different department or role inside the company, then that employee should also be transferred to a new IAM position. It's possible for one person or piece of software to fulfill many different functions. On the other hand, the Sun project could need additional tools, such as a dedicated storage bucket on Amazon S3 for all of its data. If this is the case, the policy that is linked with the Sun task has to be updated so that it includes the new bucket's location. If this new bucket is not shared with the Sun project, then the individuals who are a part of that endeavor will not have access to it.

3.4.2   ABAC Benefits over RBAC

- Innovation scales ABAC permits: It is no longer necessary for an administrator to change the existing policies in order to provide access to newly accessible resources. Consider an ABAC strategy that was developed using the access-project tag as one such example. If the team members who are working on the Heart project need more Amazon EC2 resources, the developer who is in charge of the project may create new Amazon EC2 instances and tag them with the access-project = Heart tag. Anyone working on the Heart project will have the ability to launch and terminate such instances as soon as their tags are equal to one another.
- ABAC needs fewer rules: Having a single set of rules to follow across all departments and positions means less paperwork. Such policies are less cumbersome to administer.
- ABAC helps teams evolve swiftly: This is owing to the fact that rights for newly created resources are provided automatically depending on their properties. For instance, if the firm currently supports the Heart and Sun projects utilizing ABAC, adding a new Lightning project is a simple and straightforward process. An administrator of the Identity and Access Management system will establish a new role with the access-project = Lightning tag. In order to provide support for a new initiative, it is not essential to alter the

policy. Instances that have the access-project value set to Lightning may be created and viewed by anybody who has the permissions necessary to take the role. Another possibility is that a member of the team will switch from working on the Heart project to the Lightning project. The user is given a new IAM role that has been assigned to them by the IAM administrator. There is no need to make any changes to the permissions policies.

- ABAC allows flexible privileges: When establishing the regulations, it is advised that the fewest possible people are allowed to comply with them. When using traditional RBAC, users are required to develop a policy that details the resources to which individual users are granted permission to get access. On the other hand, ABAC makes it feasible to limit access to resources based not on the principal who seeks access, but on the tags associated with those resources.
- ABAC uses corporate directory employee characteristics: Any Security Assertion Markup Language (SAML)-based or web-based identity provider is able to provide session tags for AWS. The federation of the workforce will result in the attributes of the personnel being transmitted to their AWS principal. Then, based on those qualities, ABAC might be utilized to either give or revoke access to the resource.

3.5   HANDS-ON IAM

It is possible to create new IAM users using the AWS Management Console. These are the actions to take while establishing an IAM user:

1. Open the AWS Management Console and go to the IAM console. This will show the display in Figure 3.4.
2. Select "Users" from the main menu. When ready, choose the "Add users" option.
3. In this space, type the new user's name. The user's AWS username is their means of entry. If you want to add more than one individual, you may do so by selecting "Add another user" and entering their login credentials. Currently, there is a limit of ten concurrent users. The result may be seen in Figure 3.5.
4. Decide on the new permissions for this set of users. Access may be gained either via the AWS Management Console or through code. Check out Figure 3.6.

   Programmatic access is the best option for customers that require access to the API, AWS Command Line Interface (CLI), or Utilities on Windows PowerShell. This generates a one-of-a-kind password for each user. After reaching the last page, users may be able to see or acquire the necessary access keys. If the user will need access to the AWS Management Console, they should choose this option when offered. Each sign-up is given a unique password.

   Passwords for consoles might be any of the following: Each user has a password that is generated automatically and complies with the account's password policy. After the last page is reached, the passwords are shown and may be downloaded.

FIGURE 3.4   IAM dashboard showing it's a global service.

FIGURE 3.5   Adding users to the account.

FIGURE 3.6   Specifying user details.

A user-generated password, or "custom password," is a password that the user generates. Everyone is given the password we list in the box.

If we want to force new users to change their passwords the first time they log in, we may choose "Require credential reset." If the administrator has chosen to let users change their own passwords, this will have no effect. If not, AWS will generate a new policy on its own. In accordance with the new rules, users are free to change their passwords whenever they see fit.

5. Select "Next" at the bottom right.
6. On this "Set permissions" tab, we can define the access levels for this new set of users. Figure 3.7 shows three possible answers; choose one.
   • To organize users with comparable permissions, we may use the "Add users to group" feature. With IAM, one may get a rundown of all the groups linked with a profile, in addition to the rules that pertain to each one.
   • Permissions for current users may be copied: A user's permissions are transferred from an existing user. By selecting this option, new users will be assigned the same groups, managed policies, embedded inline rules, and permissions as the original user. The account's users are shown in IAM. Find the one whose access levels correspond most closely to those needed by the new users.
   • Select "Incorporating the current policies" to get a breakdown of which policies are administered by AWS and which are set by the account's owner. Select the policies that will be imposed on the new users. After you have finished establishing the policy, you may close that tab and go back to the one you were working on before to apply it to the user's account. Trying to attach all standards to a group and then adding individuals to the appropriate group is best practice, according to experts.
7. Set a permission limit: It is up to admin to decide how restrictive they want to be with access rights. This is more advanced in terms of its functionality.

FIGURE 3.7   Setting permission.

8. Use a permissions boundary by clicking the link labeled "Set permissions boundary." IAM provides authorization for accessing account-related AWS- and customer-managed policies. Users may also start the permissions barrier selection process all over again by launching a new tab in the browser and choosing the policy that best fits their needs.

9. Next: "Tags" is the option to choose.

10. Key–value pairs (tags) are optional and may be used to offer extra information to the user.

11. Select "Next": Go through all of the prior choices. Once everything has been completed and you are ready to go, choose "Create user." Figure 3.8 depicts this.

12. There is a "Show" option next to each credential and secret access key the user may choose to show in the user list. Select "Download.csv" to get the URLs for the access keys' download locations and then save the file securely. In Figure 3.9, we can see this in action.

FIGURE 3.8   Reviewing and creating the user.

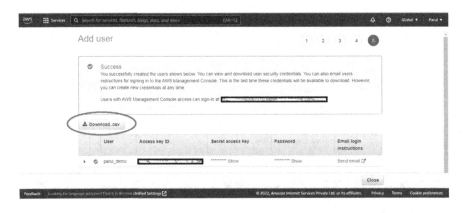

FIGURE 3.9   Access key and secret key details.

FIGURE 3.10   Successful creation of user.

13. Customers will not be able to get or download the secret access keys from the AWS API unless they are provided with the information requested below. Make a note of the user's newly generated access key ID as well as their secret access key and then use them to log in. After you have finished with this procedure, you will no longer have access to this key.

14. Everyone needs their own special set of credentials to enter the system. On the last screen, you may send an email to everyone by clicking the "Send email" button next to their name. In Figure 3.10, we can see a list of all the new users that have been added.

3.6   IAM ROLES

By using IAM roles, a user is able to bestow certain permissions on a collection of identities that are stored inside their account. An IAM role is an AWS identity that has associated authorization rules which determine what activities that identity can and cannot perform inside AWS. An IAM role is quite similar to an IAM user in this regard. On the other hand, a job is not intended to be permanently associated with a particular person; rather, it is intended to be filled by anyone who needs it at any given time. In addition, a task does not have any permanent credentials, such as a password or a set of keys, that must be used in order to access it. Users, on the other hand, are provided with a distinct set of temporary security credentials to utilize for the duration of the role session.

Through the use of roles, it is possible to provide access to AWS resources to individuals or programs who normally wouldn't have it. It is feasible, for example, to provide users with rights in an AWS account that go above and beyond those that they are ordinarily provided with, or to provide users with access in one AWS account with permissions in another AWS account. Alternatively, it might be desirable to provide permission for a mobile app to access AWS resources without mandating that the app include AWS access credentials in order to fulfill the permission request. It is possible that it will be essential to provide access to AWS resources to users whose

credentials have already been created in another location, such as a company directory. We also have the option of granting access to the account to other parties so that
they can do audits on the available resources.

3.7   CREATION OF IAM ROLES

The following steps must be followed to create an IAM role:

1. Figure 3.11 depicts the first step, which is to click the "Role" button, followed by "Create role."
2. As shown in Figure 3.12, we will be creating an AWS service role by choosing the "Trusted entity." We've chosen a role for an EC2 instance.
3. After this, the generated role's necessary permissions may be added. For
   the purpose of clarity, we're just allowing read access in this demo, and
   therefore we choose "IAMReadOnlyAccesss." Figure 3.13 shows this.
4. Now comes the phase in which we will be identifying things, going through
   them, and creating them. It contains the JSON document that we provided
   the role with to authorize its access. Figure 3.14 illustrates this point.
5. On the screen that follows, we can see that a role with the name "DemoRole"
   is being created. Figure 3.15 illustrates this point.

3.8   SAFEGUARDING THE ROOT ACCOUNT

There are different ways to safeguard the root account. They are listed below.

Password policy: The IAM password policy does not apply to the root password
or access keys for an AWS account. When the password for an IAM user has been
expired for a certain amount of time, that person will no longer be able to log in to
the AWS Management Console; however, they will still be able to utilize any access

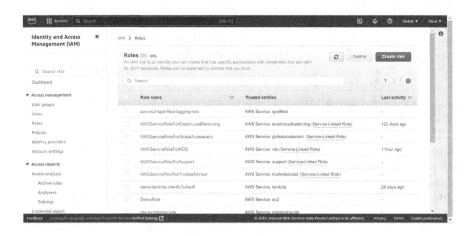

FIGURE 3.11   Beginning creation of role.

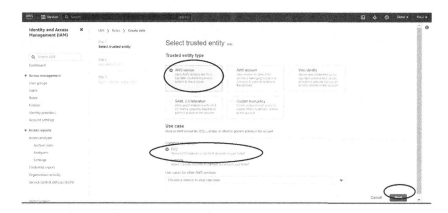

FIGURE 3.12   ASW service selection.

FIGURE 3.13   Adding permissions.

FIGURE 3.14   Details of the role to be created.

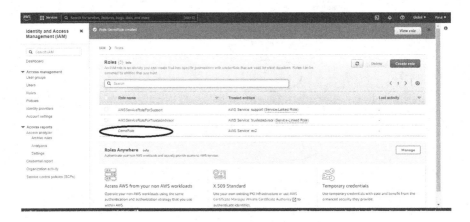

FIGURE 3.15   Successful creation of IAM role.

FIGURE 3.16   Password policy in AWS account.

keys that they have. After users have established or updated a password policy, the majority of the settings for the password policy come into effect the next time that users change their passwords. On the other hand, some choices have an immediate impact. Figure 3.16 shows the password policy in existing implementation.

When users next change their passwords, the new minimum password length as well as the character types that are required will take effect. It is not necessary to alter previously used passwords, even if such passwords do not adhere to the new password policy.

When a time limit for a password is set, that limit is immediately put into effect once it has been set. Let's assume we've selected a password expiration date of three months (90 days) from now. Every user of the Identity Access Management system whose existing password is more than 90 days old will be compelled to update it. When those individuals next log in, they will be required to choose a new password. Changing the existing password is depicted in Figure 3.17.

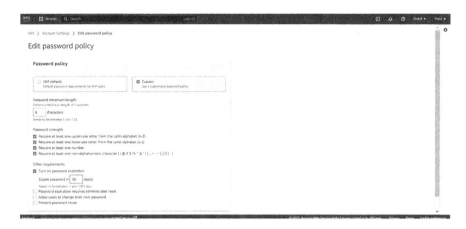

FIGURE 3.17 Changing the password policy.

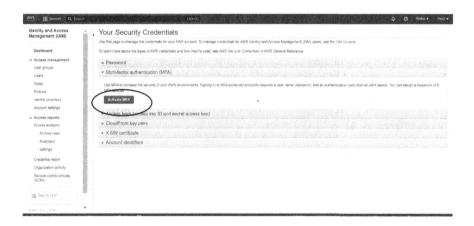

FIGURE 3.18 Activating MFA.

Virtual MFA device: This is software that may be used on any screen to simulate the appearance of a genuine thing. To be more specific, the device generates a six-digit random number using a time-synchronized one-time password. The method for logging in requires the user to go to a different page, where they will be asked to submit a valid device code. This step is necessary for the procedure. When multi-factor authentication is used, it is necessary for each user to have their own, separate authentication token. Figure 3.18 illustrates the page that must be visited in order to enable multi-factor authentication. It is not possible to validate a user's identity using a virtual MFA device that belongs to someone else. Because it may run on unprotected mobile devices, virtual MFA may not be as secure as FIDO2 or hardware MFA. This is because FIDO2 was designed to work only on computers. Customers are required to use a virtual multi-factor authentication device in the interim period between the approval of their hardware purchases and the delivery of their equipment. Figure 3.18 illustrates this.

FIDO security key: This is a peripheral that may be attached to a computer by means of a USB port on that computer. The FIDO Alliance is responsible for the maintenance of the open authentication standard known as FIDO2. Users who have activated FIDO2 security keys input their credentials and then touch their device to verify them rather than entering a code. This replaces the need for users to remember and enter a code.

Hardware MFA device: This is a piece of hardware that generates a numeric code consisting of six digits by using a time-synchronized one-time password as its method of operation. It is necessary for the user to submit a valid device code while they are signing in. If a user has more than one MFA device, each of those devices must be completely unique to the user. In order to get access, users are required to input a code that was created on their own device.

3.9   CONCLUSION

This chapter on AWS Identity and Access Management should have provided readers with a basic grounding in AWS security. AWS gives customers a wide variety of options for remote computing in addition to its security-related offerings. It has demonstrated in depth how to create an IAM user, an IAM role, and a set of policies. To keep an AWS account and customers secure while they're using the service, IAM policies are needed. IAM will handle the situation when several people use the same account. As more and more companies use the AWS cloud, there will be a strong need for qualified professionals who have an in-depth grasp of the principles and services offered by AWS.

4 EC2 Instances, Auto Scaling, and Load Balancing in AWS

4.1 INTRODUCTION

In recent years, the use of virtualization technology has become increasingly prevalent in the field of cloud computing. One of the leading providers of cloud services, AWS, offers a variety of options for virtualization through its Elastic Compute Cloud (EC2) service. In this chapter, we explore the different pricing options and EC2 instance types available in AWS, as well as the elastic load balancer and Auto Scaling features. These tools provide users with a flexible and scalable infrastructure that can meet the demands of their applications. In this section, we will dive deeper into the launching of an EC2 instance, a fundamental step in getting started with AWS. By the end of this chapter, users will have a solid understanding of the virtualization options available in AWS and how to leverage them to build a reliable and scalable cloud infrastructure.

EC2 is one of the core services of AWS that provides scalable computing resources in the cloud. It allows users to create virtual machines (instances) in the cloud with various operating systems and configurations. With EC2, users have complete control over the computing resources, such as CPU, memory, and storage. [90] EC2 also provides various instance types optimized for different use cases, such as general-purpose computing, high-performance computing, memory-intensive workloads, and storage-optimized applications.

One of the significant benefits of using EC2 is its elasticity, which allows users to scale computing resources up or down according to demand. This means that users can easily add or remove instances based on traffic or usage patterns. Auto Scaling is a powerful feature of EC2 that enables users to automatically adjust the number of instances in response to changes in demand. Auto Scaling groups allow users to define policies that specify how instances should be scaled based on criteria such as CPU usage, network traffic, or other custom metrics.

Load balancing is another important feature of AWS that helps distribute incoming traffic across multiple instances to improve performance and availability. Elastic Load Balancing (ELB) is a service that provides load balancing for EC2 instances. ELB has three types of load balancers: Application Load Balancer (ALB), Network Load Balancer (NLB), and Classic Load Balancer (CLB). ALB is optimized for HTTP and HTTPS traffic, NLB is designed for Transmission Control Protocol (TCP) and UDP traffic, and CLB is a legacy load balancer that supports both HTTP and TCP traffic.

DOI: 10.1201/9781003406136-4

49

4.2 EC2 INSTANCES

Amazon EC2 is a service inside the AWS cloud that provides elastic computing resources. Users will not have to make any upfront hardware expenditures with Amazon EC2, enabling businesses to bring their products to market faster. With Amazon EC2, a huge number of virtual servers, or just one, may be easily established, protected, networked, and managed. [34, 97, 93] Users of Amazon EC2 may simply react to fluctuating demand without fear of losing prospective clients.

4.2.1 CHARACTERISTICS OF AMAZON EC2

The following are some of the features of using Amazon EC2:

- Instances are a kind of virtual computerized environment.
- Amazon Machine Images (AMIs) are instance templates that come preconfigured with all the software and data that the server will need (including the OS and other software).
- Instance types are the various combinations of processing power, storage space, and network bandwidth that may be assigned to the instances.
- With key pairs, login information for the instances can be safeguarded (AWS stores the public key, and the user stores the private key in a secure place).
- Instance store volumes are used to store data that will be erased when the instance is stopped, hibernated, or terminated.
- Using Amazon Elastic Block Store (Amazon EBS), one may create volumes of persistent storage to keep data safe.
- There are many locations where the resources may be hosted or "Regions" and "Availability Zones" where resources such as instances and Amazon EBS volumes can be stored.
- With security groups, one may set the protocols, ports, and network address ranges that can connect the instances.
- Elastic Internet Protocol (IP) addresses, or static IPv4 addresses, are used in cloud computing to provide for more flexibility.
- Tags are a kind of metadata that may be created and applied to the resources in Amazon EC2.
- A virtual private cloud (VPC) is a network inside the Amazon cloud that is separated conceptually from the public cloud but may be connected to an external network if necessary.

Amazon EC2 provides users with access to various types of instances, each of which was developed with a specific goal in mind. There is the ability to modify the instance type to meet the requirements of the applications by choosing from a variety of configurations for the central processing unit (CPU), memory, storage, and networking. Each instance type gives customers a selection of instance sizes from which to pick. [94] This makes it possible to scale the resources to match the requirements of the task they want to accomplish.

4.2.2 TYPES OF INSTANCES

EC2 instances can be categorized into the following types. Figure 4.1 shows the same in detail.

- General purpose:
    Owing to their complete sets of compute, memory, and networking capabilities, general-purpose instances are well suited to a diverse variety of applications. This makes them very versatile. Web servers and code repositories are the applications that profit the most from these instances since they use these resources in proportionate amounts.
- Compute optimized:
    Compute-optimized instances are ideal for programs that need a lot of computing power and would benefit from having powerful processors. The instances in this family work brilliantly for tasks involving batch processing, video transcoding, high-speed web servers, high-performance computing (HPC), scientific modeling, dedicated gaming servers and ad server engines, machine learning inference, and other applications that require extensive computational work.
- Memory optimized:
    Instances with memory optimization are designed to speed up the processing of big datasets in memory-intensive applications.

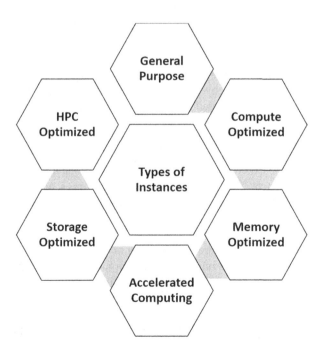

FIGURE 4.1   Types of instances.

- Accelerated computing:
    Hardware accelerators, also known as co-processors, are used in acceler-
    ated computing instances in order to facilitate the acceleration of activities
    such as the calculation of floating-point numbers, the processing of images,
    and the matching of data patterns.
- Storage optimized:
    Applications that need high-throughput, sequential read and write access
    to very large datasets on local storage are the target audience for storage-
    optimized instances. They are built with the purpose of delivering tens of
    thousands of low-latency, random I/O operations per second to applications.
- HPC optimized:
    AWS offers high-performance computing instances that are optimized
    to give the best cost performance when running large-scale HPC applica-
    tions. These instances were built expressly for this purpose. Large, complex
    simulations as well as deep learning workloads are excellent examples of the
    kinds of applications that may potentially make use of the high-performance
    CPUs that are available in HPC instances.

4.2.3   EC2 PRICING MODELS

Amazon EC2 provides users with access to cloud computing capabilities that are
both secure and scalable. Users have access to a variety of operating systems and
combinations of resources, such as RAM, CPU, and storage, from which they may
choose depending on the requirements of the application they are developing. When
users take advantage of Amazon EC2, it takes just a few minutes at most to acquire
capacity and set it up. It is possible to utilize just one, hundreds, or even thousands
of distinct server instances at the same time. [95] The cost of using Amazon Elastic
Compute Cloud is determined by a variety of parameters, including the operating
system(s), the number of scheduled server hours, the pricing scheme, the instance
type, and the total number of instances.

Users only need to pay for the resources they actually use when pricing is done
on a per-second basis. Customers benefit from this EC2 per-second payment model
since it eliminates the expense of any minutes or seconds that are unused.

On-Demand Instances, Reserved Instances, Spot Instances, and Dedicated Hosts
are the four distinct pricing models that are available for use with Amazon EC2
instances.

- On-Demand Instances: There is no need for an upfront payment when using
    this method. Instead, customers will be charged for computing capability
    on a per-hour or per-second basis (just for Linux instances) based on the
    instances that they choose. Because of flexible scaling, businesses only
    have to pay for the instances that they actually utilize, regardless of how
    many of them they employ. This configuration is useful for prototyping
    apps with transitory or variable usage patterns and testing such applications.

On-Demand Instances are an option that should be considered by those who are interested in making use of EC2 Instances at a low cost and with a great degree of flexibility, all without having to make any significant initial expenditures or sign up to extended service contracts. Users have the ability to increase or decrease their processing capacity according to the requirements of the apps they use.

- Reserved Instances: If the price of an Amazon EC2 Reserved Instance is compared with the price of an On-Demand Instance, as much as 75 percent of the difference could be saved. It is also possible to reserve available capacity when it is used in a certain Availability Zone. This is made possible by the fact that it is used in that zone. Compared to On-Demand Instances, the cost reductions that are available via Reserved Instances may be more than sufficient for applications that have workloads that are predictable. The capacity to forecast use patterns ensures access to computing resources whenever they are required. Customers have the option of committing to using EC2 for either one or three years, which will result in considerable reductions in the total costs of their computing operations. Because of the high degree of flexibility in its pricing model, Amazon EC2 may benefit from it being used at a reduced cost.

- Spot Instances: Spot Instances on Amazon Elastic Compute Cloud are resources in the AWS cloud that are not being used. The price of an identical On-Demand Instance may be reduced by up to 90 percent if a Spot Instance is purchased instead. The cost of Amazon EC2 Spot Instances is subject to regular changes in response to the market dynamics of fluctuating supply and demand. Depending on the requirements, users may be charged by the hour or even by the second (although this only applies to Linux instances). Customers who have pressing computing needs for large-scale dynamic workloads and applications with changeable start and completion times may find that using Spot Instances on Amazon EC2 is an excellent choice. Spot Instances are at their best when they are put to use for highly viable apps that need just a small amount of computing power and that also have flexible start and shutdown times.

- Dedicated Host: By using a Dedicated Host, users have the opportunity to acquire some EC2 hardware that may be used only for their own needs. By leveraging their existing server-bound software licenses for things such as Windows Server, SQL server, and so on with dedicated hosts, businesses may be able to save money. Moreover, by using dedicated hosts, it will be much simpler for users to satisfy compliance requirements. Customers that go with the Dedicated Hosts option will be charged the On-Demand pricing for each hour that their host is actually put to use. This service does not support billing on a per-second basis and only supports billing on an hourly basis. A Dedicated Host in EC2 is a physical server that is configured specifically for the needs of a single user.

Figure 4.2 shows different pricing models available for EC2 Instances.

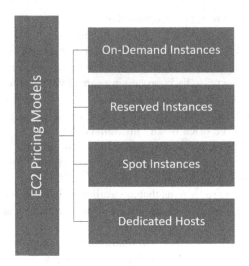

FIGURE 4.2   Different pricing models in EC2 instances.

4.3   ELASTIC LOAD BALANCER (ELB)

Elastic Load Balancing allows for the possibility of incoming traffic being automatically redistributed to a variety of EC2 instances, containers, or IP addresses located inside one or more Availability Zones. [91] It monitors the states of the targets that users have registered with it and only sends traffic in their direction if it determines that they are ready to receive it. When we make use of Elastic Load Balancing, the resources of the load balancer will increase or decrease automatically in response to the number of requests that are sent to it.

4.3.1   ADVANTAGES OF A LOAD BALANCER

- A piece of software known as a load balancer assists in distributing work among a number of servers or other types of computer resources. There is a possibility that the deployment of a load balancer will increase the reliability and fault tolerance of the applications.
- One may quickly adjust the amount of computing resources that are allocated by a load balancer to meet the changing needs of the applications without disrupting service to those applications.
- It is possible to configure the load balancer with health checks so that it will only serve requests to computing resources that are functioning. The load balancer can handle encryption and decryption, allowing the computer resources to concentrate on what they are good at.

4.3.2   TYPES OF LOAD BALANCER

With Elastic Load Balancing, the incoming traffic to any EC2 instances, containers, or IP addresses located in one or more Availability Zones is automatically spread

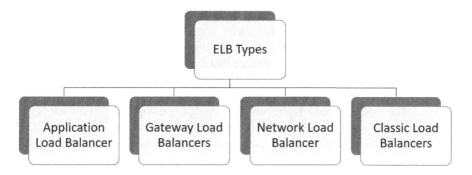

FIGURE 4.3   Types of elastic load balancer.

over all of those zones. It monitors the status of the registered targets and only sends traffic in their direction if those targets are online and able to process it. If we're using Elastic Load Balancing, the load balancer may expand or contract in size according to the number of requests that are coming in. [91, 92] Scalability for the vast majority of workloads is already included in the solution. It's important to note that Elastic Load Balancing is compatible with more than one variety of load balancers, including Application Load Balancers, Network Load Balancers, Gateway Load Balancers, and Classic Load Balancers. Figure 4.3 shows the various types of load balancers in AWS.

- Application Load Balancer:

An Application Load Balancer is responsible for distributing network traffic across servers and is located at Layer 7 of the Open Systems Interconnection (OSI) model, which is where applications are maintained. Upon receipt of a request from the load balancer, it will first sort the listener rules in order of priority to determine which rule should be implemented, and then it will choose a target from the target group in order to carry out the action that the rule specifies. It may be possible to set up listener rules to route requests to certain recipients, but this will depend on the nature of the communications that the application offers. Even if a single target is registered with several target groups, the routing for each group is managed independently of the others. The technique that is utilized while routing traffic may have its parameters changed according to the target group. While round-robin is the strategy that will be used by default, users have the option of switching to the routing method that has the fewest requests that are still pending if they like.

There is the ability to quickly add or remove targets from the load balancer without causing any disruptions to the service in order to accommodate shifting load needs. Elastic Load Balancing offers the ability to automatically expand or reduce the size of the load balancer in response to changes in the amount of traffic that the application receives over time. By the use of Elastic Load Balancing, a significant number of workloads are capable of being automatically scaled.

It is possible to set up health checks that will monitor the state of the registered targets in order to ensure that the load balancer will only send requests to targets that are fully functional.

- Network Load Balancer:

The Open Systems Interconnection design is composed of four levels, and a Network Load Balancer is located and operates inside the fourth layer. Even with hundreds of thousands of requests per second, there will be no discernible slowdown. The load balancer will choose a single target from the pool of available targets whenever it receives a connection request for an incoming connection. This will be done according to the default rule. It makes an attempt to set up a Transmission Control Protocol connection with the specified host using the listener port that has been defined.

When an Availability Zone has been declared active for a load balancer, Elastic Load Balancing will deploy a load balancer node to the zone. By default, only destinations located inside a load balancer node's own Availability Zone are offered for traffic distribution by that node. If cross-zone load balancing is turned on, each load balancer node will distribute traffic across all of the registered targets in each of the available Availability Zones.

A load balancer that has several Availability Zones can be utilized in order to increase the fault tolerance of the applications. To do this, the load balancer would need to be configured in such a way that each target group has at least one member in each Availability Zone. If the IP address for the appropriate subnet is removed from the Domain Name System (DNS) when one or more target groups in an Availability Zone do not have a healthy target, but the other load balancer nodes in the other Availability Zones are still able to route traffic, this provides a nice demonstration of this concept. If a client continues to use an IP address after the time to live (TTL) for that address has passed, the request will fail because the IP address has been removed from the DNS database.

A target for TCP traffic is selected by the load balancer on the basis of the protocol, IP address, port, IP address of the destination, and TCP sequence number. Client TCP connections may be distinguished from one another based on the one-of-a-kind source ports and sequence numbers they use, which enables flexible routing to a variety of destinations. TCP connections are only ever routed to a single destination, no matter how long the connection lasts.

The load balancer decides which node will be the destination for UDP traffic based on the protocol, the IP address of the sending node, the source port, the IP address of the receiving node, and the port on the receiving node. As a UDP flow's origin and destination are the same place, the flow will always be directed toward the same endpoint. Since the source IP address and port number of each UDP flow are different from one another, it is possible to route each flow to a particular location.

When activating an Availability Zone with Elastic Load Balancing, a new network interface will be generated for use with that Availability Zone. In order to get a persistent IP address, each load balancer node in the Availability Zone makes use of this particular network interface. In the case of load balancers that are exposed to the internet, users have the option of allocating a single IP address from Elastic Load Balancing to each subnet.

The manner in which targets are registered differs according to the kind of target that was selected when the target group was established. A number of different items, including instance IDs, IP addresses, and Application Load Balancers, are examples of things that may be registered. The kind of target determines, as well, whether or not the client's IP address is kept. There are more specifics about the protection of clients' intellectual property.

The load balancer allows targets to be simply added or removed whenever business needs call for it, and this can be done without the requests to the application being disrupted in any way. With Elastic Load Balancing, we are able to modify the size of the load balancer in reaction to changes in the amount of traffic that is being sent to the application. In the event that the workload is normal, Elastic Load Balancing will automatically scale to accommodate the additional demand. After the load balancer's health checks have been configured, it will only send requests to destinations that are currently functioning.

- Gateway Load Balancers:

Gateway Load Balancers make it easy to set up, scale, and regulate the operation of numerous different kinds of virtual appliances, such as firewalls, Intrusion Detection System (IDS)/Intrusion Prevention System (IPS), and IPS/IDS/IPS. Gateway Load Balancers also make it possible to control the operation of physical appliances. Both traffic distribution and dynamic scaling of the virtual appliances to meet peak loads are features. Traffic distribution allows for a transparent network gateway, which is a single point of entrance and departure for all traffic.

To provide more clarity, the Gateway Load Balancer plays a role in the OSI paradigm at the level of the network layer. It checks any open ports for incoming IP packets and then sends them on to the specified group after monitoring those ports. It does this by using either the 5-tuple (for TCP/UDP flows) or the 3-tuple (for non-TCP/UDP flows) to ensure that flows remain attached to a single device.

Gateway Load Balancers use Gateway Load Balancer endpoints to provide the secure exchange of traffic across VPC boundaries. Users can use a Gateway Load Balancer endpoint, which is a virtual private cloud endpoint, to make a private connection between the virtual appliances of their service provider and the application servers of the service consumers. In addition to the other virtual appliances, a Gateway Load Balancer is installed in the private cloud that is being used. It is essential when using a Gateway Load Balancer that we link each of the virtual appliances with a particular user or group.

Routing tables are responsible for directing traffic to and from the exit point of a Gateway Load Balancer. To interact with the Gateway Load Balancer endpoint in the service provider VPC, the endpoint in the service consumer VPC must first connect with the Gateway Load Balancer endpoint in the service provider VPC. It is necessary to configure the application servers and the Gateway Load Balancer endpoint on distinct networks. With this configuration, the Gateway Load Balancer has the potential to be configured as the next hop for the routing table of the application subnet.

- Classic Load Balancers:

With a load balancer, incoming application traffic is distributed over a large number of Amazon EC2 instances that are situated in a variety of Availability Zones. Because of this, the error tolerance of the applications will significantly increase. When Elastic Load Balancing detects that one of the instances is down with an issue, it will reroute all of the traffic to the instances that are still operating normally.

A load balancer performs the function of a central hub via which all clients are able to communicate with the system. The number of users who are able to use the app has just increased. If the needs of the application change, the load balancer will make it possible for users to add or remove instances without the service being disrupted in any way. With Elastic Load Balancing, the load balancer may expand or contract in response to changes in the amount of work being done by the application. Elastic Load Balancing gives users the ability to autonomously scale the majority of their workloads.

A listener is a kind of service that is used to monitor a particular port and protocol for connection requests arriving from clients. These requests are then routed to one or more registered instances of the service. A load balancer may have only one listener or numerous listeners all working together.

If we add health checks to check on the state of the instances, the load balancer may be configured to only serve requests to those that are actively executing.

4.4   AUTO SCALING GROUPS

By using Amazon EC2 Auto Scaling, one can guarantee that the application will always have sufficient Amazon EC2 instances to meet the requirements of the current demand. We are responsible for creating Auto Scaling groups, which are groupings of EC2 instances. Amazon EC2 Auto Scaling will never let the group size drop below the threshold set for the minimum number of instances that may be contained in an Auto Scaling group. This minimum number of instances can be configured for each Auto Scaling group individually. [93, 94] Users have the ability, when using Amazon EC2 Auto Scaling, to specify the maximum number of instances that should be used for each group, and Amazon will never expand the size of the group above that specified number. Amazon EC2 Auto Scaling will always have the group's instances match the capacity set, regardless of whether this is done at the initial establishment of the group or at a later time. One may set the scaling parameters that will be used by Amazon EC2 Auto Scaling, and depending on those parameters, it may start and stop instances automatically in response to spikes and dips in application utilization.

For example, the size of an Auto Scaling group may range from one to four instances, depending on how big the group has to be. The scaling rules that are designed may increase or decrease the number of instances as required, according to the criteria specified, as long as they are contained within the boundaries of the minimum and maximum number of instances that have been defined.

4.4.1 BENEFITS OF AUTO SCALING GROUPS

Amazon Elastic Compute Cloud Auto Scaling is used as part of the application's overall architecture to make the most of the AWS cloud. [96, 98] This is one way to get the most out of using the AWS cloud. The following benefits are available to users when Amazon EC2 Auto Scaling is integrated into any application:

- Improved resistance to the effects of failure: In the event that Amazon EC2 Auto Scaling concludes that a specific instance is not functioning properly, it will terminate the instance and begin a new one in its place. With Amazon EC2, automatic scaling may be configured to span several Availability Zones. In the event that it is necessary to do so, Amazon EC2 Auto Scaling may deploy new instances to a different Availability Zone.
- More easily accessible to the public: It is possible to ensure that the application is able to handle the demand at any given moment by using Amazon EC2 Auto Scaling.
- Better budgeting: The size of the instance can be automatically scaled up or reduced using Amazon EC2 Auto Scaling, depending on the strain that is being placed on the system. Creating Amazon EC2 instances just when they are needed, and shutting them down when they are not, helps businesses save money since they only have to pay for the instances they actually use.

4.5 LAUNCHING AN EC2 INSTANCE

To begin installing an EC2 instance, we must first log in to our Amazon account and then follow the procedures below:

1. Click "EC2" under "All services" to see the EC2 instance dashboard, then click "Launch instance" from there. Figure 4.4 shows how to do this.
2. To begin, we need to give this instance a name. Here, we're using the label "First EC2" to describe the instance. More labels may be added if desired. We can refer to Figure 4.5 to illustrate our point.

FIGURE 4.4 Beginning of launching an EC2 instance.

FIGURE 4.5 Naming the instance.

3. Selecting the OS and Application Images is the next step. There is a selection menu where we can see all of the possibilities. As an AMI, we've decided on Amazon's Linux-2. Thorough descriptions of all the available options are provided here. Figure 4.6 illustrates the process in action inside an AWS environment.

4. The next step is to choose the "Instance type." The settings for the active instance are shown here. The listing will be shown in our chosen region only if it is currently accessible there. Instances of many kinds may be found here. For the sake of this demonstration, we have chosen t2.micro since they are part of the plan's free tier. If we click the "Compare instance" button next to the drop-down list, as in Figure 4.7, we can use it to see how one instance compares to another. The 370 choices in the list are clearly visible.

FIGURE 4.6   Selecting AMI for the instance.

FIGURE 4.7   Selecting instance type.

5. The next step in launching an EC2 instance should be the generation of a key pair. In this instance, the private and public key pair will be encrypted using Rivest–Shamir–Adleman algorithm (RSA). The system we're utilizing will determine the private key file format we use. We must choose either Mac OS X or a Windows version later than Windows 10. We require the .ppk file format for Windows 7 and 8, and the .pem file format is not suitable. As may be seen in Figure 4.8, we settled on the .ppk extension.

6. The next phase of launching this EC2 instance will include configuring the network. An instance needs a security group to regulate incoming and outgoing connections. Then, a choice must be made from the menu on the current page. In addition, we must enable HTTP connections from the internet. Even the Secure Shell (SSH) traffic may be tailored to user specifications. We've set up our system such that any IP address may send and receive data. In the real world, this can be observed in detail in Figure 4.9.

FIGURE 4.8 Key pair generation.

FIGURE 4.9 Network configuration for the instance.

7. The next step is setting up the volume for storage. In this section, we'll choose the EBS (Elastic Block Storage) volume that will be associated with the instance. Choose the single 8 GB gp2 root drive depicted in Figure 4.10.
8. At this stage, we'll configure the user information in the advanced settings. The first command to be run when starting an instance is user data. At the start of our EC2 instance, we have placed our code here.

We must see whether our chosen instance's summary checks out. The last step is a verification of our instance data. We double-checked, and it is indeed part of the basic package for the free account. Thus, we won't have to pay anything to use this EC2 instance. We just hit "Launch instance" when we're ready to start using it.

FIGURE 4.10 EBS volume selection.

FIGURE 4.11 Successful launching of EC2 instance.

9. The newly formed instance will have two IP addresses: a public one that can be accessed from anywhere on the internet, and a private one that can be used to pinpoint its exact location inside Amazon. When the instance is stopped and restarted after a period of time, the public IP address changes. Figure 4.11 displays this phenomenon. In the event that the instance is restarted, the private IP address will stay unchanged, but the public IP address will be reset.

4.6 CONCLUSION

Virtualization in AWS was the topic of discussion in this chapter. This discussion covered the various price options that are accessible under EC2 instances. In this chapter, we have gone through the various EC2 instance types. The concept of the elastic load balancer as well as its many forms have been covered. The AWS infrastructure makes extensive use of Auto Scaling. There is an extensive discussion on the function of Auto Scaling groups. This chapter has also implemented the launching of an EC2 instance in an AWS account.

5 Storage in S3 and Database in AWS

5.1 INTRODUCTION

As more organizations migrate to cloud computing, the need for dependable and scalable storage solutions has grown. AWS offers a comprehensive set of storage choices to fulfill the demands of its customers. AWS provides a solution for any use case, from basic object storage to high-performance block storage.

Amazon Simple Storage Service (S3) is one of AWS's core storage services. S3 is a highly scalable object storage service with limitless storage space for any sort of data. S3 is useful for a wide range of applications, including data lakes, backup and recovery, and content delivery. S3 also offers many storage classes, including Standard, Infrequent Access, and Glacier, which allows customers to manage their storage costs depending on data use patterns.

AWS offers both relational and non-relational databases, each designed to meet specific application requirements. Amazon Relational Database Service (RDS) is a fully managed relational database service that supports popular database engines such as MySQL, PostgreSQL, Oracle, and SQL Server. RDS is designed to provide high availability, durability, and security, with automated backups, software patching, and scalable storage options.

5.2 AMAZON S3

Amazon Simple Storage Service is a component of AWS that gives customers the ability to store and retrieve anything on a vast scale and to access their data from anywhere in the world. Images, videos, documents, and even log files may be saved securely on S3, in addition to a great deal of other data types.

When information is stored using S3, this is done in the form of "objects," which are collections of data that each have their own unique key, value, and metadata. Buckets, which are S3's highest-level containers, are used for the purpose of organizing and storing things. [99] A bucket may be accessed from any location on the planet using the AWS Management Console, the AWS Command Line Interface (CLI), or the AWS Software Development Kits (SDKs). Each bucket has a name that is unique throughout the whole world. S3 has a number of storage levels accessible to its users, some of which are Standard, Infrequent Access (IA), and Glacier. We can see the details in the following sections and in Figure 5.1.

Amazon S3 provides various storage classes that cater to different data access patterns and offer different levels of durability, availability, and cost. [102] The storage classes available in S3 are:

DOI: 10.1201/9781003406136-5

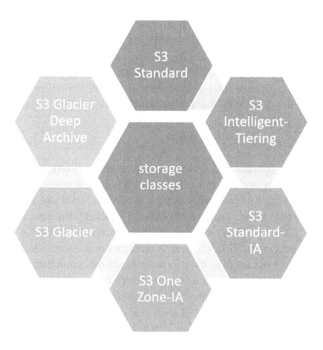

FIGURE 5.1 Storage classes in Amazon S3.

- S3 Standard: S3 Standard is intended for data that is regularly accessed and needs excellent durability, availability, and performance. Data saved in S3 Standard is duplicated across several Availability Zones (AZs) within a region, delivering durability and availability of 99.999999999 percent (11 nines).
- S3 Intelligent-Tiering: With S3 Intelligent-Tiering, data is automatically relocated to the lowest-priced access tier when use patterns change. Data is shifted between the more often accessed "hot" layer and the less frequently accessed "cold" tier based on machine learning analysis of object access patterns. The reliability and accessibility of this storage tier are 99.999999999 percent and 99.9 percent, respectively.
- S3 Standard-Infrequent Access (S3 Standard-IA): S3 Standard-IA is intended for seldom-accessed data that has to be accessible quickly. This storage tier is cheaper than S3 Standard while still offering the same reliability and accessibility. Data may be moved to S3 Glacier Deep Archive for long-term storage with the use of lifecycle rules, which are supported by S3 Standard-IA.
- S3 One Zone-Infrequent Access (S3 One Zone-IA): Data in S3 One Zone-IA is stored in a single AZ as opposed to being distributed over many AZs, as in S3 Standard-IA. Data that is easily reproduced or is not mission-critical is a good fit for this storage tier, which boasts an availability of 99.5 percent.

- S3 Glacier and S3 Glacier Deep Archive: Both S3 Glacier and S3 Glacier Deep Archive are intended for storing inaccessible data indefinitely. The retrieval of data stored in S3 Glacier may take minutes to hours, whereas retrieval of data stored in S3 Glacier Deep Archive might take up to 12 hours. Both types of storage have a durability of 99.999999999 percent, making them perfect for meeting legal, regulatory, and compliance standards.

5.2.1 S3 BUCKET

Images, movies, documents, and database backups are just some of the file types that may be stored in S3's limitless space. The service is a great option for storing crucial data and guaranteeing its availability since it is reliable, safe, and scalable.

The primary data storage unit in S3 is called a "bucket." Buckets, a kind of named object storage, allow users to store an unlimited amount of data of any sort. The bucket name is used in the S3 URL; thus, it must be unique across all AWS accounts. Data stored in an S3 bucket may have its access controls configured on a per-bucket basis. [100] A bucket's permissions may be restricted to certain AWS accounts or IAM users, or they can be made universally available. When versioning is turned on, the bucket may store many versions of the same object.

S3 buckets may be accessed using a number of methods, including the AWS Management Console, the CLI, SDKs, and application programming interfaces (APIs). [102] S3 also facilitates the development of reliable and scalable software by allowing integration with other AWS services such as EC2, Lambda, and CloudFront.

5.2.2 S3 OBJECTS

The smallest unit of data storage in Amazon S3 is an object, which includes both content data and metadata. Documents, images, videos, audio files, and other media are all examples of object types.

Whenever we put anything into an S3 bucket, we need to give it a name—the object key. The object key serves as a means of subsequent retrieval. Additionally, key–value pairs may be used to attach metadata to objects in S3. Additional details about the item, such as its content type, creation date, or creator, may be provided by means of this metadata.

An S3 object's URL will always consist of the bucket's name and the object key. The S3 interface, SDKs, and APIs enable users to save, retrieve, and remove objects.

The items in the bucket may be managed and protected using S3's capabilities such as versioning, lifecycle rules, and object locking. As an example, versioning may be used to store different iterations of an object and safeguard against deletion or overwriting. [100] Objects may be automatically moved between storage classes or deleted after a certain amount of time because of lifecycle rules.

An object in Amazon S3 is made up of numerous components that make up the stored data and metadata. The following are the major components of an S3 object:

1. Object key: An object key is a one-of-a-kind identifier for an item inside a bucket. It may be any string of Unicode characters with a maximum length of 1,024 bytes.
2. Object data: The stuff saved in S3 is referred to as object data. It may be any sort of file up to five terabytes (TB) in size, such as a document, picture, video, or audio file.
3. Metadata: Object metadata is a collection of name–value pairs used to describe an item. It may comprise information such as the object's content type, creation date, update date, and author.
4. Version ID: If versioning is enabled for the S3 bucket, each item will be assigned a unique version ID. We may get past versions of the item using this ID.
5. Access control list (ACL): An ACL is used to control object access. Using the ACL, one may give or remove rights to AWS accounts, IAM users, or roles.
6. Object lock configuration: An object lock setting prevents an item from being removed or rewritten for a certain length of time.
7. Tags: Users may use tags to help identify and organize things in S3. Tags are key–value pairs that may be used to categorize and track objects.
8. Storage class: S3 offers numerous storage classes from which customers may choose the sort of storage that best meets their requirements. Each storage class has a distinct amount of durability, availability, and performance, as well as a varied cost.

Overall, these components work together to create S3 objects, a versatile and scalable method of storing and managing data in the cloud.

5.2.3 S3 VERSIONING

Amazon S3 allows us to store distinct iterations of the same file with distinct revisions within a single bucket. If we enable versioning for a bucket, S3 will save every iteration of every item eternally. A version ID is a persistent identifier for a single version of a releasable or erasable item. [102] The advantages of versioning can be seen in Figure 5.2. Versioning is useful for a few different reasons:

| Data protection | Compliance | Collaborative editing | Rollback |

FIGURE 5.2 Advantages of S3 versioning.

1. Data protection: Versioning protects against accidental deletion or modification of objects. Even if a user deletes or edits an item, it is always possible to revert back to the prior version.
2. Compliance: If it is required by law or regulation to keep all previous iterations of an object, versioning can enable this.
3. Collaborative editing: Collaborative editing is feasible owing to the versioning function. Each user may submit a new version of the item, and all versions will be saved.
4. Rollback: If the current version of an item is corrupted or includes defects, it is possible to revert to a prior version thanks to versioning.

Versioning may be easily enabled for a bucket. This can be achieved with the use of the AWS CLI, SDKs, or APIs. When versioning is enabled, a unique ID is assigned to each new addition to the bucket. The version ID of an object may be used to obtain or delete that version, and lifecycle rules can be set up to move objects to other storage classes or remove them after a certain amount of time has passed.

It's important to note that versioning can increase the cost of storing data in S3, as each version of an object counts as a separate object. [100] When it comes to applications that need data security, compliance, or collaborative editing, however, the advantages of versioning frequently exceed the added expense.

The act of moving data from one place to another inside a cloud computing system is referred to as data migration in the cloud. Moving data from on-premises storage to cloud storage, or from one cloud provider to another, may be part of this process.

5.3   DATA MIGRATION IN THE CLOUD

Data transfer in the cloud often entails numerous processes, which can be seen in Figure 5.3, including the following:

1. Planning: This includes identifying the data to be moved, defining the data's source and destination, and analyzing any possible risks or obstacles involved with the migration.
2. Preparation: This includes cleaning and arranging the data for migration and ensuring that it is in a format that can be readily transferred to the destination.
3. Execution: This entails physically moving data from the source to the destination, which may be accomplished via a number of means such as direct network transfer, physical data transfer, or a third-party tool.
4. Validation: This entails ensuring that the data has been correctly migrated and is available and usable in the new place.
5. Testing: The migrated data is tested to confirm that it is working properly and that there are no bugs or mistakes.

Some of the advantages of cloud data transfer include enhanced scalability, lower expenses, and better performance and dependability. However, there are certain

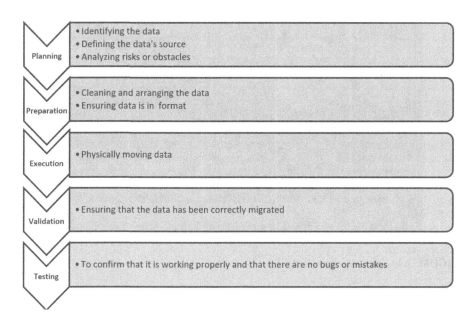

Planning
- Identifying the data
- Defining the data's source
- Analyzing risks or obstacles

Preparation
- Cleaning and arranging the data
- Ensuring data is in format

Execution
- Physically moving data

Validation
- Ensuring that the data has been correctly migrated

Testing
- To confirm that it is working properly and that there are no bugs or mistakes

FIGURE 5.3   Process of data migration in cloud.

possible difficulties and hazards involved with cloud data transfer, such as data loss, security threats, and compatibility problems. As a result, it is critical to properly plan and execute any cloud data transfer project to reduce these risks and ensure a successful end.

5.4   DATA MIGRATION IN AWS

Moving information from a local server or another cloud service into AWS cloud storage or other AWS services is known as a data migration. [101] Data migration in AWS can be seen in Figure 5.4.

To facilitate businesses' transition to the AWS cloud, AWS offers a number of data migration services, as follows:

5.4.1   AWS STORAGE GATEWAY

With AWS Storage Gateway, organizations can save data in the AWS cloud while still maintaining a copy on-premises for easy access. [102] File gateways, volume gateways, and tape gateways are all supported.

- File gateway: This sort of gateway allows companies to store and retrieve files in Amazon S3 as objects. This is beneficial for applications requiring low-latency data access, such as backups or media sharing. Network File System (NFS) and Server Message Block (SMB) are two file-based protocols that file gateways support.

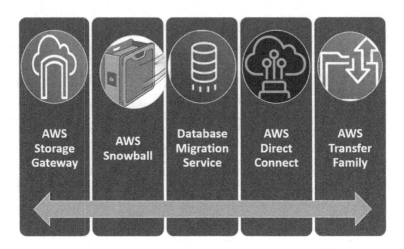

FIGURE 5.4   Data migration in AWS.

- Volume gateway: This gateway allows businesses to store data in Amazon S3 as Amazon Elastic Block Storage (EBS) snapshots. It gives cloud access to block storage, which is beneficial for applications that need low-latency data access, such as databases or virtual machines. iSCSI (Internet Small Computer System Interface) storage volumes are also supported by volume gateways.
- Tape gateway: This sort of gateway allows enterprises to store backup data as virtual tapes on Amazon S3. It connects backup software to a virtual tape library (VTL), which is beneficial for enterprises with a huge volume of backup data to transfer to the cloud.

5.4.2   AWS Snowball

The AWS Snowball solution is a physical data migration solution that enables businesses to transport enormous amounts of data to the AWS cloud using a physical device. The durable and tamper-resistant device known as the Snowball can be made available to businesses by AWS. After that, they may copy their data onto the device and then upload it to AWS for secure cloud storage. The AWS Snowball comes in two different sizes, 50 TB and 80 TB, and it may be used for data migration, disaster recovery, and data transport.

5.4.3   Database Migration Service

With the help of the AWS Database Migration Service, moving databases to the cloud is a breeze. It may be used to move databases from on-premises to the cloud, or from one cloud provider to another, and it supports both homogeneous and heterogeneous migrations. MySQL, PostgreSQL, Oracle, SQL Server, and more are just some of the databases it works with. Automatic schema conversion, continuous data replication, and low downtime are just some of the benefits of using the AWS Database Migration Service, which employs a replication technique to move data to the cloud.

5.4.4 AWS TRANSFER FAMILY

To safely move files between Amazon S3 and Amazon EFS, businesses may use AWS Transfer Family, a fully managed file transfer service. File Transfer Protocol (FTP), File Transfer Protocol Secure (FTPS), and Secure File Transfer Protocol (SFTP) are all supported. Organizations may control which users have access to the transfer service by virtue of the feature's compatibility with AWS IAM.

5.4.5 AWS DIRECT CONNECT

AWS Direct Connect is a private high-speed network connection that lets businesses link their on-premises data center with AWS. The network performance is more stable and consistent than a standard internet connection. In addition to facilitating data transfer, database replication, and hybrid cloud installations, AWS Direct Connect serves a wide range of other uses. It may be used to set up a dedicated network connection to one or more AWS services, and it offers connection speeds ranging from 50 Mbps to 10 Gbps.

5.5 PRICING IN DIFFERENT STORAGE CLASSES

AWS provides a number of storage tiers for its S3, with varying prices for each tier depending on how much emphasis is placed on performance, durability, and availability. Here are several types of storage:

- Amazon's default storage class, S3 Standard, is optimized for data that is accessed regularly. It's ideal for use in applications that need constant access to data because of its high levels of durability, availability, and performance. The cost of using S3 Standard depends on how much information needs transport, access, and storage.
- Data with irregular or unpredictable access patterns do well with S3 Intelligent-Tiering. Using machine learning, data may be dynamically shifted between high- and low-use tiers as usage patterns change. Automatic tiering is an extra cost for S3 Intelligent-Tiering, which is priced according to storage capacity, data transmission, and requests.
- S3 Standard-Infrequent Access is a storage tier created for infrequently used data that nonetheless has to be highly available and durable. It's just as fast as S3 Standard, but it costs more to retrieve data. There is a fee for retrieval in addition to the storage, transfer, and request costs associated with S3 Standard-Infrequent Access.
- S3 One Zone-Infrequent Access is intended for data that is viewed rarely and may be rebuilt in the event of deletion. In comparison with S3 Standard

and S3 Standard-Infrequent Access, cost is reduced, but just one AZ is used. Costs for S3 One Zone-Infrequent Access begin at US$0.01 per month and increase with the quantity of data stored, the number of transfers, and the number of queries made.

- With retrieval periods of minutes to hours, S3 Glacier is best suited for preserving data and keeping it safe for the long haul. The retrieval prices are greater than in other S3 storage classes, but the storage costs are the lowest. There are extra costs for retrieval and early deletion on top of the standard pricing for S3 Glacier, which is determined by the total quantity of data stored, the total number of data transfers, and the total number of queries.

With retrieval durations ranging from hours to days, S3 Glacier Deep Archive is best suited for long-term data preservation. The retrieval prices are the highest of all the S3 storage classes, while the storage costs are the lowest. The cost of Amazon's S3 Glacier Deep Archive service rises with the size of the data, the number of times it is accessed, and the number of times users delete it.

5.6 SECURITY AND ACCESS MANAGEMENT

To aid businesses in keeping their data safe, AWS offers a number of security and access control tools for Amazon S3. For example:

- Organizations may control which employees have access to their stored data thanks to Amazon S3's integration with AWS IAM. In order to control access to S3 resources, businesses may use IAM to set up and control IAM users, groups, and roles.
- Amazon S3 allows for end-to-end encryption of data while it is being sent and while it is stored. By default, data is encrypted while in transit; when it is at rest, encryption may be accomplished using either server-side encryption (SSE) or client-side encryption (CSE).
- Amazon S3 has an audit log feature that lets businesses keep track of who accessed what files in their S3 storage accounts. Amazon S3 is used to store access logs, while Amazon CloudWatch and Amazon Simple Notification Service (SNS) are used to send them to other AWS services.
- Amazon S3 has the potential to help users comply with a number of rules and regulations, including the Health Insurance Portability and Accountability Act (HIPAA).

5.7 DATABASES IN AWS

Managing databases may be difficult and time-consuming, and yet they are a crucial part of many contemporary systems. A variety of AWS-managed database services simplify cloud database deployment, management, and scalability. These services are built to accommodate several database engines and data models, in addition to being highly available, scalable, and secure. Amazon RDS, Amazon Aurora,

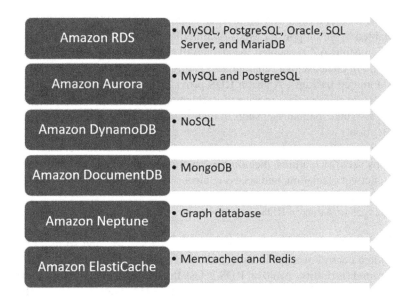

FIGURE 5.5   Databases in AWS.

Amazon DynamoDB, Amazon DocumentDB, Amazon Neptune, and Amazon ElastiCache are all examples of databases offered by AWS. [103] AWS takes care of the underlying infrastructure and administrative responsibilities, freeing up IT departments to concentrate on applications and data. Organizations may construct cloud-based data solutions that are scalable, versatile, and dependable with AWS database services. Figure 5.5 shows the databases supported in AWS.

5.7.1 Amazon RDS

Amazon Relational Database Service is a cloud-based, fully managed service that enables clients to set up, maintain, and expand relational databases. It works with not only popular options such as MySQL and PostgreSQL, but also SQL Server, MariaDB, and Oracle. [103] With Amazon RDS, clients may save time and energy on routine administrative tasks such as database installation, upgrade, and backup. Depending on traffic and business needs, users may expand their databases without experiencing any downtime.

Advantages of Amazon RDS:

1. Fully managed: As Amazon RDS is a fully managed service, customers can focus their attention where it belongs—on developing their applications—instead of worrying about infrastructure, patches, or backups.
2. Scalable: Amazon RDS is highly scalable, and users can scale their databases up or down based on their traffic patterns and business needs without any downtime.

3. Multi-AZ: The high availability and fault tolerance of Amazon RDS are enabled by its support for Multi-Availability Zone (Multi-AZ) deployment. When Multi-AZ is enabled, Amazon will automatically generate a copy of the main database in a separate AZ, giving a backup in case of disaster.

4. Automated backups: Amazon RDS provides automated backups, making it easy to recover data in case of accidental data loss or corruption. Users can also take manual snapshots of their databases for long-term backup and retention.

5. Security: Data may be stored safely using Amazon RDS because of its many security features, including encryption both while at rest and in transit, network isolation, and access control.

Disadvantages of Amazon RDS:

1. Limited control: Amazon RDS is a managed service, and so users have limited control over the infrastructure and configuration settings.

2. Limited flexibility: Amazon RDS is less flexible than operating a database on an Amazon EC2 instance. Users are restricted to the supported database engines and versions by Amazon RDS.

3. Cost: Comparatively, Amazon RDS can be more expensive than operating a database on an EC2 instance. For smaller volumes, the cost of the managed service and the underlying infrastructure may be prohibitive.

4. Performance limitations: The efficacy of Amazon RDS is inferior to that of operating a database on an EC2 instance. Compared with operating a database on an EC2 instance with optimized configuration settings, users may experience increased latency and decreased throughput.

5. Scaling limitations: Compared with operating a database on an EC2 instance, Amazon RDS has scalability limitations. To scale a database beyond Amazon RDS's limitations, users may need to migrate to a larger instance type or a different database engine.

5.7.2 AMAZON AURORA

Amazon Aurora is a relational database that is compatible with MySQL and PostgreSQL and is meant to deliver excellent speed and availability. It also supports automated scalability and failover, making it ideal for mission-critical applications requiring low latency and high availability. [103] It employs a distributed storage technology, which enables it to grow storage capacity without requiring any downtime. Amazon Aurora also includes security measures including encryption at rest and in transport.

Advantages of Amazon Aurora:

1. High performance: Amazon Aurora is optimized for maximum performance and minimal latency. It employs a distributed storage system and is optimized for contemporary hardware, resulting in quicker processing times and reduced costs.

2. Scalability: Amazon Aurora is highly scalable and can scale up to 64 TB of storage and thousands of read replicas. It can automatically add or remove replicas based on demand, making it an ideal choice for applications that experience unpredictable traffic patterns.
3. Availability: Amazon Aurora provides high availability and fault tolerance through Multi-AZ deployment. In the event of a failure, Amazon Aurora automatically fails over to the standby instance, ensuring that data is always available.
4. Compatibility: Amazon Aurora is compatible with MySQL and PostgreSQL, enabling users to migrate existing applications to Amazon Aurora without modifying their source code.
5. Security: As sensitive data may be encrypted both at rest and in transit, the network can be isolated, and access can be controlled, both of which Amazon Aurora delivers.

Disadvantages of Amazon Aurora:

1. Cost: When compared with Amazon RDS, Amazon Aurora is more costly. If consumers need more memory, disk space, or advanced capabilities such as Multi-AZ deployment, the price of Amazon Aurora may rise fast.
2. Limited availability: Amazon Aurora is not available in all regions and AZs. This can limit the choice of regions for deploying applications and can lead to higher latency for some users.
3. Limited control: Amazon Aurora, like Amazon RDS, is a managed service, meaning that end users have restricted access to the system's configuration and underlying infrastructure.
4. Migration challenges: Migrating to Amazon Aurora can be challenging, especially for applications that use features that are not supported by Amazon Aurora. This can require significant changes to the application code and database schema.
5. Learning curve: Using Amazon Aurora requires a certain level of expertise and knowledge of the underlying database engine. This can require additional training and resources for users who are not familiar with MySQL or PostgreSQL.

5.7.3 Amazon DynamoDB

Amazon DynamoDB is a fully managed NoSQL database service that offers high-throughput applications, predictable performance, seamless scalability, and minimal latency. It supports both key–value and document data formats, making it useful for a variety of applications including gaming, advertising, and the Internet of Things. Amazon DynamoDB has a flexible pricing structure that allows customers to pay only for the desired throughput, with no upfront costs.

Advantages of Amazon DynamoDB:

1. High performance: Amazon DynamoDB's architecture prioritizes high throughput and low latency for optimal performance. It can process millions of requests per second and grow automatically to meet future demands.
2. Scalability: Amazon DynamoDB can easily expand or contract in response to fluctuating demand. Because of this, it is a great option for programs with fluctuating data loads or irregular traffic patterns.
3. Flexibility: Users of Amazon DynamoDB are free to choose the data model that works best for their applications from among document and key–value storage. It is possible to refine the search results by applying filters, sorting them, and even using pagination.
4. Serverless: Users who use Amazon DynamoDB in a serverless setting don't have to worry about maintaining any of the underlying hardware or software. As a result, this cuts down on unnecessary expenses and improves efficiency.
5. Security: Data in Amazon DynamoDB may be encrypted both while in storage and while in transit, and access can be restricted and audited. Because of this, it's a safe bet for keeping private information secure.

Disadvantages of Amazon DynamoDB:

1. Cost: Amazon DynamoDB can be more expensive than other database services such as Amazon RDS or Aurora. The cost can increase quickly if users require larger tables or additional features such as backups and global tables.
2. Limited control: Users have restricted access to the underlying infrastructure and configuration options in Amazon DynamoDB since it is a managed service. Users who need granular control over their databases may find this limiting.
3. Query limitations: Amazon DynamoDB has some limitations in terms of querying capabilities. For example, it does not support JOIN operations or secondary indexes with multiple attributes.
4. Learning curve: Using Amazon DynamoDB requires a certain level of expertise and knowledge of NoSQL databases. This can require additional training and resources for users who are not familiar with NoSQL databases.
5. Migration challenges: Migrating to Amazon DynamoDB can be challenging, especially for applications that use features that are not supported by Amazon DynamoDB. This can require significant changes to the application code and database schema.

5.7.4 Amazon DocumentDB

Amazon DocumentDB is a fully managed document database that is MongoDB compatible. It has built-in security, backup, and recovery tools, as well as quick and scalable performance. Amazon DocumentDB is intended to provide highly available, scalable applications with minimal latency and high throughput. It also has a flexible pricing approach that enables users to pay for just the resources they utilize.

Advantages of Amazon DocumentDB:

1. Compatibility: Amazon DocumentDB is fully compatible with MongoDB, which means that applications that are built using MongoDB can be easily migrated to Amazon DocumentDB without requiring any code changes. This makes it a convenient option for users who are already using MongoDB.
2. Scalability: Amazon DocumentDB can easily expand or contract in response to fluctuating demand. Because of this, it is a great option for programs with fluctuating data loads or irregular traffic patterns.
3. Performance: Amazon DocumentDB's speed, scalability, low latency, and high throughput make it an ideal database solution. Supporting read-intensive workloads at a rate of millions of requests per second is within its capabilities.
4. Security: Security measures in Amazon DocumentDB include access control, audit logging, and encryption, both while data is in transit and while it is at rest. Because of this, it's a safe bet for keeping private information secure.
5. Managed service: Amazon DocumentDB is a fully managed service, which means that users don't need to manage any servers or infrastructure. This reduces operational overheads and can lead to cost savings.

Disadvantages of Amazon DocumentDB:

1. Cost: Amazon DocumentDB can be more expensive than other database services such as Amazon RDS or Aurora. The cost can increase quickly if users require larger clusters or additional features such as backups and encryption.
2. Limited features: Amazon DocumentDB does not support all of the features that are available in MongoDB. For example, it does not support sharding or geospatial indexing.
3. Query limitations: Amazon DocumentDB has some limitations in terms of querying capabilities. For example, it does not support JOIN operations or secondary indexes with multiple attributes.
4. Learning curve: Using Amazon DocumentDB requires a certain level of expertise and knowledge of MongoDB. This can require additional training and resources for users who are not familiar with MongoDB.
5. Migration challenges: Migrating to Amazon DocumentDB can be challenging, especially for applications that use features that are not supported by Amazon DocumentDB. This can require significant changes to the application code and database schema.

5.7.5 Amazon Neptune

Amazon Neptune is a service for storing and retrieving large amounts of interconnected data that is totally controlled by Amazon. It's great for applications that need intricate data links since it supports popular graph models such as property graphs and Resource Description Framework (RDF). [103] Amazon Neptune is lauded for its lightning-fast, scalable speed, as well as its high levels of availability and durability. Additionally, it has built-in safety measures, including encrypted storage and transmission.

Advantages of Amazon Neptune:

1. Graph database capabilities: Amazon Neptune is designed specifically for storing and querying highly connected data, making it an ideal option for graph databases. It supports both property graph and RDF data models.
2. Scalability: Amazon Neptune is capable of dynamically expanding or contracting to meet fluctuating demand. Because of this, it is a great option for programs with fluctuating data loads or irregular traffic patterns.
3. Performance: With Amazon Neptune, customers can expect excellent throughput and minimal latency at scale. Supporting read-intensive workloads at a rate of millions of requests per second is within its capabilities.
4. Security: Encryption both at rest and in transit, together with access control and audit monitoring, are just some of the security capabilities available in Amazon Neptune. Because of this, it's a safe bet for keeping private information secure.
5. Managed service: With Amazon Neptune, customers can forget about taking care of their own servers and other infrastructure since it is a completely managed service. As a result, this cuts down on unnecessary expenses and improves efficiency.

Disadvantages of Amazon Neptune:

1. Cost: Amazon Neptune can be more expensive than other database services such as Amazon RDS or Aurora. The cost can increase quickly if users require larger clusters or additional features such as backups and encryption.
2. Limited features: Amazon Neptune does not support all of the features that are available in other graph databases such as Neo4j. For example, it does not support some graph traversal or analysis capabilities.
3. Query limitations: Amazon Neptune has some limitations in terms of querying capabilities. For example, it does not support JOIN operations or complex aggregation queries.
4. Learning curve: Using Amazon Neptune requires a certain level of expertise and knowledge of graph databases. This can require additional training and resources for users who are not familiar with graph databases.

5. Migration challenges: Migrating to Amazon Neptune can be challenging, especially for applications that use features that are not supported by Amazon Neptune. This can require significant changes to the application code and database schema.

5.7.6 AMAZON ELASTICACHE

Memcached and Redis are both supported by this fully managed in-memory data storage. Fast and scalable performance, smart scalability, and failover are all features it provides. Games, advertising tech, and real-time analytics are just a few examples of applications that may benefit from Amazon ElastiCache's low latency and high throughput. It supports a wide range of use cases, such as caching, session management, and pub/sub messaging, and comes equipped with security features, including encryption at rest and in transit.

Advantages of Amazon ElastiCache:

1. High performance: ElastiCache from Amazon uses in-memory caching to provide lightning-fast performance. As a result, it's perfect for programs that need both fast response times and low latency.
2. Scalability: Amazon ElastiCache is easily scalable, expanding or contracting as needed. Because of this, it is a great option for programs with fluctuating data loads or irregular traffic patterns.
3. Easy to use: Amazon ElastiCache is easy to set up and use, with a simple API and management console. It is also compatible with many popular caching engines such as Memcached and Redis.
4. Cost-effective: Amazon ElastiCache can help reduce costs by reducing the load on the back-end database. This can help lower the number of read and write operations required, leading to cost savings.
5. Managed service: Amazon ElastiCache is a fully managed service, which means that users don't need to manage any servers or infrastructure. This reduces the operational overhead and can lead to cost savings.

Disadvantages of Amazon ElastiCache:

1. Data loss risk: Since Amazon ElastiCache is an in-memory data store, there is a risk of data loss if the cache is restarted or if there is a failure. This can be mitigated by using persistence options such as Redis RDB or Redis AOF.
2. Limited features: Amazon ElastiCache does not support all the features that are available in open-source caching engines such as Memcached or Redis. This can be a challenge for applications that require specific features.
3. Learning curve: Using Amazon ElastiCache requires a certain level of expertise and knowledge of caching engines. This can require additional training and resources for users who are not familiar with caching engines.

4. Integration challenges: Integrating Amazon ElastiCache with applications can be challenging, especially for applications that were not designed to use caching. This can require significant changes to the application code and architecture.

5. Cost: The cost of using Amazon ElastiCache can increase quickly if users require larger clusters or additional features such as backups and encryption. This can make it less cost-effective for some applications.

5.8   CONCLUSION

AWS provides storage and database services such as Amazon S3, RDS, Aurora, DynamoDB, DocumentDB, Neptune, and ElastiCache. Amazon S3 is a scalable, dependable, and low-cost object storage service. It has the ability to store and retrieve any amount of data from any place. RDS provides fully managed relational databases, while Aurora is a high-performance, high-availability relational database. Amazon DynamoDB is difficult to top in terms of speed and stability, as well as ease of scaling. Amazon Neptune is a fully managed graph database service meant for heavily connected data, while Amazon DocumentDB is a fully managed document database that is MongoDB compatible. Finally, Amazon ElastiCache, a fully managed in-memory data storage service with lightning-fast scalability, is available. Users should carefully assess their requirements and choose the service that best matches their demands, since each service has its own set of advantages and disadvantages. Customers may easily implement and scale cloud-based storage and database services using AWS, freeing up resources for more strategic pursuits.

6 AWS Approach for Cloud Integration and Monitoring

6.1 INTRODUCTION

Cloud integration and monitoring are essential aspects of managing and optimizing resources in the cloud environment. Amazon Web Services (AWS) provides a comprehensive set of tools and services to facilitate seamless integration and effective monitoring of the cloud infrastructure. This chapter will explore various topics related to AWS cloud integration and monitoring, covering a wide range of aspects that are crucial for successfully leveraging the AWS ecosystem.

The chapter begins by delving into the different methods of cloud formation. AWS CloudFormation allows users to define and deploy infrastructure as code (IaC), enabling them to provision and manage a collection of AWS resources in a predictable and efficient manner. We will explore the various techniques and benefits of creating and managing CloudFormation templates to automate the deployment of the cloud infrastructure.

Next, we will dive into AWS CloudWatch, a powerful monitoring and observability service provided by AWS. CloudWatch enables us to collect and track metrics, collect and monitor log files, set alarms, and automatically react to changes in the AWS resources. Additionally, we will delve into CloudWatch Logs, a service that enables users to centralize, monitor, and analyze logs from various sources within their AWS infrastructure.

The chapter will also explore the AWS Personal Health Dashboard, a service that provides personalized information about the performance and availability of AWS services. In addition, we will have a dedicated section on important messaging services such as Amazon Simple Queue Service (SQS) and Amazon Simple Notification Service (SNS). We will gain insights into how SQS can help decouple and scale microservices by allowing asynchronous communication between components. We will also explore SNS, which facilitates publishing and subscribing to topics, enabling event-driven architectures and real-time notifications.

6.2 CLOUD FORMATION IN AWS

CloudFormation is a service provided by AWS that allows users to define and manage their infrastructure as code. It enables them to create a collection of AWS resources in a declarative template format, eliminating the need for manual provisioning and configuration.

With AWS CloudFormation, infrastructure can be described using either JavaScript Object Notation (JSON) or YAML Ain't Markup Language (YAML) templates. These templates define the desired state of their AWS resources, such as Amazon EC2 instances, Amazon S3 buckets, Amazon RDS databases, security groups, networking components, and more. [104] Figure 6.1 explains the benefits of cloud formation. By using CloudFormation templates, users can achieve the following benefits:

1. Automation: CloudFormation enables users to automate the provisioning and management of AWS resources. The infrastructure is defined in a template, which can be version-controlled and deployed repeatedly, ensuring consistent configurations across different environments.

2. Infrastructure as code: CloudFormation treats infrastructure as code, allowing users to version, review, and iterate on the infrastructure changes. This approach promotes best practices such as code review, testing, and collaboration.

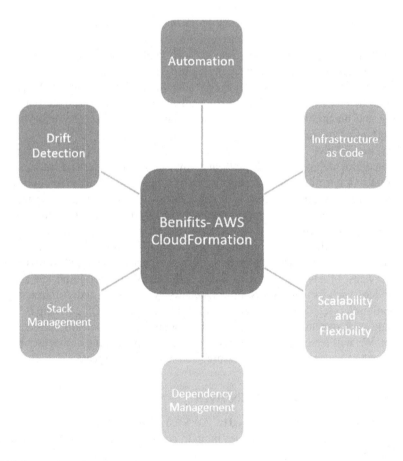

FIGURE 6.1 Benefits of cloud formation.

3. Scalability and flexibility: CloudFormation supports the creation of complex architectures, including the ability to create nested stacks and use conditions, parameters, and mappings within the template. This flexibility allows resources to be modeled and provisioned to match the specific requirements.

4. Dependency management: CloudFormation automatically manages resource dependencies. It analyzes the template and provisions resources in the correct order, taking into account dependencies between resources. This ensures that resources are created and configured in the proper sequence.

5. Stack management: CloudFormation organizes resources into logical groups called stacks. Stacks can be created, updated, and deleted as a single unit, simplifying management and enabling changes to the infrastructure to be easily tracked and controlled.

6. Drift detection: CloudFormation can detect any configuration changes made outside of the CloudFormation stack and identify them as "drift." This feature helps maintain the desired state of the infrastructure and provides insights into any manual modifications that need to be incorporated into the template.

CloudFormation provides a powerful and efficient way to provision and manage AWS infrastructure. It simplifies the process of creating and maintaining complex architectures, improves repeatability and consistency, and helps with the management of infrastructure as part of the overall development and deployment process.

In AWS, there are several ways to perform cloud formation, which involves defining and deploying infrastructure as code. [105] These methods enable users to provision and manage the AWS resources in a consistent and automated manner. Here are some of the different methods of cloud formation in AWS, which can also be seen in Figure 6.2.

1. AWS CloudFormation templates: AWS CloudFormation provides a declarative way to define infrastructure using JSON or YAML templates. It is possible to specify the desired state of the resources, such as EC2 instances, VPCs, load balancers, and more, in the template. CloudFormation takes care of provisioning and managing the resources based on the template, ensuring consistent deployments.

2. AWS Cloud Development Kit (CDK): The AWS CDK is an open-source software development framework that allows cloud infrastructure to be defined using familiar programming languages such as TypeScript, Python, Java, and more. Code can be written to create and manage AWS resources, leveraging the power of programming constructs and reusable components. The CDK generates CloudFormation templates behind the scenes and provisions the resources accordingly.

3. AWS CloudFormation Designer: CloudFormation Designer is a visual tool that helps users create, view, and modify CloudFormation templates using a drag-and-drop interface. It provides a graphical representation of

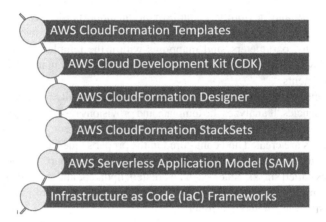

FIGURE 6.2   Different ways of cloud formation.

infrastructure, making it easier to understand and visualize the relationships between resources. The Designer can be used to visually design the
templates or import existing templates for editing.

4. AWS CloudFormation StackSets: StackSets allows a CloudFormation stack
   to be deployed across multiple AWS accounts and regions simultaneously.
   This is particularly useful for managing and maintaining consistent infrastructure across multiple environments, such as development, staging, and
   production. With StackSets, a template can be defined once and deployed to
   multiple accounts and regions with a single action.

5. AWS Serverless Application Model (SAM): SAM is an extension of
   CloudFormation that simplifies the deployment of serverless applications.
   It provides a simplified syntax for defining serverless resources, such as
   AWS Lambda functions, API Gateway endpoints, and DynamoDB tables.
   SAM templates can be transformed into CloudFormation templates for
   deployment, allowing users to leverage the benefits of both SAM and
   CloudFormation.

6. IaC frameworks: Apart from AWS-specific tools, there are also general-
   purpose IaC frameworks, such as Terraform, that support AWS. Terraform
   enables users to define their infrastructure using a declarative language and
   manage resources across multiple cloud providers, including AWS. It provides a consistent workflow for provisioning and managing infrastructure
   in a multi-cloud or hybrid environment.

These are some of the different ways cloud formation can be performed in AWS.
Each method offers its own set of advantages and may be suitable for different scenarios. The choice depends on users' familiarity with programming languages, pref-
erence for visual interfaces, need for multi-account deployments, and the complexity
of their infrastructure requirements.

6.3 AWS CLOUDWATCH

A service offered by AWS for monitoring and observability is called CloudWatch. Metrics, logs, and events from existing AWS resources and applications may be collected, monitored, and analyzed in real time. [106, 107] The AWS environment's health, performance, and efficiency in operation can all be monitored and analyzed with the help of CloudWatch.

Key features of AWS CloudWatch:

1. Metrics: Metrics, or numerical data points that measure the efficiency of the AWS resources, are gathered and stored by CloudWatch. CPU load, network throughput, disk I/O, and other similar quantities are all possible examples of such measures. These key performance indicators (KPIs) may be tracked in real time, and alerts can be set up to initiate predetermined courses of action should they be breached.

2. Alarms: With CloudWatch Alarms, customers can establish thresholds for metrics and have them activate responses when they are exceeded. Alarm actions may be used to proactively react to changes in the system by doing things such as sending alerts, scaling AWS resources, or running AWS Lambda functions. Alarms are useful for spotting and fixing problems in performance or operations.

3. Dashboards: Unique representations of data, logs, and alarms may be built for AWS resources using CloudWatch Dashboards. In order to keep an eye on crucial indicators and spot trends or problems immediately, users may build interactive dashboards that give a consolidated view of the apps and infrastructure.

4. Logs: It is possible to gather, store, and examine log files from several AWS services and applications with the help of CloudWatch Logs. Logs may be sent to CloudWatch Logs from Amazon EC2 instances, AWS Lambda functions, and AWS CloudTrail. CloudWatch Logs may be used to analyze performance and solve issues by searching, filtering, and gaining insights from log data.

5. Events: One can keep an eye on what's happening in the AWS environment and take action in response to specific triggers using CloudWatch Events. Filter-based matching events may be used to construct rules that can then lead to automated responses. As a result, users may construct event-driven architectures and automate activities in response to changes made to AWS resources.

6. Application Insights: Users may get extensive knowledge about the apps and perform troubleshooting with the help of CloudWatch Application Insights. It can automatically identify out-of-the-ordinary patterns, including faults or slowdowns, and suggest fixes. Third-party programs such as Microsoft SQL Server and Apache HTTP Server, in addition to popular AWS services such as EC2, RDS, and Lambda, are supported by Application Insights.

Users can monitor and control the entire AWS environment from a centralized location with CloudWatch since it is compatible with many other AWS services. By offering insights and the capacity to adapt to changes in real time, it plays a critical role in keeping business applications and infrastructure running smoothly, reliably, and securely.

6.4   CLOUDWATCH LOGS

CloudWatch Logs is a feature of Amazon CloudWatch that enables customers to collect, monitor, and analyze log files from multiple sources inside their AWS infrastructure. It offers a consolidated and scalable solution for storing and managing logs, making it simpler to solve problems, get operational insights, and satisfy regulatory needs. [108] We can see the key features of CloudWatch Logs in Figure 6.3. The following are the key features of CloudWatch Logs:

1. Log collection: CloudTrail, AWS Lambda, and AWS EC2 instances are just a few of the log sources that may be collected by CloudWatch Logs. Using log streams, you may set up near-real-time logging to CloudWatch Logs.
2. Centralized log storage: CloudWatch Logs uses extremely reliable and scalable storage for all of its log data. Streams of logged information are included in log groups. Logs may be organized into categories according to the applications and services being monitored.

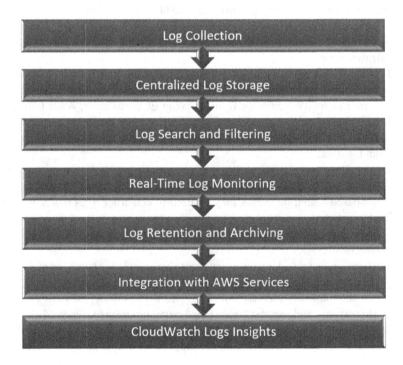

FIGURE 6.3   Features of CloudWatch Logs.

3. Log search and filtering: Users can easily find the information they're look-ing for in CloudWatch Logs, owing to its robust search and filtering fea-tures. A search may be limited to a certain log group, a certain time period, or all log groups simultaneously.

4. Real-time log monitoring: Users can keep tabs on events as they happen using CloudWatch Logs' real-time monitoring capabilities. Using metric filters, they can parse numerical data from log events for use in CloudWatch Dashboard alerts and visualizations.

5. Log retention and archiving: Retention periods can be defined for log groups to set a limit on how long each set of logs should be kept. Amazon S3 may be used for archiving logs for legal and regulatory compliance storage.

6. Integration with AWS Services: The integration between CloudWatch Logs and other AWS services is smooth. CloudWatch Logs may be used for a wide variety of purposes; some examples include storing logs created by Amazon VPC Flow Logs and capturing log events from AWS CloudTrail, as well as monitoring and troubleshooting AWS Lambda function invocations.

7. CloudWatch Logs Insights: Log analytics have never been easier than with CloudWatch Logs Insights. Users may run complex queries on the logs to pull out relevant information, perform aggregates, and spot trends and patterns.

With CloudWatch Logs, customers can easily monitor application performance, solve problems, and obtain operational insights by storing and analyzing logs from all AWS services in one place. [108] Users may improve the observability of the sys-tem and save time on log management by switching to CloudWatch Logs.

6.4.1 HANDS-ON CLOUDWATCH LOGS

1. CloudWatch Logs requires users to first go to the CloudWatch section and then, once within the logs, to the log groups. As can be seen in the screen-shot in Figure 6.4, a log group has already been formed when working with Lambda, and that group has been linked to this account.

2. Figure 6.5 is what users will see if they click through to get information about the log group associated with their account. This clearly includes all group information, including creation time, retention, stored data protec-tion, detected data sensitivity, and so on. Here, we can see that the log group chosen has a single associated log stream.

3. The information on the log events is available here. Going back to the last example run when the Lambda function was built, every little detail can be seen. See Figure 6.6 for an illustration of this. The exact times and durations of each command's execution, down to the minute, are included. Consider a scenario in which the user wishes to modify the same lambda code and call it again. Log event shown in Figure 6.6 contain the updated modification timestamp that will be appended to the changed function and be recorded here as shown.

FIGURE 6.4   Working with CloudWatch Logs.

FIGURE 6.5   Log group details.

FIGURE 6.6   Information on the log events.

6.5 AWS PERSONAL HEALTH DASHBOARD

The AWS Personal Health Dashboard is a service provided by AWS that offers personalized information about the performance and availability of AWS services that customers are currently using. It provides a consolidated view of the health of their AWS resources, helping them stay informed about any issues or events that may impact their applications or infrastructure. [109] Features of the AWS Personal Health Dashboard can be seen in Figure 6.7.

Key features of the AWS Personal Health Dashboard:

1. Service health notifications: The Personal Health Dashboard sends proactive and customized alerts on the health of the AWS services being used. It delivers real-time notifications on service outages, scheduled maintenance events, and other critical information that may have an effect on AWS resources.
2. Personalized health insights: The dashboard provides the user with tailored insights and suggestions depending on how they're using the AWS assets. It aids in assessing the possible effects that service disruptions might have on the assets and suggests solutions to these problems.

FIGURE 6.7 Features of AWS Personal Health Dashboard.

3. Event history: The Personal Health Dashboard keeps a log of all alerts and notifications that have been issued with regard to AWS resources. Examining earlier incidents and how they were fixed may shed light on AWS's stability and dependability in the long run.
4. Trusted Advisor integration: AWS Trusted Advisor, a tool that offers advice on how to get the most out of AWS investment in terms of performance, security, and cost-effectiveness, is tightly coupled with the Personal Health Dashboard. Existing AWS infrastructure can be improved with the help of Trusted Advisor's insights and alerts about any problems that may arise.
5. Customizable notifications: The alerts that arrive from the Personal Health Dashboard may be set up in any way the user chooses. The user selects the AWS services that they want to keep an eye on, the sorts of alerts that they want to receive, and the methods of contact they prefer (email, SMS, or a personal health API, for example).

Customers can reduce the negative effects of service interruptions by keeping an eye on the status of their AWS resources with the aid of the AWS Personal Health Dashboard. It helps businesses keep their AWS-hosted apps up and running smoothly by giving them actionable insights and alerts so that they can respond quickly to issues that arise. It's a helpful resource for keeping tabs on the AWS setup and making educated choices. If users want to know how AWS is doing in general, they can check out the Service Health Dashboard, as shown in Figure 6.8, and if they want to know how their specific AWS resources are doing, they can check out the Personal Health Dashboard. Figure 6.9 illustrates this point.

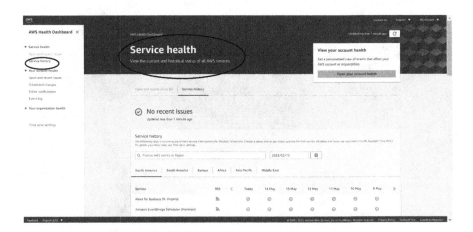

FIGURE 6.8   Service Health Dashboard.

FIGURE 6.9   AWS Personal Health Dashboard.

6.6   MESSAGING SERVICES

AWS provides various messaging services that enable reliable and scalable communication between different components of users' applications or distributed systems. Figure 6.10 shows the messaging services offered by AWS. Some of the key messaging services offered by AWS are:

1. Amazon SQS: managed message queuing service for decoupling components.
2. Amazon SNS: publish-subscribe messaging for sending notifications to subscribers.
3. Amazon MQ: managed message broker supporting Apache ActiveMQ and RabbitMQ.

FIGURE 6.10   Messaging services offered by AWS.

4. Amazon EventBridge: event bus service for integrating and routing events.
5. AWS Messaging for IoT: messaging capabilities for IoT applications.
6. AWS AppSync: managed service for real-time APIs and data synchronization.

6.6.1 Amazon Simple Queue Service

Amazon SQS is a fully managed message queuing service provided by AWS. It enables decoupling and asynchronous communication between different components of an application or distributed systems. SQS allows users to send, store, and receive messages, providing reliable and scalable communication between various parts of their application architecture.

Characteristics of Amazon SQS include:

1. Scalability and reliability: SQS has an almost infinite capacity for processing messages because of its scalable architecture. It can manage varying workloads since it scales automatically in response to the number of messages in the queue. By duplicating messages across various Availability Zones within a Region, SQS guarantees message persistence.
2. Simple API: SQS's message-sending and message-receiving API is intuitive and easy to use. It's simple to include with the apps since it works with a number of languages and software development kits (SDKs).
3. Message storage: For maximum reliability and accessibility, SQS messages are stored in various Availability Zones inside a single AWS Region. Messages' lifespans may also be managed by setting a custom retention duration.
4. Queues and message order: Messages may be organized and prioritized in SQS via the use of several queues. While First-In-First-Out (FIFO) queues provide rigorous ordering and exactly-once processing for each message, standard queues provide high throughput with best-effort ordering.
5. Message visibility: A message is briefly unavailable to other consumers when it is retrieved from a queue. This prevents many consumers from concurrently processing the same message. A message will expire after a certain amount of time (its visibility timeout) if a consumer does not act on it.
6. Dead-letter queues: With SQS's dead-letter queues, developers may separate and examine messages that were not properly processed. Dead-letter queues are used to automatically forward failed communications for further investigation and debugging.
7. Integration with AWS services: Customers may construct versatile and scalable systems by combining SQS with other AWS services such as AWS Lambda, Amazon Simple Notification Service, and Amazon EventBridge.

Decoupling an application's components using of Amazon SQS improves fault tolerance and makes asynchronous processing possible. It excels in environments where distributed systems, microservices, and event-driven architectures need high levels of loose coupling, scalability, and dependability.

6.6.2 Amazon Simple Notification Service

Amazon SNS is a fully managed publish-subscribe messaging service provided by AWS. It enables messages or notifications to be sent to a large number of subscribers or endpoints, including applications, individuals, and other services. SNS simplifies the design and implementation of event-driven architectures and allows for efficient and flexible communication between components of distributed systems.

Characteristics of Amazon SNS include:

1. Publish-subscribe model: The communications structure used by SNS is known as publish-subscribe. Publishers post to themes, and readers follow those subjects to read new content. Subscribers may be anything from an HTTP endpoint or email address to a mobile push notification platform or an AWS Lambda function.

2. Topic-based communication: Topics are used by social networking sites to classify and organize communications according to their subject matter. Publishers post to certain "topics," and readers who have signed up for those subjects will then get any new posts sent to those topics. This provides publishers and subscribers with more communication freedom and scalability by decoupling them.

3. Simple API and protocols: To post and subscribe to topics, SNS offers a simple application programming interface. It's compatible with a wide range of protocols, including HTTP/HTTPS, email, short message service (SMS), mobile push notifications (APNS, Google Cloud Messaging), and AWS Lambda function invocations.

4. Message filtering: Topic-based message filtering rules are available in SNS. This allows users to send messages to selected subscribers depending on criteria such as their interests or other qualities of the messages themselves. Message delivery efficiency is increased, and the amount of time spent processing messages is decreased, via the use of filtering.

5. Fanout and multi-protocol support: The fanout functionality of SNS allows for the simultaneous delivery of a single message submitted to a subject to a large number of subscribers. SNS also offers multi-protocol compatibility so that users may choose to receive messages in whatever protocol or format best suits them.

6. Message attributes: Using SNS, users may add metadata to messages by attaching custom characteristics. Messages may be filtered, redirected, or otherwise processed depending on these properties.

7. Integration with AWS services: Connecting to other AWS services is simple using SNS. This includes the likes of AWS Lambda, Amazon Simple Queue Service, Amazon EventBridge, and more. This allows users to construct event-driven architectures and connect SNS to other parts of the AWS setup.

Amazon SNS simplifies the process of sending notifications and messages to a large number of recipients or services. It enables flexible and scalable communication, making it suitable for various use cases, such as application-to-person (A2P) messaging, mobile app push notifications, event-driven architectures, and system alerts.

6.6.3 AMAZON MQ

Amazon MQ is a managed message broker service provided by AWS. It offers a reliable and scalable solution for decoupling applications and systems by facilitating messaging between different components. Amazon MQ supports two popular open-source message brokers, Apache ActiveMQ and RabbitMQ, providing compatibility with existing applications and familiarity to developers.

Characteristics of Amazon MQ include:

1. Fully managed service: The operational details, such as infrastructure provisioning, maintenance, patching, and scaling, are all taken care of by AWS with Amazon MQ since it is a fully managed service. This frees users from worrying about the underlying message broker architecture so they can concentrate on making apps.
2. Compatibility with Apache ActiveMQ and RabbitMQ: Amazon MQ supports Apache ActiveMQ and RabbitMQ, two widely used open-source message brokers. This enables seamless migration of existing applications or integration with systems that are already built on these message brokers.
3. Message durability and persistence: Messages in Amazon MQ are persistent because they are replicated across many brokers in various Availability Zones within a given Region. In the face of failures, this aids in keeping data intact and accessible. As an additional measure against message loss, they may persist on disk.
4. Flexible protocols and connectivity: Advanced Message Queuing Protocol (AMQP), Message Queuing Telemetry Transport (MQTT), OpenWire, and Stomp are just some of the messaging protocols that Amazon MQ supports. This facilitates interoperability with several software programs, hardware components, and service platforms.
5. High availability and scalability: Amazon MQ ensures message delivery reliability by simultaneously duplicating messages across different Availability Zones within a single geographic area. With its horizontal scalability features, it can adapt to different message volumes and workloads, guaranteeing consistent and efficient communication.
6. Security and compliance: For granular authentication and authorization, Amazon MQ works with AWS Identity and Access Management. It also allows for encryption both while in motion and when stored. HIPAA, the Payment Card Industry Data Security Standard, and General Data Protection Regulation are just a few of the rules and standards with which Amazon MQ complies.

7. Monitoring and management: Message broker metrics may be monitored and tracked with the help of Amazon MQ thanks to its compatibility with AWS CloudWatch. To be notified of any performance concerns or threshold violations, users may set up alerts and notifications. Amazon MQ also has logging features for debugging and auditing purposes.

Amazon MQ is a managed, scalable message broker service that ensures applications and their components can communicate reliably with one another. It's adaptable and simple to integrate because of its support for industry-standard protocols and interoperability with widely used message brokers. Amazon MQ provides a solid foundation for messaging in an AWS environment, making it ideal for both application migration and system development.

6.6.4 AMAZON EVENTBRIDGE

Amazon EventBridge is a serverless event bus service provided by AWS. It allows users to connect various AWS services, SaaS applications, and custom applications in a loosely coupled and scalable manner. EventBridge simplifies the process of building event-driven architectures by providing a central hub for event routing and processing.

By defining rules, users may direct events from one source to another, whether it is an AWS Lambda function, an Amazon SNS topic, an Amazon SQS queue, or an AWS Step Function. AWS services, bespoke apps, and even third-party SaaS applications may all create events. EventBridge mediates between event producers and event consumers, transporting events according to predetermined rules.

EventBridge works with a broad variety of partner integrations and AWS services, including Zendesk, Datadog, and Segment, in addition to Amazon S3, AWS CloudFormation, AWS CloudTrail, and AWS CodeBuild. To manage unique event formats or domain-specific use cases, it is also possible to design bespoke event buses and specify bespoke event schemas.

The key benefits of using Amazon EventBridge include:

1. Simplified event-driven architecture: EventBridge simplifies the process of creating event-driven systems by providing a standardized and extensible framework for routing events.
2. Decoupled and scalable event processing: Decoupling event producers from event consumers with EventBridge paves the way for effective event processing at scale.
3. Event transformation and enrichment: EventBridge rules allow for the alteration and enrichment of data prior to routing events to targets.
4. Integration with AWS services and SaaS applications: Easy event integration throughout the system is made possible by EventBridge's support for a wide range of AWS services and third-party SaaS apps.
5. Event replay and history: For up to 90 days, EventBridge stores event data, letting users relive and evaluate prior happenings.

Amazon EventBridge provides a flexible and scalable event-driven architecture solution, simplifying the development of event-driven applications and systems by acting as a central event bus.

6.6.5   AWS Messaging for IoT

Several of AWS's messaging services are tailored to the needs of Internet of Things programs. These services make it possible for IoT devices, cloud services, and other parts of IoT systems to communicate in a safe and scalable manner. Some of the most important AWS message services utilized in the IoT are:

1. AWS IoT Core: AWS IoT Core is a managed cloud service that facilitates communication between and among IoT devices. For quick and easy device-to-device interaction, it supports the MQTT, MQTT via WebSocket, and HTTP protocols. Authentication of devices, encrypted data transfer, and message routing are all services provided by IoT Core. It also supports Device Shadow, which lets gadgets update their cloud-based saves to reflect their current state for easier app integration.

2. Amazon Simple Notification Service: With SNS, users may send messages to a wide audience thanks to its publish-subscribe architecture, which is totally controlled by the service itself. Notifications, warnings, and event-driven messages may be sent to IoT devices or other services using its push-based messaging and integration with IoT apps. Besides the standard HTTP/HTTPS, SNS also works with other protocols such as email, SMS, mobile push notifications, and more.

3. Amazon Simple Queue Service: SQS is a fully controlled message queuing service that allows for the separation of a distributed system's individual parts. It can store and send messages reliably and at scale. SQS may be utilized in IoT situations that call for dependable message queuing and buffering, such as those involving device-to-cloud and cloud-to-device communication. It is compatible with traditional queues as well as FIFO queues.

4. AWS IoT Events: Users can monitor and react to events generated by IoT devices and other data sources using AWS IoT Events. It offers a rule-based method for defining event patterns and then triggering actions or alerts. Monitoring device data, finding abnormalities, launching automated processes, and sending out warnings are all possible with the help of IoT Events.

5. AWS IoT Analytics: The IoT Analytics service allows businesses to handle and analyze massive amounts of IoT data. It allows for the processing, storage, querying, and presentation of data collected from internet-connected devices. When combined with other AWS services, such as IoT Core and Amazon S3, IoT Analytics enables the creation of comprehensive IoT data processing pipelines.

6.6.6 AWS APPSYNC

When it comes to communication inside IoT ecosystems, these messaging services offer a foundation for it to be dependable, secure, and scalable. To effectively manage device-to-cloud and cloud-to-device communications, event processing, and data analysis, users may use these services in the development of dependable Internet of Things applications:

1. GraphQL API: GraphQL application programming interfaces may be developed using AppSync, allowing for rapid and versatile data querying and manipulation. With GraphQL, customers can request just the information they really need, eliminating unnecessary data requests. In addition, users may mutate data for further customization and get continuous updates by subscribing to the service.
2. Real-time data: Through its compatibility with services such as AWS Lambda, Amazon DynamoDB, Amazon Elasticsearch, and AWS IoT Core, AppSync enables the seamless synchronization of data in real time. Clients and back-end systems may now update and communicate in real time with one another.
3. Data sources: AppSync supports integration with a wide range of data sources, including HTTP endpoints, bespoke data sources, and AWS services such as DynamoDB, Aurora Serverless, and Lambda functions. The result is a uniform GraphQL API that provides access to aggregated data from many sources.
4. Offline support: When a user's internet connection is interrupted, they may still use their mobile or web app thanks to AppSync's built-in offline features. AppSync's client-side SDKs allow for local data storage and subsequent synchronization with the server when an outage has been resolved.
5. Authorization and authentication: AppSync's support for several authentication techniques, such as AWS Identity and Access Management, Amazon Cognito, and OpenID Connect, allows for granular control over who has access to what data. Customers may restrict access to sensitive information by defining permission rules at the field level.
6. Real-time and batch resolvers: Both real-time and batch resolvers are available in AppSync. While real-time resolvers allow for instantaneous updates and push alerts, batch resolvers streamline the process of querying several data sources with a single network request.
7. Caching: AppSync's caching layer may be tweaked to suit users' needs, allowing them to boost speed and lessen the strain on their back-end systems. It allows for the caching of individual data fields and automated caching depending on request patterns.

By harnessing the potential of GraphQL and connecting with numerous AWS services, AWS AppSync streamlines the creation of scalable and real-time apps. Developers are freed from the difficulties of back-end data retrieval, synchronization, and real-time changes, allowing them to concentrate on front-end client applications.

6.7   CONCLUSION

When it comes to managing and integrating cloud resources, AWS has customers covered. Its services include strong monitoring capabilities for performance, security, and compliance, and they allow for easy on-premises-to-cloud communication. By using AWS, businesses are able to improve the performance of their cloud installations without sacrificing reliability, scalability, or safety. Businesses may achieve faultless connection, effective resource management, and powerful monitoring capabilities in the cloud with AWS's approach to cloud integration and monitoring. Through these means, they may maximize the advantages of their cloud installations in terms of performance optimization, compliance assurance, and problem prevention.

7 An Introduction to Serverless Computing Services

7.1 INTRODUCTION

Serverless computing has transformed how firms design and deploy cloud applications. Serverless architecture has become more popular owing to its scalability, low cost, and low maintenance requirements. AWS stands out among the top serverless computing service providers owing to the breadth and depth of its serverless solutions.

When it comes to building and deploying apps, serverless computing on AWS is a strong paradigm because it eliminates the need for developers to manage servers and infrastructure. With serverless computing, AWS does all of the heavy lifting behind the scenes, allowing developers to concentrate on building applications and implementing business logic. [110, 116] A variety of serverless services, such as AWS Lambda for event-driven code execution, Amazon API Gateway for developing APIs, AWS Step Functions for constructing serverless workflows, and AWS AppSync for creating GraphQL APIs, are available from AWS. Developers can concentrate on innovation rather than infrastructure administration thanks to AWS serverless computing's high scalability, pay-per-use model, and quick application development and iteration.

The purpose of this chapter is to introduce readers to serverless computing and the different serverless services offered by AWS. To begin, we will examine what serverless computing is and how it differs from more conventional forms of computing. We will next examine AWS's serverless offerings, which free developers from the tedium of managing infrastructure and servers while they focus on building and releasing new software.

7.2 SERVERLESS COMPUTING

Serverless computing frees up developers from infrastructure administration and allows for faster iterations throughout both the development and deployment phases. Figure 7.1 shows the features of serverless computing. The cloud service provider is responsible for infrastructure upkeep, security, and patching; serverless designs also improve fault tolerance and resilience. [111] Serverless computing allows developers to focus on the application's core business logic by shifting the burden of infrastructure management to the cloud provider. However, developers should be aware that the underlying servers and infrastructure still exist.

DOI: 10.1201/9781003406136-7

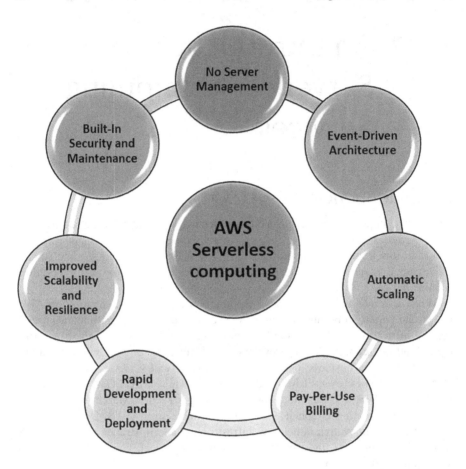

FIGURE 7.1   Features of AWS serverless computing.

1. No server management: Serverless computing frees developers from infrastructure and server management responsibilities. By outsourcing infrastructure provisioning, scalability, and maintenance to the cloud provider, developers and company owners are free to concentrate on what really matters: developing code and executing business logic.
2. Event-driven architecture: Serverless apps are built from the ground up as a set of stateless functions that are triggered by external events. Some examples of such events include HTTP requests, database updates, file uploads, and even user-defined events. Each function is responsible for a unique operation or piece of logic and may be used, deployed, and scaled in isolation.
3. Automatic scaling: The serverless operations are automatically scaled by the cloud provider in response to an increase in demand. The supplier will automatically provide more resources to the function as the demand for it increases. In contrast, during times of low activity, resources are reduced or perhaps removed entirely, resulting in savings.

4. Pay-per-use billing: In serverless computing, developers are billed based on the actual usage of their functions rather than paying for idle resources. Billing is typically calculated in terms of execution time and the number of invocations. This pay-per-use model allows for cost-efficiency, as resources are allocated and billed only when needed.

5. Rapid development and deployment: Serverless designs allow for quicker iterations of both development and deployment. Developers are liberated from infrastructure management tasks and may instead concentrate on creating new code and implementing business logic. Because of this, productivity rises and application release times decrease.

6. Improved scalability and resilience: With serverless computing, applications may automatically expand to meet fluctuating user demand, maintaining peak performance even during peak use times. Serverless apps benefit from increased scalability and robustness since the cloud provider handles the underlying infrastructure scaling.

7. Built-in security and maintenance: The security procedures, such as infrastructure patching, monitoring, and threat detection, are all handled by the cloud provider. This frees developers up to concentrate on the core features of the program, safe in the knowledge that the cloud service provider is handling security.

Reduced administration burden, scalability, cost-effectiveness, quick development, and enhanced resilience are just some of the benefits that serverless computing provides to developers. [112] Serverless services allow developers to concentrate on creating useful applications for end users while leaving the underlying infrastructure and management to the cloud service provider.

7.3   AWS SERVERLESS OFFERINGS

AWS provides a comprehensive suite of serverless services that enable developers to build and deploy applications without managing servers. [116] Figure 7.2 shows the serverless offerings of AWS. Here are some of the key serverless services offered by AWS:

1. AWS Lambda: With AWS Lambda, users can execute code without having to provision or manage servers. Code written in one of the supported languages may be set to run on a variety of triggers, including file uploads, database updates, API calls, and scheduled events.

2. Amazon API Gateway: Amazon API Gateway enables the creation, management, and deployment of secure APIs. It integrates seamlessly with AWS Lambda, allowing users to build serverless APIs that trigger Lambda functions. API Gateway provides features such as authentication, caching, and rate limiting for the APIs.

3. AWS Step Functions: Users may coordinate and organize a number of Lambda functions as a sequence of stages using AWS Step Functions, a serverless workflow tool. By facilitating the visualization, monitoring, and debugging of the application's process, it streamlines the creation of even the most complicated workflows.

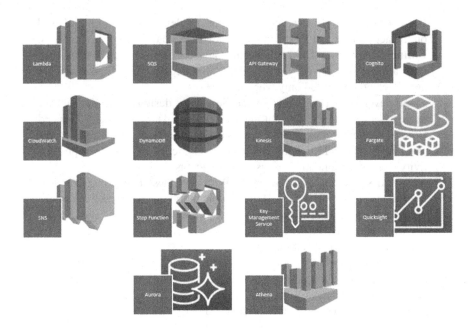

FIGURE 7.2   Serverless offerings of AWS.

4. AWS AppSync: The creation of real-time, data-driven apps is made much easier with the help of AWS AppSync, a fully managed service offered by AWS. The databases, AWS Lambda functions, and other services may all be accessed using its GraphQL API. AppSync manages background processes such as caching and offline access.

5. Amazon S3: Amazon Simple Storage Service isn't technically a serverless service, but it's often utilized in serverless designs as a place to save static assets, file uploads, and persistent data. The object storage solution it offers is extremely scalable, reliable, and safe.

6. Amazon DynamoDB: When it comes to storing and retrieving data, serverless apps often use DynamoDB, a managed NoSQL database service. It provides consistent performance at any size, is easily scalable, and works well with other AWS services.

7. Amazon SQS: Decoupling the parts of a distributed system is made possible using Simple Queue Service, which is a fully controlled message queuing service. It enables dependable and asynchronous communication between components, which is essential for the decoupling and scalability of microservices and serverless systems.

8. Amazon EventBridge: Creating event-driven architectures is a breeze using Amazon's serverless event bus service, EventBridge. It makes it easier to respond to events and initiate actions across a wide variety of AWS services and SaaS apps.

These are some of the many serverless services that AWS provides. In addition, AWS offers services such as AWS Cognito for user identification and authorization, AWS Glue for serverless data integration, and AWS Step Functions for state machine-based processes. Without worrying about managing infrastructure, developers can focus on creating scalable, efficient, and cost-effective apps with the help of AWS's many serverless services.

7.4 AWS LAMBDA

AWS offers a serverless computing solution known as Lambda. Software may be executed without the need for the developer to set up or manage any servers. [117] The code is uploaded to Lambda and told what events (or "triggers") should cause it to run, and Lambda handles running it when those events occur. Here are some key aspects of AWS Lambda:

1. Event-driven execution: Lambda functions are triggered to act based on the occurrence of a predefined event. HTTP requests, data changes in Amazon S3 or DynamoDB, Amazon SNS messages, and application-specific events are all examples of suitable triggers.
2. Supported languages: AWS Lambda is compatible with several other languages, such as Python, Java, C#, PowerShell, and Go, as well as JavaScript (Node.js). This provides developers with the freedom to build their own functions in the programming language of their choice.
3. Automatic scaling: Lambda will automatically increase the capacity of the functions as needed. When a function is triggered by an event, Lambda prepares the required resources to carry out the function's execution and scales up to meet increased demand. Without any human involvement, this autonomous scaling guarantees both excellent availability and performance.
4. Pay-per-use pricing: Lambda charges customers solely for the time the functions actually spend using the computing resources. AWS calculates the cost by factoring in the total time spent on all of those requests. The elimination of costs associated with unused capacity is a major benefit of the pay-as-you-go pricing model.
5. Integration with AWS services: With Lambda, users can easily construct serverless architectures because of its tight integration with other AWS services. Integration with other AWS offerings is possible, including API Gateway, Amazon Simple Storage Service, Amazon DynamoDB, Amazon Kinesis, and AWS Step Functions. These connections make it possible to create serverless apps that process data and respond to events using many AWS services.
6. Serverless Application Model: The SAM is a framework offered by AWS that may be used in conjunction with Lambda to create serverless apps. By offering a declarative framework for specifying resources, functions, and event triggers, SAM makes it easier to build and operate serverless applications.

AWS Lambda allows developers to create scalable, event-driven apps without worrying about servers or infrastructure. It's a potent instrument for constructing serverless architectures and allowing quick application development because of its adaptability, low cost, automated scalability, and tight connection with other AWS services.

7.4.1 How Lambda Works

To further understand how a Lambda function works, we must first dissect its structure. First, let's go to the AWS Lambda web page. [113] We can see that, besides .Net (formerly NET Core), there are other options such as Go, Java, Node.js, Python, Ruby, and even a custom runtime. The "Hello from Lambda" application, written in Python, will be run to demonstrate Lambda's capabilities. Figure 7.3 clearly demonstrates this.

Let's run this code to see what it produces and to use the Lambda functions it contains. Figure 7.4 shows the code. Figure 7.5 shows the output of the code "Hello from Lambda!" If we click the "Next: Lambda responds to events" link after we get this result, we'll be taken to a new page that shows us how Lambda works in action.

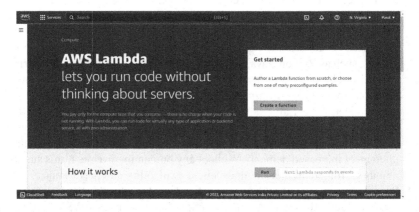

FIGURE 7.3 Beginning with Lambda.

FIGURE 7.4 How Lambda works.

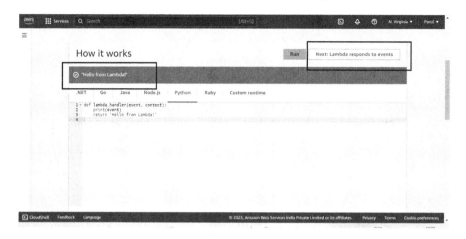

FIGURE 7.5   Output from Lambda screen.

FIGURE 7.6   Cost calculations of Lambda.

Figure 7.6 depicts the Lambda function in action. The act of clicking a camera is analogous to clicking a cell phone, since both will ultimately provide data to data processing buckets, whereupon the Lambda function will be activated through the IoT back end. As we can see, the cost per invocation of a Lambda function is quite low (only a few cents), even when the number of invocations exceeds 1 million.

7.5   AMAZON API GATEWAY

Developers may build, publish, and control their apps' Application Programming Interfaces with the help of Amazon API Gateway, a service offered by AWS. [114] It provides a safe and scalable entry point to the application's features for client apps, acting as a gateway or proxy between them and the back-end services. Here are some key features and functionalities of Amazon API Gateway, as shown in Figure 7.7:

FIGURE 7.7 Key features of Amazon API Gateway.

1. API creation and management: With API Gateway, users can build RESTful APIs or WebSocket APIs with little effort thanks to its user-friendly setup. An API can be created by defining resources, methods, request/response models, headers, and more.
2. Integration with back-end services: A range of back-end services, including AWS Lambda, AWS Step Functions, AWS Elastic Beanstalk, HTTP endpoints, and even our own on-premises servers, may be integrated via APIs using API Gateway. Requests and answers can easily be mapped across services, and it offers a variety of integration possibilities.
3. Security and authentication: To ensure the safety of the APIs, API Gateway includes a number of different safeguards. AWS Identity and Access Management, Amazon Cognito, and custom authorizers are just a few of the options for configuring authentication and authorization. Secure communications using secure sockets layer and transport layer security (SSL/TLS) are also supported.

4. API monitoring and logging: The API Gateway has built-in logging and monitoring features. Amazon CloudWatch allows users to set thorough logging of API calls and answers, as well as monitor API use, latency, error rates, and other data. This information can be used to learn about use trends, diagnose problems, and improve performance.

5. Caching and throttling: To ease the burden on the back-end services and speed up response times, API Gateway allows users to cache API replies at several levels. One may limit the frequency of API calls and safeguard the back-end services from traffic spikes and misuse with the throttling features it offers.

6. API versioning and deployment: API Gateway allows users to handle various API releases. It simplifies the deployment of changes and the management of the API lifecycle by letting them design and manage several stages or environments (such as development, testing, and production) for the APIs.

7. API Gateway Developer Portal: To help developers find, explore, and try out their APIs, API Gateway includes a fully customizable and publishable Developer Portal. Making it simpler for third-party developers and partners to include their offerings, it allows for self-service API consumption and documentation.

Amazon API Gateway simplifies the process of creating, deploying, and managing APIs, allowing developers to focus on building their applications while offloading the complexities of infrastructure management and scaling.

7.6   STEP FUNCTIONS

To coordinate and orchestrate the execution of distributed applications and microservices as a sequence of steps or processes, users may make use of AWS Step Functions, a fully managed solution offered by AWS. [115] It provides a visual interface for building and executing workflows that comprise discrete tasks or actions, allowing users to construct scalable and robust applications. Here are some key features and concepts related to AWS Step Functions:

1. State machines: State machines are used in the definition and execution of workflows in AWS Step Functions. A state machine is an abstract representation of a program's execution structure, consisting of states, transitions, and conditions. In a workflow, each state stands for a distinct operation.

2. Task-based execution: Each step in a Step Functions process is an individual activity or action that fulfills some need. These operations may include any number of AWS services, such as Lambda functions, Batch jobs, ECS operations, SNS alerts, or notifications.

3. Visual workflow designer: The AWS Step Functions console offers a visual tool for designing and visualizing procedures in Step Functions. As a result, the logic of the application is simpler to follow and control.

4. Error handling and retry logic: Error handling and retry logic may be defined for certain workflow stages or the whole process using Step Functions. Timeouts may be configured for states that take too long to complete, and users can also tell it how to handle mistakes.

5. Parallel execution: Users may perform numerous operations concurrently thanks to Step Functions' capability for parallel execution of tasks or states. As a result, users may run many processes simultaneously, which increases productivity.

6. State transitions and conditions: In Step Functions, the criteria for moving between stages are rules created by users. Conditional branching and decision-making in the processes are possible to provide criteria depending on input data or prior state output.

7. Integration with AWS Services: A number of AWS services, including AWS Lambda, AWS Batch, Amazon Elastic Container Service, AWS Glue, and the AWS Step Functions Data Science SDK, are fully compatible with Step Functions. As a result, the features of these services may be incorporated into current processes.

8. Monitoring and logging: The monitoring and logging capabilities of Step Functions are built in. Workflows may be monitored for execution time and performance, and execution history can be recorded. For centralized logging and monitoring, Step Functions may connect to AWS CloudWatch.

9. Workflow versioning and deployment: Users can keep track of updates to the procedures and deploy new versions with the help of the tools provided by Step Functions. As a result, the application's logic may undergo rapid iteration and improvement.

Using AWS Step Functions, developers of distributed applications and complicated processes have a dependable and scalable tool at their disposal. Figure 7.8 shows the features of Step Functions. It streamlines state and execution flow management, freeing up developers to concentrate on creating the core functionality of their applications.

7.7 AWS APPSYNC

AWS AppSync is a fully managed service that facilitates safe data synchronization and communication between client applications and back-end data sources, making it easier to construct real-time and offline-capable apps. [116] Figure 7.9 shows the features of AWS AppSync. It enables the development of GraphQL APIs with native support for connecting to a wide variety of AWS and third-party services. Here are some key features and concepts related to AWS AppSync:

1. GraphQL API: AppSync is compatible with GraphQL, an API query language and runtime that allows users to execute GraphQL queries on current information sources. GraphQL schemas and resolvers, which may be defined in AppSync, allow clients to connect with the sources of data in a manner that is both flexible and efficient.

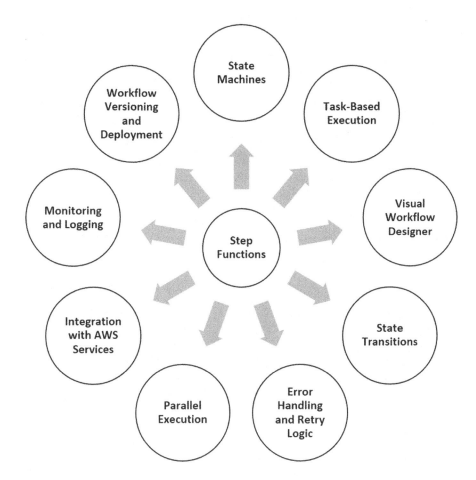

FIGURE 7.8   Features of Step Functions.

2. Real-time and offline capabilities: AppSync allows for the synchronization of data between clients and servers in real time. It makes use of WebSocket-based subscriptions to notify users instantly of any data changes. AppSync also has built-in offline functionality, enabling mobile and web clients to cache data locally before syncing with the server when an internet connection is established.

3. Data sources and resolvers: The AWS services Amazon DynamoDB, Amazon Aurora Serverless, Amazon Elasticsearch Service, AWS Lambda, and more can all be accessed with AppSync. It also allows users to interface with custom APIs or other services by using HTTP resolvers for access to their own bespoke data sources.

4. Fine-grained authorization: Users may restrict access to the information down to the field level using AppSync's fine-grained permission features. Using AWS Identity and Access Management and Amazon Cognito User Pools, users may establish sophisticated authorization rules according to user role, group membership, or custom logic.

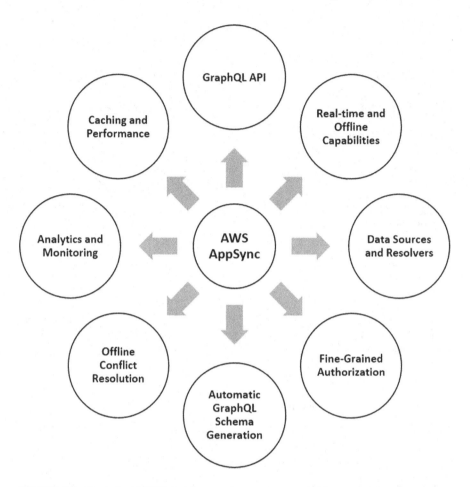

FIGURE 7.9   Features of AWS AppSync.

5. Automatic GraphQL schema generation: If many data sources are set up, AppSync can automatically produce a GraphQL schema which is ready to use. The information model's structure and connections are analyzed, and a schema is created to describe them. The schema is also adaptable and extensible.

6. Offline conflict resolution: For offline updates, AppSync has built-in dispute resolution techniques. It is possible for conflicts to arise during synchronization with the server if numerous clients make modifications to the same data item while offline. To manage these collisions and preserve data integrity, AppSync allows users to set their own resolution algorithms.

7. Caching and performance: AppSync's caching features will help the application run faster and use fewer server resources. They allow users to manage cache behavior and enhance data retrieval on both the server and client sides.

8. Analytics and monitoring: When it comes to monitoring and debugging the GraphQL APIs, AppSync works with AWS CloudWatch to provide businesses with the metrics and logs they need. CloudWatch provides dashboards and alerts to measure and monitor performance, latency, and issues related to API use.

Developing real-time and offline-capable apps that rely on effective data synchronization and communication is a challenging task, but AWS AppSync makes it easier than ever. It simplifies the process of developing reliable and responsive apps by hiding the difficulties involved in maintaining data sources.

7.8   AMAZON S3

Amazon Simple Storage Service is not a server-free service, although it is widely used in serverless frameworks. The term "serverless" describes a kind of architecture that frees programmers from administrative duties in favor of coding. Figure 7.10 shows the features of Amazon S3. So that code can be executed in response to events without the need to create or manage servers, AWS offers a serverless computing solution called AWS Lambda.

The many ways in which AWS Lambda may interact with Amazon S3 in a serverless architecture include processing files, reacting to events in S3, and getting data

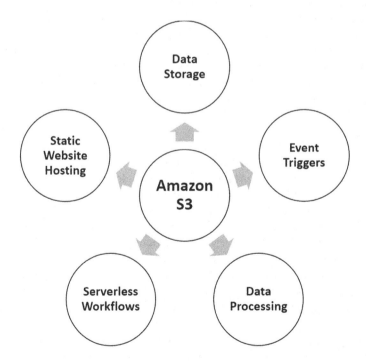

FIGURE 7.10   Features of Amazon S3.

from S3 for further processing. In a serverless system, Amazon S3 functions as follows:

1. Data storage: Amazon S3 is a flexible and reliable object storage solution that can store media of all shapes and sizes. It's a great option for serverless apps that require a flexible data storage and retrieval solution.
2. Event triggers: When certain actions take place in Amazon S3, such as when a file is uploaded or removed, or its metadata is modified, AWS Lambda functions may be triggered. Serverless functions that handle data in S3 may be set to run in response to these events.
3. Data processing: Data in Amazon S3 may be processed by Lambda functions hosted on AWS. For instance, whenever a new file is uploaded to S3, a custom Lambda function may be set to run and perform any number of useful functions on it, such as data extraction, thumbnail generation, and analytics.
4. Serverless workflows: When many serverless services are used together to complete a business activity, Amazon S3 may be a component of the workflow. An AWS Step Functions workflow may, for instance, call a Lambda function to process data from S3, followed by another Lambda function to either save the processed data back to S3 or take some other action.
5. Static website hosting: Static web pages may also be hosted in a serverless manner on Amazon S3. Users may bypass the requirement for a separate server in order to serve static web content such as HTML, CSS, and JavaScript by enabling static website hosting on an S3 bucket.

   Developers may create scalable, event-driven, low-cost applications by integrating the serverless capabilities of AWS Lambda with the storage capabilities of Amazon S3. With this method, businesses can concentrate on developing the application and executing the business logic, while AWS handles infrastructure maintenance and scalability.

7.9   DYNAMODB

Amazon DynamoDB is a NoSQL database service offered by AWS that is completely managed by Amazon. Although DynamoDB does not operate without servers, it is often used as such in serverless systems. The term "serverless" describes a kind of architecture that frees programmers from administrative duties in favor of coding. So that code can be executed in response to events without the need to create or manage servers, AWS offers a serverless computing solution called AWS Lambda. Figure 7.11 shows the characteristics of DynamoDB.

As part of a serverless architecture, AWS Lambda may communicate with Amazon DynamoDB to perform tasks such as storing and retrieving data. Here's how serverless computing makes use of Amazon DynamoDB:

1. Data storage: Amazon DynamoDB serves as a highly scalable and fully managed NoSQL database. Automatic scalability and low-latency data access make it suitable for processing heavy loads. DynamoDB is flexible because it can store both structured and semi-structured data.

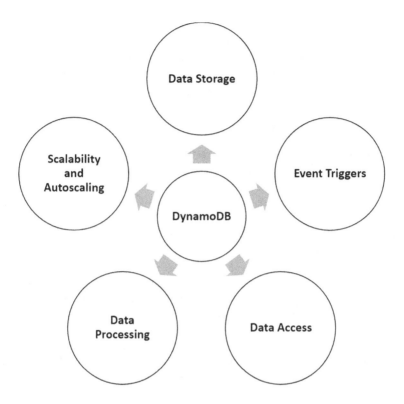

FIGURE 7.11   Characteristics of DynamoDB.

2. Event triggers: DynamoDB events, such as the creation, modification, or removal of a record, may trigger AWS Lambda operations. When the DynamoDB data changes, serverless operations can be executed owing to these triggers.
3. Data access: Data in DynamoDB may be read, written, and modified using AWS Lambda functions. Lambda functions may be used to run complicated searches against DynamoDB and get the desired data for further processing.
4. Data processing: Serverless workflows, in which various serverless services are coupled to accomplish certain business operations, might include DynamoDB. A Lambda function may be triggered by a Step Functions workflow to do things such as get data from DynamoDB, process it, and then put it back into DynamoDB or another storage service.
5. Scalability and Auto Scaling: The Auto Scaling feature of DynamoDB allows it to dynamically modify its capacity in response to demand. Since there is no need to deploy or manage the database's underlying infrastructure, this fits into the serverless paradigm well. The scalability requirements of serverless applications are easily met with DynamoDB.

Developers may create extremely scalable and responsive apps by combining the serverless features of AWS Lambda with the scalability and speed of Amazon DynamoDB. The serverless design frees users to concentrate on coding and executing business logic while AWS handles database growth, maintenance, and infrastructure management through the DynamoDB service.

7.10   SIMPLE QUEUE SERVICE

When it comes to message queuing, look no further than AWS Simple Queue Service (SQS). Even while SQS isn't serverless on its own, it's often used in serverless architectures to facilitate component decoupling and asynchronous communication between services. The term "serverless" describes a kind of architecture that frees programmers from administrative duties in favor of coding. So that code can be executed in response to events without the need to create or manage servers, AWS offers a serverless computing solution called AWS Lambda. Figure 7.12 shows the features of Amazon SQS.

When it comes to integrating Amazon SQS into a serverless architecture, AWS Lambda may be utilized to interface with SQS queues for asynchronous message processing. Here's how Amazon SQS fits into a serverless architecture:

1. Message queuing: The Amazon SQS is a dependable and extensible queuing system. By enabling one component to submit a message to an SQS queue and another component to receive and process the message asynchronously, in its own time, it facilitates the decoupling of components within an application.
2. Event-driven processing: Event sources, such as SQS, may be utilized to initiate AWS Lambda operations. Lambda functions may be set up such that they are automatically called whenever a new message arrives in an SQS queue.
3. Scaling and resilience: Scalability and availability are both handled mechanically by SQS. It can store and transmit messages successfully despite a high volume, and it can store a lot of them. SQS enables reliable message storage and delivery, which works well with the serverless architecture in which services such as Lambda scale automatically to manage demand surges.
4. Asynchronous communication: SQS facilitates the asynchronous interaction of the various parts of a serverless application. An application's front end may initiate its back end's processing by posting a message to an SQS queue, and the back end can then process the message without needing to wait for an instant response.
5. Fault tolerance: SQS ensures reliability by storing messages in several data centers and servers. This guarantees that messages will always be received and handled, even in the case of a failure.
6. Dead letter queues: Dead letter queues are supported by SQS and are used to process messages that were not successfully delivered despite many attempts. Using dead letter queues, unsuccessful messages may be captured and processed independently for use in error investigation and debugging.

FIGURE 7.12   Features of Amazon SQS.

Developers may create highly scalable and decoupled apps by combining the serverless features of AWS Lambda with the asynchronous message processing of Amazon SQS. While AWS handles infrastructure maintenance and scalability, users can concentrate on developing the application and executing business logic using a serverless design. SQS offers dependable and asynchronous communication between components, which improves the serverless architecture's adaptability and reliability.

7.11   EVENTBRIDGE

When it comes to event bus services, AWS offers Amazon EventBridge, which is entirely managed by Amazon. It provides a centralized event-routing service that makes

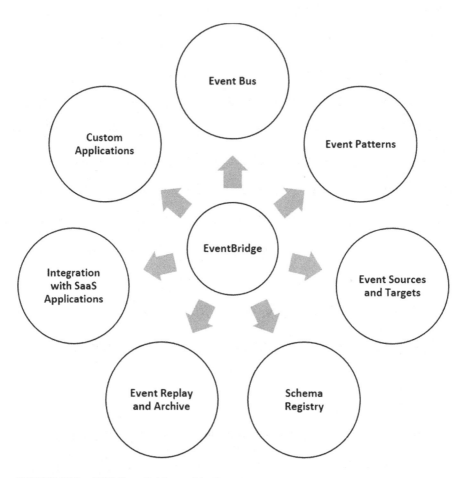

FIGURE 7.13 AWS EventBridge and its features.

it easier to integrate and coordinate numerous AWS services, SaaS apps, and bespoke applications, letting users create serverless architectures. Figure 7.13 shows the features of AWS EventBridge. With EventBridge, developers can design event-driven architectures in which various parts of the program may exchange information and respond to triggers. Here are some key features and concepts related to Amazon EventBridge:

1. Event bus: Amazon EventBridge is like a central bus for events or a router for happenings. In this way, subscribers from various systems and services may respond to events published on the event bus. AWS services, bespoke apps, and SaaS applications are just a few examples of where events could be generated.
2. Event patterns: Rules can be designed that apply to certain kinds of events or situations with the help of EventBridge's event pattern support. According to these guidelines, some events will be routed to designated destinations. Properties of events, event structures unique to each AWS service, and user-defined patterns may all form the basis of event patterns.

3. Event sources and targets: Several AWS services are supported by EventBridge as event sources that may provide data to the event bus. AWS Lambda, S3, CloudWatch, Step Functions, and others are all instances of event sources. EventBridge's API allows for user-created event sources to be used. The components that respond to events are represented by targets, and they may be anything from an AWS Lambda function to an Amazon SNS topic to a state machine implemented using AWS Step Functions.

4. Schema registry: It is possible to design and maintain the event's schemas with the help of EventBridge's schema registry. To guarantee uniformity and interoperability across event generators and consumers, schemas specify the event's structure, format, and validation standards. Users may enforce event structure and verify event data with the help of the schema registry.

5. Event replay and archive: To recreate the current state or analyze the past, users may use EventBridge to replay events from the event bus. For long-term archiving and auditing, they may set up an event archive, which maintains a replica of all events in an S3 bucket.

6. Integration with SaaS applications: Pre-built event providers allow EventBridge to connect to a wide range of SaaS services. Providers such as Zendesk, Datadog, Auth0, and more may provide the events so that an event-driven architecture can make use of data from other services.

7. Custom applications: With EventBridge's API and SDKs, users may connect existing programs as event sources or receivers. To take part in the event-driven architecture, they may integrate EventBridge with personal systems or those of a third party.

Using Amazon EventBridge, users can create event-driven serverless architectures that provide benefits including scalability, modularity, and loosely coupled components. Because EventBridge streamlines event integration, routing, and processing, users can direct the focus where it belongs: on constructing business logic and effectively responding to events.

7.12 CONCLUSION

The chapter on AWS serverless computing introduces key services and concepts for building scalable, event-driven applications. AWS Lambda offers serverless computing triggered by events such as API Gateway requests and S3 uploads. Amazon API Gateway provides secure API endpoints with features such as authentication and rate limiting. AWS Step Functions orchestrates complex workflows across multiple services. AWS AppSync simplifies real-time and offline-capable app development. Amazon S3 is a scalable storage solution with event notifications and data lifecycle management. Amazon DynamoDB offers scalable NoSQL data storage. Amazon SQS enables decoupling with reliable message queuing. Amazon EventBridge serves as a central event bus for event routing and integration. These services empower developers to focus on code and build scalable, responsive applications.

8 AWS and Machine Learning—An Integrated Approach

8.1 INTRODUCTION

In today's hyper-technological world, two of the most potent and widely available technologies are machine learning (ML) and cloud computing. Both of these areas of study are based on the concept that computers can learn from their own mistakes. These two technologies have the potential to have a tremendous influence on businesses of all sizes, from sole proprietorships to multinational corporations. Utilizing data from the past, algorithms that are capable of self-education via the process of machine learning may be constructed. Dealing with the storage needs of various machine learning algorithms, such as linear regression and logistic regression, is one of the most difficult tasks that a data scientist or an expert in machine learning must carry out. This is one of the most significant obstacles they confront. Cloud computing has the potential to bring about significant changes in the field of machine learning. Applications that employ machine learning might be augmented and improved with the help of cloud computing. The term "intelligent cloud" refers to the combination of machine learning with cloud computing that has been developed recently.

Pattern recognition, computational learning, and machine learning are all forms of "learning" that make use of principles from artificial intelligence, and they are closely connected to one another. The idea that computers should be able to teach themselves has been around for quite some time; in fact, it was first proposed in 1959. Since then, it has been developed further and further.

The vast majority of businesses are able to make use of this technology as public cloud providers are beginning to explore the possibility of offering machine learning services.

8.2 MACHINE LEARNING

The study of strategies that may "learn" from data in order to improve performance on a predetermined set of tasks is the primary focus of the field of study known as machine learning, which seeks to understand these approaches and create new ones. [59] It is commonly acknowledged that it is an important component of artificial intelligence. The use of training data allows machine learning algorithms to develop a model, which in turn allows them to produce predictions or judgments without being explicitly programmed. [60] For instance, conventional algorithms are not used in areas such as health, email filtering, speech recognition, and machine vision because it is either not feasible or not practicable to construct such algorithms. [61]

DOI: 10.1201/9781003406136-8

Although computational statistics is a subfield of machine learning, machine learning as a whole does not center on generating predictions via the use of computers. Computational statistics, however, do. The study of mathematical optimization offers tools, theory, and application fields for the field of machine learning, which is a subdiscipline of computer science. Data mining is a subfield of computer science that focuses on using unsupervised learning techniques in order to perform exploratory data analysis. [63] In specific applications of machine learning, data and neural networks are used to simulate the processes that occur inside the human brain. When it is applied to the resolution of problems encountered in business, machine learning is also known as predictive analytics. [64, 65]

Algorithms for learning are founded on the concept that what has worked in the past will likely continue to work in the future. For example, "since the sun has risen every morning for the preceding 10,000 days, it is probable that it will do so again tomorrow."

It is feasible for machine learning systems to carry out a task without being specifically instructed to do so. It is a technique in which computers are taught to accomplish particular tasks using data that they have been provided with. Algorithms may be designed that tell computers how to solve simple issues; the computer doesn't have to learn anything in order for this procedure to operate. Humans may have trouble designing complicated algorithms on their own for more complex professions. In actuality, it may be more effective to permit the computer to design its own algorithm rather than depending on human programmers to describe every step. [66]

Machine learning is a discipline of computer science that employs a number of approaches to educate computers on how to execute activities for which there is no ideal answer. It's typical in scenarios where there are a lot of alternative answers to label some of them as real. As a consequence, the computer's algorithms may be enhanced by utilizing this data as training data.

8.3   OTHER DISCIPLINES AND ML

Arthur Samuel, who worked at IBM at the time, came up with the concept of "machine learning" in 1959 as a name to describe the burgeoning area of online gaming and artificial intelligence. [67] During this same period, the phrase "self-teaching machines" was also often used. [68, 69] In his book *Learning Machines*, Nilsson details the work he did in the 1960s, when pattern recognition was the primary focus of machine learning. [70] Even in the 1970s, Duda and Hart contended there was still a significant amount of interest in pattern recognition. [71] A paper that was released in 1981 analyzed various different instructional methods for training students to recognize 40 characters shown on a computer screen. These 40 characters included 26 letters, ten figures, and four special symbols. [72]

8.3.1   ARTIFICIAL INTELLIGENCE

An artificial intelligence project served as the academic impetus for the development of machine learning. Early on, several academics working in the field of artificial intelligence were intrigued by the idea of letting robots learn from their own experiences by providing them with training data. In an attempt to find a solution to the problem, several symbolic methods and something called "neural networks" were used. These models, which were later found to be based on generalized linear models, were referred to as "neural networks." [74]

However, a division has emerged between AI and machine learning as a result of an increasing emphasis on the application of a knowledge- and logic-based approach to both of these technologies. In both theory and practice, probabilistic systems struggled with problems related to the collection and representation of data. [75] In the 1980s, expert systems had supplanted AI, and statistics had become a rather unimportant field of study. [76] In the field of AI, symbolic and knowledge-based learning persisted, which eventually led to inductive logic programming. On the other hand, the more statistical line of research in pattern recognition and information retrieval moved beyond the field of AI proper. [75] Both the field of artificial intelligence and the field of computer science gave up on neural network research at the same time. Researchers from different areas, in addition to those in the domains of artificial intelligence and computer science, such as Hopfield, Rumelhart, and Hinton, have taken up the "connectionism" issue. In the mid-1980s, back propagation was given a new lease of life, and this proved to be their most important advance. [75]

The decade of the 1990s saw the beginning of rapid growth in a relatively new field known as machine learning. The goal of the discipline has shifted from the development of artificial intelligence to the resolution of actual problems. The symbolic approaches that it had gotten from AI were replaced with methods that were borrowed from statistics, fuzzy logic, and probability theory. This change was executed. [76]

Machine learning and artificial intelligence are often confused with one another, leading to widespread confusion. Learning and prediction in machine learning are based on passive observation, but learning and action in artificial intelligence are founded on active engagement with the environment and are designed to maximize a system's chances of success. [77]

ML was expected to still be a subfield of artificial intelligence in 2020, according to a variety of sources. [76, 78, 79] Some people believe that AI encompasses just a portion of ML, contrary to popular belief. [62, 80, 81]

8.3.2 DATA MINING

Data mining and machine learning often make use of the same methods and have a lot in common. The primary difference between the two, however, is that data mining is focused on finding previously unknown features within the data, while machine learning is focused on producing predictions based on the properties learned from the training data (this is the analysis step of knowledge discovery in databases). On the other hand, data mining may be used as a preprocessing phase in machine learning to improve learner accuracy while simultaneously using a broad variety of machine learning methodologies. This can be accomplished by employing a wide range of machine-learning techniques. Confusion between these two research communities arises from the fact that machine learning is frequently evaluated based on its ability to reproduce known knowledge, whereas knowledge discovery and data mining (KDD) is focused on discovering knowledge that has never been discovered before. In other words, KDD is more concerned with uncovering previously unknown information. When compared with known information, supervised methods easily outperform unsupervised approaches; however, supervised methods can't be used in normal KDD since there isn't enough data to train them.

8.3.3 OPTIMIZATION

Many learning issues are formulated as the minimization of a loss function on a training set of samples, and machine learning has close ties to optimization as well. In classification, for example, the aim is to give a label to instances, and models are trained to accurately predict the pre-assigned labels of a group of examples. Loss functions reflect the disparity between the predictions of the model being trained and the actual problem instances.

8.3.4 GENERALIZATION

Rather than striving to minimize loss on a training set, optimization approaches seek to lower loss on all samples, while machine learning focuses on data that has not been seen before. Deep learning algorithms, in particular, are currently being studied to see how generalization works across various learning approaches.

8.3.5 STATISTICS

The primary objective of statistics is to draw conclusions about a population based on a sample, whereas the primary objective of machine learning is to discover generalizable predictive patterns. Although the two fields of study share many similarities, the primary objective of each is quite different. [82] The work done by Michael I. Jordan is considered to be the beginning of a long and illustrious history of machine learning in the field of statistics. [83] He also brought up the possibility of using the term "data science" to refer to the more general field of study. [83]

When we refer to an "algorithmic model," we are referring to machine learning methods such as random forest. According to Leo Breiman, [78] algorithmic models and data models are the two paradigms that make up machine learning algorithms.

Statistics and machine learning have come together to establish a new field that is now known as statistical learning. Some statisticians refer to this field by its previous name. [79]

8.4 MACHINE LEARNING APPROACHES

In general, the "signal" or "feedback" available to the learning system may be divided into three categories:

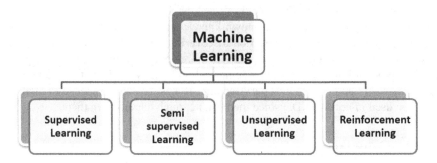

FIGURE 8.1   Types of machine learning.

- Supervised learning: By giving the computer examples of inputs and the intended outcomes they represent, supervised learning teaches the computer a general rule that maps inputs to outputs.
- Unsupervised learning: An unsupervised learning system seeks structure on its own without any labels to help it. Unsupervised learning may be used to obtain a desired output as a goal in and of itself (finding previously unknown patterns).
- Reinforcement learning: To attain a certain goal, a piece of software interacts with a constantly changing environment. The program is given input in the form of incentives, which it tries to maximize while navigating its problem domain. [62]

Figure 8.1 shows the types of ML available to us.

8.4.1 SUPERVISED LEARNING

Mathematical models are used to represent the inputs and outputs of supervised learning techniques, which use collections of data to train machines. [84] In the context of this discussion, the term "training data" refers to a collection of examples. It is possible for any number of inputs to result in the production of a supervisory signal, which is also known as a training example output. A matrix is used to represent the training data, and each trial is represented by an array of vectors that are referred to as feature vectors. It is possible to utilize supervised learning algorithms to train a function that can then be used to predict the output that is connected with new inputs via the iterative optimization of a goal function. [85] An optimal function will allow an algorithm to properly compute its output for inputs that were not included in the training data. This will allow the algorithm to be more general. An algorithmic improvement is a process that gradually becomes more efficient at doing a given task over the course of its lifetime. [73]

Active learning, classification, and regression are all types of algorithms that may be used for learning under supervision. [77] In situations in which the outputs may take on any numerical value within a certain range, regression techniques are used, while classification methods are utilized in situations in which the outputs can only take on a specific set of values. A classification algorithm for emails, for instance, may receive an email and then state the name of a folder to which the email needs to be sent as an example of what it might do.

Similarity learning aims to learn from examples by comparing the degree of likeness or connection between two things. Although it is closely tied to regression and classification, similarity learning seeks to learn from instances. In addition to rating and recommendation systems, some of its numerous applications include monitoring for visual identification, verification of faces and speakers, and verification of speakers' voices.

8.4.2 Unsupervised Learning

Methods of unsupervised learning determine the structure of data by grouping or clustering data points from a collection of data that consists simply of inputs. This data might come from any source. The algorithms are able to learn from the data even when it is not labeled, categorized, or classified in any way. Unsupervised learning algorithms search the data for patterns and base their decision-making on the existence or absence of such patterns, in contrast to supervised learning algorithms, which react to the input provided by the user. One of the most significant applications of unsupervised learning is density estimation in statistics. This may be done by estimating the probability density function, for example. [86] Unsupervised learning is often used in other domains as well, and one of its functions includes the summing up and explanation of various data features.

Cluster analysis, as its name indicates, involves breaking a dataset up into smaller groups (called clusters) on the basis of specified criteria, with the intention of determining the degree to which the data in each cluster shares commonalities with, or diverges from, the data in the others. If the data structure is characterized by a similarity metric and evaluated, for instance, by internal compactness or the similarity between members of the same cluster and separation, then the difference between clusters may be determined. Internal compactness is an example. The estimated density of, and connections between, nodes in a network are the foundation of certain alternative methods.

8.4.3 Semi-supervised Learning

Methods of learning that fall between being wholly unsupervised and fully supervised include semi-supervised learning (with completely labeled training data). Certain training instances do not have any associated training labels despite the fact that a large number of researchers in the field of machine learning have demonstrated that the accuracy of learning can be significantly improved by combining unlabeled data with even a small quantity of labeled data.

It is more cost-effective to collect training labels in poorly supervised learning, which results in larger effective training sets. This increases the size of the training sets. [87]

8.4.4 Reinforcement Learning

When it comes to software agents, reinforcement learning focuses on how such agents could function most effectively in a particular circumstance so that they can get the greatest potential advantage from the environment as a whole. In machine learning, the environment is shown as a Markov decision process (MDP) almost all of the time. Approaches based on dynamic programming are used quite often in reinforcement learning algorithms. [88] It is not necessary to have a mathematical model of the MDP in order to utilize strategies related to reinforcement learning. Reinforcement learning algorithms are used in both autonomous vehicles and video games in which the player competes against a human adversary.

8.5 MACHINE LEARNING IN AWS

Making better predictions, understanding more about the data, reducing operating expenses, and enhancing the overall user experience of a website may all be achieved using AWS ML. AWS provides the most complete set of AI and machine learning services, infrastructure, and deployment tools available.

It is possible to construct machine learning applications using AWS Free Tier, which includes a variety of products. We'll take a look at a few of them now. Figure 8.2 explains these services at a glance.

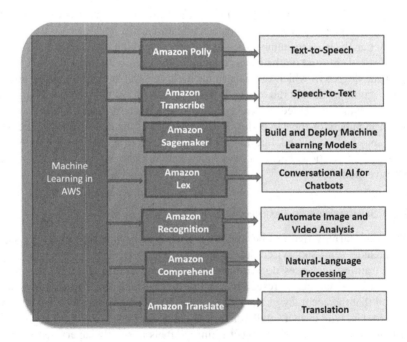

FIGURE 8.2 Free Tier-available ML services in AWS.

8.5.1 Amazon Polly

If we've ever dreamed of creating an app that can speak or a whole new category of speech-enabled products, Amazon Polly is the solution. Polly's text-to-speech (TTS) service uses deep learning algorithms to produce human speech that sounds natural. Developing speech-enabled apps that function in several countries is possible because of the wide range of genuine voices available.

A new machine learning technology called neural text-to-speech (NTTS) is used in Polly to increase the quality of the speech. NTTS technology developed by Polly is able to mimic the speaking manner of newscasters for use in news narration. Figure 8.3 explains the benefits of Amazon Polly.

A company's unique voice may now be developed with Amazon Polly Brand Voice. The Amazon Polly team will collaborate with a customer to create a distinctive NTTS voice for its organization as part of this one-of-a-kind collaboration.

8.5.2 Amazon Transcribe

To rapidly and easily turn audio into text, Amazon Transcribe, an AWS service, is available to users. Customers may utilize Amazon Transcribe for a variety of commercial purposes, including the transcription of audio-based customer service interactions, the creation of subtitles for audio/video content, and the analysis of audio/video data (text-based).

As a text-to-audio converter, Amazon Transcribe opens the door to a wide range of voice-to-text applications. With Amazon Comprehend, sentiment analysis of text data processed by Amazon Transcribe may be performed, as well as the extraction of important words from text data. Additionally, customers may use Amazon Translate and Amazon Polly to receive voice input in one language, translate it into another language, and produce voice output, allowing for multilingual interactions. Amazon Transcribe, Amazon Kendra, or OpenSearch (the successor to the Amazon

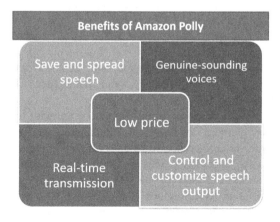

FIGURE 8.3 Amazon Polly and its benefits.

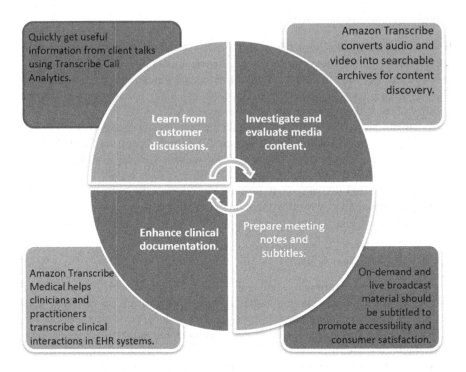

FIGURE 8.4   Use cases for Amazon Transcribe.

Elasticsearch service) may also be used to index and search across an audio/video collection. The use cases for Amazon Transcribe are listed in Figure 8.4.

Speech and acoustic aspects such as variable intensity, tone, and spoken rate may all be handled by this service. Ambient noise, many speakers, accented voices, and transitions between various languages may all be found in a single audio sample. The accuracy of the service output may be affected by the circumstances.

8.5.3   Amazon SageMaker

ML models can be created, trained, tested, and deployed using the Amazon SageMaker service, which is an all-in-one service that includes all of the necessary tools and procedures.

Amazon SageMaker is designed from the bottom up, with high availability in mind. There are no planned downtimes or maintenance periods for companies. Therefore, it can offer fault tolerance when a server dies or an Availability Zone is unavailable because the SageMaker APIs are housed in Amazon's high-availability data centers. In order to offer fault tolerance for the service, the replication stack is spread over three different AWS Regions.

Amazon SageMaker does not utilize or distribute any of the designs, datasets, or algorithms it acquires from its customers. The safety and security of its consumers are two of the most important concerns it has. It is as a consequence of this that AWS

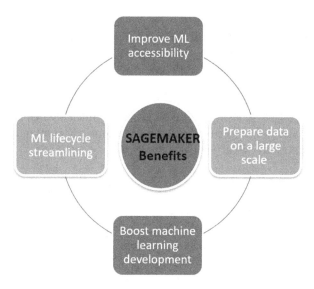

FIGURE 8.5   SageMaker and its benefits.

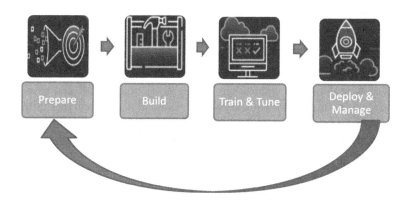

FIGURE 8.6   SageMaker—steps to build a service.

provides simple but effective solutions that enable businesses to pick where their data is kept and how it is encrypted while it is in transit and at rest. Figure 8.5 shows details of SageMaker and its benefits. Responsible and advanced physical and technological safeguards are used to keep user information safe from unwanted access. It's up to customers to decide which AWS services are utilized to process, store, and host their content since they have full ownership over the material.

To run an ML notebook, train the model, create predictions, and store all outputs in a database, all of the computing, storage, and data processing capabilities required must be supplied. Other services may be hosted on Amazon SageMaker instances, such as hosting a notebook or conducting training. Customers are only charged for what they really use, with no minimum or up-front expenses. Figure 8.6 explains the steps involved in building a service.

Amazon SageMaker Studio enables a unified, web-based graphical user interface via which all aspects of ML development may be executed. SageMaker Studio gives complete access to every step that is required to create, train, and deploy models, as well as control over those steps and insight into how they work. Users can simply enter data, generate fresh notebooks, train and adjust models, move to and fro between stages to fix tests, compare end results, and push models; all of these functions are available in a single location, which significantly increases productivity. The single visual interface of SageMaker Studio is where all machine learning development tasks may be carried out.

8.5.4 Amazon Lex

Amazon Lex is powered by the same deep learning technology that powers Alexa, and so it can perform activities such as voice search and language interpretation for users. Businesses may automate back-end business logic, such as data extraction and update, using Amazon Lex and AWS Lambda. Chat, phone, and IoT devices may be introduced when the bot's development is complete. To keep an eye on the bot's development, users may utilize the reports that are available to them. The end-to-end solution provided by Amazon Lex is scalable, safe, simple to use, and secure. Details of the use cases of Amazon Lex are listed in Figure 8.7.

8.5.5 Amazon Rekognition

Amazon Rekognition, a tool offered by Amazon, makes it simple to integrate strong visual analysis into applications. Rekognition Image's fast and easy search and organizing tools let users quickly search, evaluate, and categorize millions of photos. With the help of Rekognition Video, it is possible to extract kinetic context from recorded or live-streamed videos. Figure 8.8 explains the features of Amazon Rekognition.

In addition to being able to identify celebrities and recognize items, Rekognition Image can also generate text and detect scenarios. In addition, the app allows users to search for and compare the faces of other users. Rekognition Image is built on Amazon's specialist image recognition engine, which analyzes billions of photographs every day for Prime Photos.

Rekognition Image uses deep neural network models to recognize and classify millions of items and scenarios in user photographs, and Amazon is continually adding new categories and learning-based capabilities to the platform. Rekognition Image customers only pay for the photographs analyzed and the face information that is preserved. Use cases related to Amazon Rekognition have a broad coverage and are depicted in Figure 8.9 in detail.

Using Rekognition Video, it is possible to detect activities, assess the movement of people in the frame, and recognize items such as celebrities and improper material in films saved in Amazon S3 and live video broadcasts from Acuity, among other things. With Rekognition Video's powerful technology, people may be recognized and tracked, even if their identities are concealed or if they enter and exit an area as a

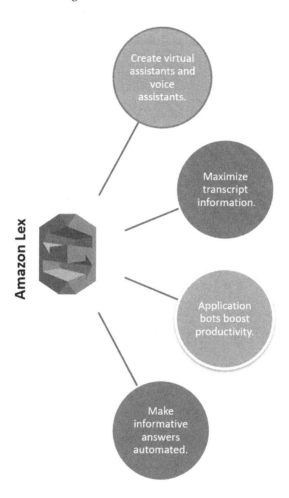

FIGURE 8.7 Use cases of Amazon Lex.

full person immediately. An app that promptly tells clients when an item is delivered to their front door may use this information. The Rekognition Video function allows for the indexing of objects, activities, surroundings, celebrities, and faces, making video search considerably easier.

8.5.6 AMAZON COMPREHEND

Machine learning and natural language processing are used in Amazon Comprehend, a service that deciphers and interprets text. The use cases that can be covered under this topic can be found in Figure 8.10.

Instead of reading content, Amazon Comprehend lets users get an idea of how customers feel about a company's goods or services by analyzing the language used and extracting key phrases, locations, people, and corporations mentioned in the

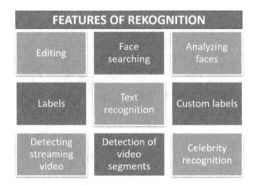

FIGURE 8.8 Features of Amazon Rekognition.

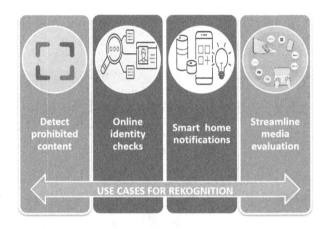

FIGURE 8.9 Use cases of Amazon Rekognition.

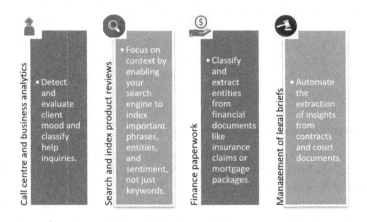

FIGURE 8.10 Use cases of Amazon Comprehend.

text. All the use cases in Figure 8.10 are possible sources of this kind of information, as are websites, social media feeds, emails, and news articles. Additionally, Amazon Comprehend may be provided with a broad range of text documents in order for it to better understand the information being presented. It is possible to leverage Amazon Comprehend's output to understand user comments, improve search results using search filters, and organize documents according to common topics.

8.5.7 Amazon Translate

Amazon Translate is a service that uses neural machine translation. Deep learning algorithms may now be used by engineers to read corporate and user-authored content and to create apps that need support for several languages. Translating languages has never been easier thanks to deep learning algorithms. The API makes it possible to utilize the service for one-time or batch translations of material from one language to another. Any of Amazon Translate's 75 supported languages may be used to translate any document.

Amazon Translate is a great option if users have a lot of material to translate, need it done quickly, and don't mind a little bit of ambiguity in the translation. Survey and questionnaire results may be summarized using Amazon Translate raw output. It can also be used to construct a first draft from a large amount of material in several languages. Amazon Translate's raw output can also be used to allow customers to search for their app in their preferred language. Figure 8.11 shows the major benefits of Amazon Translate.

Customer service experts may use Amazon Translate in a variety of ways, including translating documents created by their firm, such as product descriptions and comparisons of alternatives, user FAQs, and support materials. Amazon Translate may be used for more comprehensive post-editing when translating high-value, branded content such as marketing and advertising materials, contracts, and other papers.

8.6 OTHER ML-BASED SERVICES IN AWS

8.6.1 Amazon CodeGuru

This is a tool for developers that provides insightful suggestions to improve code quality as well as pinpointing the lines of code in an application that are the most expensive to maintain. CodeGuru may be integrated into an existing software development process in order to automate code reviews, continuously monitor the performance of a program while it is running in production, and provide visual advice on how to improve software reliability, application performance, and overall cost.

CodeGuru Reviewer makes use of machine learning and automated reasoning in order to identify significant weaknesses, security weaknesses, and difficult-to-find issues in the development of applications. It then offers ideas to improve the quality of the code in those areas.

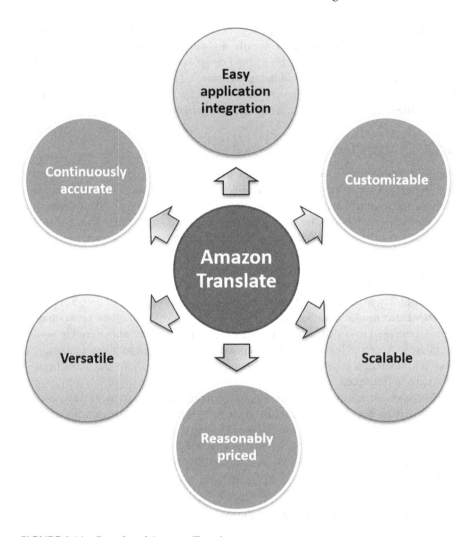

FIGURE 8.11   Benefits of Amazon Translate.

CodeGuru Profiler enables developers to understand the runtime behavior of their programs, which enables them to discover and remove inefficiencies in their code, boost performance, and substantially cut the expenses associated with calculation.

8.6.2   Amazon DevOps Guru

Amazon DevOps Guru is a product driven by ML that makes it easy to improve the operations and maintenance of an application. Using DevOps Guru, users may identify any departures from a business's typical operating patterns in order to protect its consumers from experiencing the negative effects of any operational troubles.

DevOps Guru is able to identify abnormal application behavior and bring to light critical issues that could lead to service outages or breakdowns by utilizing machine learning models that have been informed by AWS's operational excellence over the years. When DevOps Guru identifies a significant problem, an alert is instantly sent to the appropriate parties. This alert not only details the associated anomalies but also the most likely source of the issue, as well as the date, time, and location at which it occurred. Where it is possible to do so, DevOps Guru will provide recommendations on how the issue may be resolved.

The operational data generated by AWS applications is ingested by DevOps Guru, which then provides users with a centralized dashboard from which any operational issues can be diagnosed and fixed. By selecting coverage from CloudFormation stacks or the AWS account, DevOps Guru can be used to improve the availability and dependability of an application without users having to do any manual setup or have prior experience with machine learning.

8.6.3 AMAZON ELASTIC INFERENCE

The low-cost GPU-powered acceleration connected to Amazon EC2 and Amazon SageMaker instances allows customers to cut the cost of running deep learning inference by as much as 75 percent using Amazon Elastic Inference.

Inference, the act of using a trained model to make predictions, may account for up to 90 percent of the assistance to improve the overall expenses of a deep learning application. There are two reasons for this. When it comes to training models, separate graphics processing unit (GPU) instances are best suited. The bulk of inference is conducted in real time on a single input and uses just a tiny amount of GPU computing capacity, whereas training methods analyze a large number of data samples in parallel. Also, when demand is great, it is conceivable that a GPU's entire computing power will not be used, which is both inefficient and expensive. As a second consideration, the amount of GPU, CPU, and memory capacity required by various models varies. While it may be possible to satisfy the requirements of one resource with a GPU instance that is large enough, this nearly always results in underutilization of other resources, which increases expenses.

Amazon's answer to these issues is Amazon Elastic Inference. EC2 and SageMaker instance types may now benefit from GPU-accelerated inference acceleration without needing any modifications to the source code. With Amazon Elastic Inference, the application's total CPU and memory needs may now be taken into account when selecting an instance type. To make the most effective use of resources and to lower the cost of conducting inference, users may specify their own level of inference acceleration.

8.6.4 AMAZON FORECAST

One of the most accurate forecasting services on the market is supplied by Amazon Forecast. In today's business environment, organizations employ everything—starting from easy spreadsheets to complicated business planning systems—to estimate future corporate outcomes such as product demand, resource needs, or financial success. These sorts of data are known as time-series data and are often used to produce forecasts. As an example, a raincoat's future sales may be forecasted using merely its historical sales data, on the assumption that the upcoming situation is dictated by the previous data. Large datasets with chaotic patterns may be difficult to reliably estimate using this approach. The data series that change over time (such as cost, offer price, and online traffic) and critical independent variables (such as product quality and retail locations) are not easily incorporated into this approach.

Amazon Forecast leverages machine learning to integrate time-series data with supplementary parameters before producing forecasts. This technique is the same as that employed by Amazon.com. Amazon Forecast does not require any previous expertise in machine learning. There is no need for users to submit supplementary data that they believe would alter their forecasts. There may be seasonal and regional differences in the demand for a shirt in a certain color. Machine learning is especially suited to discover these subtle relationships, which are tough for an individual to notice on their own. Supplying this with data will enable it to evaluate it for meaning, identify what is significant, and construct a forecasting model that is up to 50 percent more accurate than looking at time-series data only.

Using Amazon Forecast, users don't need to establish servers or create or train machine learning models; everything is done for them. As a consequence, there are no minimal fees or long-term commitments necessary.

8.6.5 Amazon Fraud Detector

Users will be able to identify potentially fraudulent actions via the use of machine learning and Amazon's more than 20 years of expertise in the identification of fraudulent activity. This will allow users to capture more online fraud more rapidly. Clients will have an easier time reaping the benefits of the technology if the laborious and expensive processes of designing, training, and deploying a machine-learning model for fraud detection are simplified by automation. Because each model it generates is tailored to the particular dataset of a client, the accuracy of the models that are produced by Amazon Fraud Detector is far higher than that of previous ML solutions that are designed to work for everyone. In addition, when users just pay for the things that they really utilize, they end up saving money in the long term.

8.6.6 Amazon HealthLake

Amazon HealthLake is a HIPAA-compliant service that stores massive amounts of health data and allows users to perform queries on that data. It is designed for use by healthcare practitioners, health insurance companies, and pharmaceutical companies.

It is quite usual for there to be anomalies and shortcomings in the data on health. Unstructured data includes things such as clinical notes and lab results, insurance claims and medical images, recorded interviews, and time-series data, among other types of data.

HealthLake is a cloud-based platform that medical professionals may use to keep, process, query, and analyze patient data that is hosted on AWS Cloud. The extensive medical natural language processing (NLP) capabilities of HealthLake allow for the examination of unstructured clinical content originating from a number of sources. HealthLake is able to convert unstructured data and provide broad query and search capabilities because it uses approaches that are based on natural language processing. It is possible to utilize HealthLake to store, index, and organize patient data in a manner that is secure, compliant, and verifiable.

8.6.7 AMAZON KENDRA

Amazon Kendra is a search engine that uses machine learning to function. Users and customers of company websites and applications will have no problem discovering the information they want thanks to Kendra's redesigned approach to enterprise search. This is true even if the information they require is spread across different places and content repositories inside the company.

It saves a great deal of sorting through reams of unstructured data by assisting users to obtain the answers they want at the exact moment they require them. Because Amazon Kendra is a fully managed service, customers won't have to bother about learning and implementing machine learning models before utilizing it. This frees them up to focus on more important tasks.

8.6.8 AMAZON LOOKOUT FOR EQUIPMENT

Prior experience with machine learning is not necessary to utilize Amazon Lookout for Equipment, which gathers information from various sensors installed on machinery and creates a machine-learning model based only on that information. Lookout for Equipment performs an analysis of sensor data in real time, using its own machine-learning model, in order to identify probable equipment issues before they occur. This indicates that abnormalities in the equipment can be spotted immediately, faults can be swiftly diagnosed, and steps to minimize expensive downtime can be taken immediately.

8.6.9 AMAZON LOOKOUT FOR METRICS

Amazon Lookout for Metrics is able to discover and analyze abnormalities in commercial and operational data, such as a sudden decline in sales income, using ML. It gives users the ability to quickly and easily link it to well-known data stores such as Amazon S3, Redshift, and RDS, as well as third-party SaaS, so that they can start tracking metrics that are important to their company. These data sources are subjected to an automated inspection and preparation for anomaly detection by Amazon Lookout for Metrics, which is characterized by greater speed and precision in comparison with earlier methods. Users are also welcome to provide advice on any noticed abnormalities, which will help improve results and their accuracy with time. When this is utilized, detected irregularities are grouped together, and an alert is provided with a description of the likely root cause. This makes it simpler to identify any issues that may have arisen. A severity score is assigned to each anomaly in order to assist customers in concentrating on the problems that are most important to the firm.

8.6.10 AMAZON LOOKOUT FOR VISION

Amazon Lookout for Vision is an application that makes use of computer vision (CV) and machine learning in order to identify mistakes and irregularities in graphical representations. It helps industrial organizations enhance quality while simultaneously reducing operational expenditure by immediately identifying inconsistencies in photographs of items taken at scale. Using this, customers may be able to identify, among other things, missing functional parts in products, damage to automobiles or buildings, irregularities in production lines, and minute faults on silicon wafers. Amazon Lookout for Vision uses machine learning to perceive and understand pictures at a very high degree of accuracy and scale. This allows it to see and interpret photographs from any camera in the same manner that a person would, regardless of the camera's brand or model. Amazon Lookout for Vision enables businesses to enhance their quality control and save money by doing away with the need for time-consuming and error-prone human inspections. The software also lets organizations evaluate flaws and damage in a more precise and legally acceptable manner. Just a few minutes are needed to get started automatically analyzing photographs and objects with Amazon Lookout for Vision, and users don't even need any previous experience or expertise in machine learning to do so.

8.6.11 AMAZON MONITRON

Amazon Monitron uses ML from beginning to end to recognize aberrant behavior in industrial equipment. This enables users to undertake predictive maintenance and, as a result, reduces the amount of unplanned downtime that occurs.

Installation of sensors and the accompanying infrastructure for data connection, storage, analysis, and accommodating changes is the first step in predictive maintenance. (Predictive maintenance is also known as condition-based maintenance.) Because of this, it has never been possible to construct the solution from the bottom up without the assistance of skilled professionals from the fields of technology and data science. In order to do this, they are required to locate and acquire suitable sensors for the use cases, as well as connect those sensors to an Internet of Things gateway (a device that aggregates and transmits data). Because of the challenges involved in putting this into practice, only a select few businesses have had success in using predictive maintenance.

Amazon Monitron analyzes vibration and temperature data from equipment to discover unusual patterns using machine learning. An accompanying mobile app allows users to set up the sensors and get information on operational behavior as well as notifications about potential issues in the equipment. They may begin monitoring the health of the equipment in just a few minutes without the need for any prior knowledge of programming or machine learning if they utilize the same technology that Amazon use in its fulfillment centers to monitor the equipment there.

8.6.12 AWS Panorama

AWS Panorama is a machine learning appliance and software development kit that enables computer vision for on-premises IP cameras. This functionality has recently been made accessible. Because AWS Panorama may automate processes that formerly required human interaction, it may be feasible to get a better understanding of potential issues using this tool.

Computer vision has the potential to automate a variety of visual inspection tasks, including ensuring the accuracy of orders at quick-service restaurants, monitoring assets to improve the efficiency of supply chain operations, and analyzing customer behavior to better design retail store layouts. In environments with limited network bandwidth or for businesses with data governance rules that necessitate on-premises processing and storage of video, it may be difficult or even impossible to deploy computer vision in the cloud. These settings include: AWS Panorama, which is a machine learning service that allows businesses to create predictions locally with high accuracy and low latency by employing computer vision. On-premises cameras may be outfitted with the AWS Panorama software to make this possible.

The AWS Panorama appliance allows computer vision to be added to IP cameras and analyzes video feeds from a large number of cameras using a single administrative interface. This is possible because AWS allows this appliance to be utilized. Users will be notified within milliseconds of any potential issues, such as broken products on a production line running at high speed or a vehicle that has strayed into a potentially dangerous off-limits area at a warehouse. These alerts will be sent out automatically. As a consequence of this, further cameras and gadgets that are equipped with AWS Panorama are being created by third-party manufacturers to cater to users' particular requirements. Applications for computer vision that are developed using AWS Panorama may make use of AWS machine learning models or work in conjunction with a partner from the AWS Partner Network to create CV applications more quickly.

8.6.13 Amazon Personalize

Customer-specific recommendations may be created quickly and simply with Amazon Personalize, a machine-learning tool.

Personalized product and content recommendations, tailored search results, and targeted marketing efforts are all being driven by machine learning. Machine learning, however, has proved to be a hurdle for most firms because of the difficulties of establishing machine learning technologies. Amazon Personalize makes it feasible for programmers with no previous understanding of machine learning to easily incorporate substantial personalization capabilities into their applications using machine learning technology that has been honed through years of use on Amazon.com.

Using Amazon Personalize, articles, items, movies, and music may be recommended depending on users' historical behavior. Amazon Personalize may use additional information from consumers, such as their age or geography, to better serve them. Using data analysis, Amazon Personalize will assess what information is significant and then utilize that knowledge to train and build a customization model particular to the data.

The information obtained by this is kept totally secret and is only used to give users ideas that are unique to themselves. The service maintains a virtual private cloud where users may start selling their customized predictions by making a simple API call. There are no minimum charges or responsibilities, and customers only pay for what they use. Using this service is like customers having their own in-house ML customization team ready around the clock, seven days a week.

8.6.14 AMAZON TEXTRACT

Amazon Textract is a service which can automate the process of extracting text from scanned documents. Amazon Textract is an advanced kind of optical character recognition (OCR) that can recognize information in various fields on forms.

Manual data entry is still the technique of choice for many companies when it comes to the extraction of data, despite the fact that it is time-consuming and expensive, similar to OCR. Rules and procedures need to be hard-coded and regularly updated whenever a form is changed, and this is especially important if there are several forms to deal with. When the form is not filled out in accordance with the regulations, the usual outcome is the production of results that are disorganized and pointless.

Amazon Textract is able to "read" practically any document using machine learning, and as a result, it can get accurate data from such documents without the need for any human intervention or specialized code, therefore addressing a number of challenges. Textract allows users to quickly automate document activities, which in turn enables businesses to manage millions of pages of documents in a matter of hours. Following the collection of the necessary information, customers will be able to start the processing of an application for a loan or a medical claim inside the software used by the organization. Intelligent search indexes may also be developed, automated approval processes may be implemented, and compliance with document archiving rules may be better managed by the identification of items that may need redaction. All of these things can be accomplished by identifying items that may need redaction.

8.6.15 AWS DEEPCOMPOSER

Machine learning powers AWS DeepComposer, the world's first musical keyboard, allowing developers of all skill levels to learn about generative AI while concurrently producing unique musical outputs. One of the components of the DeepComposer system is a USB keyboard connected to the programmer's PC, as well as an AWS

Management Console-accessible service named DeepComposer. It provides users with instructions, code generators, and testing sets, all of which may be used to get generative model development off the ground.

8.6.16 AWS DeepLens

AWS DeepLens puts the power of deep learning directly into the hands of software developers by providing them with a video camera that is fully programmable, as well as code, tutorials, and models that are pre-trained.

8.6.17 AWS DeepRacer

Learning about reinforcement learning (RL) in a way that is both interesting and thrilling may be accomplished with the help of a one-eighteenth-scale racing car known as AWS DeepRacer. Roughly stated, reinforcement learning refers to an advanced technique of ML that makes use of an unorthodox strategy for the training of models.

Users now have the ability to play with RL, learn via autonomous driving, and get their hands dirty all thanks to AWS DeepRacer. They may get started with the cloud-based 3D racing simulator using the virtual car and courses provided, or they can deploy their learned models to AWS DeepRacer and compete with friends or in the international AWS DeepRacer League.

8.6.18 AWS Inferentia

A machine learning inference chip known as Inferentia was created by the cloud computing firm AWS. It's possible that using a machine learning model that is trained, which is referred to as inference, might account for up to 90 percent of the application's total processing expenditure. Developers may be able to minimize their inference expenses by as much as 75 percent by utilizing Amazon Elastic Inference. This is accomplished by providing Amazon EC2 as well as SageMaker with GPU-powered inference acceleration. Nevertheless, some inference work-loads need the use of a complete GPU or call for very low latency. To tackle this issue while keeping the price as low as possible, a specialized inference chip is required.

Through the use of AWS Inferentia, this inference capacity may be obtained at low cost, with high throughput and low latency. Because each processor is capable of doing hundreds of tera operations per second (TOPS) of inference throughput, complex models have the potential to provide accurate predictions in a timely manner. It is possible to use many AWS Inferentia chips in conjunction with one another to achieve hundreds of TOPS of throughput, which results in much-improved performance. AWS Inferentia will soon be accessible to SageMaker, Amazon EC2, and Amazon Elastic Inference, enabling these services to benefit from the capabilities of AWS Inferentia.

8.6.19 TENSORFLOW ON AWS

TensorFlow simplifies the process of getting started with deep learning in the cloud for software developers. The idea has extensive support from the business world because of its widespread adoption as a viable option for deep learning research and application building.

SageMaker is a platform that allows users to develop, train, and then deploy machine learning models at scale. It provides users with a service that is a fully managed TensorFlow experience on AWS. They also have the choice of designing their own one-of-a-kind environment and workflow utilizing the AWS Deep Learning AMIs, which is pre-installed with a broad variety of well-known frameworks such as Apache MXNet and PyTorch. This is another alternative.

8.7 CONCLUSION

Machine learning has made developers' lives simple. The cloud has also contributed to this. Combining the advantages of both of these is of tremendous value. This chapter has explained machine learning along with numerous features including its types and deployment models. AWS has the capacity to deploy ML too. Different AWS services that make use of ML have been covered in depth in this chapter. In Amazon Free Tier, we can access a few of the ML-driven tools, while others are banned under Free Tier usage. A few of the services that have been mentioned in depth include SageMaker, Comprehend, Translate, Transcribe, Panorama, etc.

9 Virtual Private Cloud

9.1 INTRODUCTION

Companies in today's ever-changing technology environment are always on the lookout for new ways to take advantage of cloud computing. Cloud services provide the scalability, adaptability, and efficiency that contemporary businesses need to deal with their constantly shifting needs. AWS is one of the most popular cloud computing platforms because of the wealth of services and resources it provides to businesses as they undergo digital transformation.

The Virtual Private Cloud is an essential part of the AWS suite of offerings. [125] With VPC, organizations can construct their own private, segregated network inside AWS's cloud architecture, making it a safe haven for their sensitive data, applications, and resources. By doing so, businesses may take advantage of AWS's scalability and global reach while maintaining the continuity of their on-premises network.

Businesses may tailor the design and deployment of their cloud resources to meet their unique needs with the help of VPC, which enables them to build a scalable and flexible network infrastructure. [118] This versatility enables enterprises to manage IP addresses, create network subnets, and set up routing tables and tight security policies. Businesses may easily connect to their on-premises systems or other AWS services by using VPNs or AWS Direct Connect, both of which are secure and dependable connectivity solutions made possible by VPC.

The improved network security offered by VPC is one of its main benefits. Organizations may keep sensitive data and apps safe from prying eyes by isolating them behind private subnets and exercising fine-grained control over incoming and outgoing traffic. Businesses may strengthen their networks against cybercriminals by defining and enforcing stringent access rules using security groups and network access control lists.

Furthermore, VPC provides unrivaled scalability and flexibility, enabling businesses to quickly and easily adjust their network architecture in response to evolving operational requirements. VPC allows enterprises to easily add new subnets, deploy more computing instances, and grow network capacity without degrading performance as resource demand rises. This on-demand scalability allows businesses to adapt to the needs of their growing user base and shifting workload patterns.

In addition, VPC may be easily integrated with other AWS services, giving companies access to a wide variety of cloud-based options. Several AWS services, including Amazon EC2 instances, Amazon RDS databases, AWS Lambda functions, and more, may be linked to a company's virtual private cloud. [122] Creating complete, linked cloud infrastructures is made possible by this integration, which in turn simplifies the design of large, sophisticated applications.

In this chapter, we'll set out on an adventure to learn everything there is to know about AWS's VPC service. We'll cover the basics of VPC so that readers can start using this powerful networking solution right now, including its architecture, capabilities, and advantages. They will learn how VPC fits into the AWS ecosystem and how it can help organizations create reliable, scalable, and secure cloud infrastructures by the time they reach the last section of this chapter.

9.2   UNDERSTANDING VPC

AWS's VPC is a core feature that enables companies to establish their own isolated private networks inside the AWS cloud. It provides a safe and separate environment in which businesses may deploy resources such as compute instances, databases, and storage while keeping their network structure under tight management.

VPC is a basic cloud networking service that helps organizations bring the features and advantages of their on-premises networks to the cloud. A virtual private cloud allows a business to centrally manage network resources such as IP addresses, subnets, routing tables, and security policies. [119, 120, 125] With this much freedom, companies may design their network to meet their specific needs while still working in tandem with their current IT systems and architecture.

Businesses may run their apps and keep sensitive data safely inside a VPC because it is conceptually separated from other VPCs and the underlying AWS infrastructure. The VPC's resources are safe from prying eyes thanks to this separation from the outside world. A virtual private cloud is meant to function as a private network, protecting sensitive data from other users in a public cloud.

A VPC allows for the creation of several subnets, each of which may be used to further segment and isolate resources. To better manage network traffic, enterprises may create subnets to bundle together similar resources. Using Availability Zones, which may be assigned to subnets, enterprises can create highly available architectures that can function normally despite disruptions to one zone's worth of infrastructure. Figure 9.1 shows the architecture associated with VPC.

A variety of connections both within and outside the VPC are made possible by AWS. VPNs and AWS Direct Connect are two of the available alternatives. Hybrid cloud deployments and smooth integration are made possible using VPN connections that securely link the VPC to an organization's on-premises network. With AWS Direct Connect, businesses can link their data centers directly to the AWS cloud, ensuring that their most important applications always have access to the bandwidth and latency they need.

In addition, VPC protects the resources on the virtual network with a full suite of network security capabilities. Security groups function as virtual firewalls by regulating incoming and outgoing connections to and from an instance. Protocols, ports, and IP addresses are used to set access rules that let only approved traffic through. By filtering traffic at the subnet level, network access control lists (ACLs) let businesses set fine-grained network regulations.

AWS VPC is a crucial product that enables companies to build and control their own private, isolated networks inside the AWS cloud. VPC offers a networking

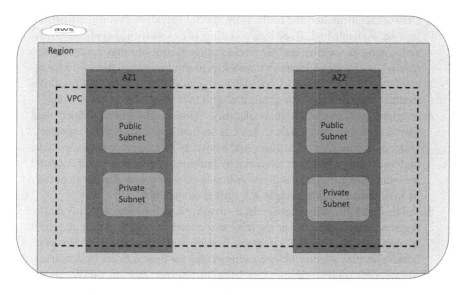

FIGURE 9.1   Virtual private cloud (VPC).

solution that is secure, isolated, and highly configurable, allowing businesses to precisely plan and implement their resource deployments for maximum efficiency, scalability, and safety. When it comes to making the most of AWS and constructing robust cloud infrastructures, knowledge of VPC's fundamental ideas and capabilities is crucial.

9.3   UNDERSTANDING SUBNETS

Subnets are an essential part of the VPC architecture, allowing for the separation and management of virtual network resources. [121] They help companies regulate data flow, set up safety protocols, and maximize use of available resources. In order to understand more about VPC subnets, let's check the following:

1. Subnet definition and purpose: A VPC subnet is a smaller IP network inside the VPC. It stands for an IP address block assigned to a particular set of resources or instances. Organizations may improve network administration, security, and performance by logically partitioning the IP address space of the VPC into smaller subnets.
2. IP addressing and CIDR notation: A range of IP addresses, written in Classless Inter-Domain Routing (CIDR) notation, is associated with each subnet. An IP address range is represented in CIDR notation by a network address followed by a slash and a number, which reflects the number of significant bits in the network mask. The notation 10.0.0.0/24, for instance, denotes a subnet whose IP addresses range from 10.0.0.0 to 10.0.0.255, with the final 8 bits (24 minus 16 network bits) accessible for host addresses.

3. Network segmentation and traffic isolation: Subnets allow businesses to divide their network into logical sections according to factors such as application hierarchy, network security, and physical location. Businesses may better manage network traffic by segmenting it into logical groups using subnets. This segmentation improves security because it reduces the vulnerability of resources to attacks and provides fine-grained control over inter-subnet connectivity.

4. Availability Zones and high availability: Within a given area, subnets may be connected to many AZs. An AZ is its own physical location, complete with its own dedicated utilities and network. Organizations may achieve high availability and fault tolerance by building subnets in several AZs and spreading resources across them. AZ redundancy ensures that services may be maintained even if a single AZ suffers an outage.

5. Routing and internet gateways: In a virtual private network, network traffic is routed according to a routing table associated with each subnet. A subnet is connected to the VPC's primary routing table automatically. However, businesses may specify unique routing rules for their subnets by constructing internal routing tables. Attaching an internet gateway (IGW) to the VPC paves the way for traffic to enter and leave the VPC from different subnets and the internet at large.

6. Network access control: Subnets delineate an area inside the VPC where network access controls may be enforced. Subnet-level network ACLs allow administrators to set up rules for regulating incoming and outgoing data packets. ACLs are used to restrict network traffic based on criteria such as protocol, port, and IP address, and they function at the subnet level. In conjunction with security groups, they offer an extra safeguard and enable granular regulation of data transmissions throughout a network.

7. Subnet associations: Subnets inside the virtual private cloud are where instances and other resources are placed. When starting an instance, businesses have the option of choosing which subnet it will use. The instance's IP address and its ability to communicate with other resources inside the VPC are both determined by this connection. Using private IP addresses, resources on the same subnet may talk to one other without any additional network routing or security measures.

Subnets in a VPC are an effective tool for controlling and organizing AWS cloud infrastructure resources. They enable logical partitioning, boost availability across many AZs, regulate access to the network, and make horizontal scalability possible. To develop safe and resilient cloud architectures that meet the needs of a given business, it is crucial to have a firm grasp on how subnets function inside a VPC.

9.3.1 TYPES OF SUBNETS

Public and private subnets in a VPC setting have various functions and degrees of access to resources. Let's have a look at the differences between public and private subnets and their applications.

Public subnets:

1. Connectivity: The route table for a public subnet must include an entry for an IGW. The resources on the public subnet may now connect directly to the internet in this way. That is to say, instances deployed on a public subnet have unrestricted access to both the internet and the rest of the world.
2. Use cases:
   - Web servers: Servers that host websites or process client requests often reside on public subnets because they need unrestricted access to the internet.
   - Load balancers: Load balancers, which split incoming network traffic across many instances, are often located on public subnets to guarantee their availability to users on the internet.
   - Bastion hosts: A bastion host, sometimes called a leap box, is a server that provides access to resources located on other, private networks. Bastion hosts are often used on public subnets to provide administrators with safe remote access.

Private subnets:

1. Connectivity: The route table for a private subnet does not include a connection to the IGW. This prevents anything on the private subnet from communicating directly with the public internet.
2. Use cases:
   - Application servers: Hosting application servers and back-end services that don't need internet connectivity is a frequent use case for private subnets. In a VPC, resources may talk to one another and to other VPC resources without the need for additional networking components such as network address translation (NAT) gateways or virtual private gateways to access the internet.
   - Databases: To prevent their data from being exposed to the public internet, databases are often housed on private subnets. Secure connections from application servers in the same VPC, or VPN connections for on-premises access, allow administrators to restrict access to databases in private subnets.
   - Back-end processing: Data processing and batch jobs are two examples of back-end processing operations that may be executed successfully in a private subnet and do not need constant access to the internet.

The main differences between public and private subnets are the routing setup and the degree to which resources are accessible from the internet. Both kinds of subnets may coexist in the same VPC, giving businesses more leeway in creating secure and adaptable network designs.

9.4   INTERNET GATEWAYS AND NAT GATEWAYS

When it comes to connecting users to the resources hosted in an AWS VPC, the service makes use of two separate networking components: internet gateways and network address translation (NAT) gateways. [123–125] Figure 9.2 shows how internet and NAT gateways work in a VPC. Let's have a look at them separately:

9.4.1   INTERNET GATEWAYS

Connecting a VPC to the outside world, an IGW is a horizontally scalable, highly available AWS-managed service. By offering public subnet resources direct access to the internet, it improves their ability to transmit and receive data.

Key characteristics of an internet gateway:

1. Public connectivity: Public subnet resources may now get public IP addresses and establish direct internet connections with the help of an IGW. It enables this by setting up a default route in the VPC's route table that sends data out into the public network.
2. Inbound and outbound traffic: An IGW facilitates communication between the VPC and the outside world, both for incoming traffic destined for VPC resources and for outgoing traffic destined for the internet. As a result, web servers and other services located in public subnets may respond to requests from customers all around the World Wide Web.

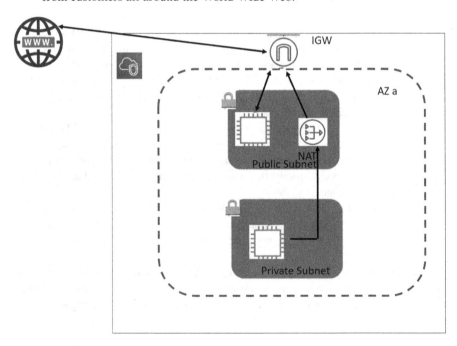

FIGURE 9.2   Internet gateways and NAT gateways.

Use cases for an internet gateway:

- Hosting public-facing applications: An IGW is typically employed when hosting publicly available web applications or services that must be visible through the internet.
- Load balancing: IGW-enabled public subnets are often coupled with load balancers, which spread incoming traffic over numerous instances or resources.

9.4.2 NAT Gateway

A managed AWS service that offers outbound internet access for resources in private subnets inside a VPC is known as a network address translation gateway. It enables instances on private subnets to create outbound internet connections while blocking direct incoming internet access.

Key characteristics of a NAT gateway:

1. Outbound connectivity: A NAT gateway allows instances on private subnets to connect to the internet for software updates, package downloads, and access to external APIs and services.
2. IP address translation: When instances in private subnets transmit traffic via a NAT gateway, their private IP addresses are converted to the NAT gateway's public IP address. This enables internet answers to reach the instances while protecting the anonymity of their private IP addresses.

Use cases for a NAT gateway:

- Outbound internet access: NAT gateways are widely used to offer internet connection for private subnet resources such as back-end servers or databases that need outbound access for software upgrades or access to external resources.
- Enhanced security: Instances in private subnets may access the internet without disclosing their private IP addresses to the external network by utilizing a NAT gateway, adding an extra degree of protection.

The functions of internet gateways and NAT gateways inside a virtual private network are distinct. While IGWs allow resources in public subnets to connect directly to the internet, NAT gateways allow resources in private subnets to access the internet from the outside while preventing unwanted traffic from entering the network. Which gateway is used in a VPC is determined by the resources' individual networking needs.

9.5 SECURITY AND ACCESS CONTROL IN A VPC

Security and access control for resources within a VPC may be managed with the help of two crucial networking technologies in AWS: network ACLs and security groups. Figure 9.3 shows this in detail. Let's have a look at them separately:

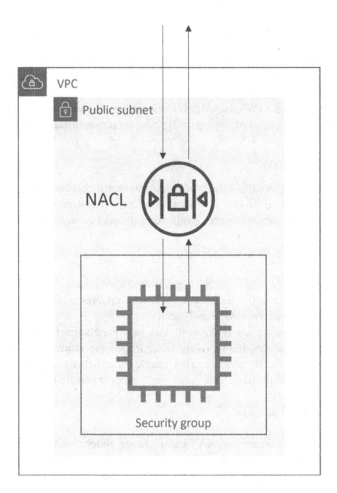

FIGURE 9.3   Security and access control in VPC.

9.5.1   NETWORK ACCESS CONTROL LISTS (ACLS)

Subnet-level traffic inside a VPC may be regulated using network ACLs, which are stateless, rules-based filters. By granting or blocking access depending on rules set for incoming and outgoing traffic flows, they give an extra line of protection to the process of safeguarding network traffic.

Key characteristics of network ACLs:

1. Subnet-level filtering: ACLs are linked to specific networks and assess incoming and outgoing traffic according to a predetermined set of criteria. They are used to restrict the flow of data into and out of a network segment (subnet).

2. Stateless: In contrast to security groups, which maintain their status, ACLs do not. This necessitates having different regulations for traffic coming in and vehicles going out. For this reason, if an incoming rule permits traffic, a similar outbound rule must also allow traffic in the other direction.
3. Rule priority: When evaluating an access control list, the rules with the smallest numbers are given priority. The proper evaluation of rules depends on the sequence in which they are configured.

Use cases for network ACLs:

* Fine-grained network traffic control: Network ACLs enable enterprises to create fine-grained restrictions over incoming and outgoing traffic at the subnet level. This allows users to limit traffic from particular IP addresses, restrict access to certain protocols or ports, and generally impose security regulations.
* Compliance and regulatory requirements: By enabling filtering and access restrictions at the network level, ACLs assist companies in meeting certain compliance needs. They offer a new level of protection and management for mission-critical or regulated workloads.

9.5.2 SECURITY GROUPS

In a virtual private cloud, communication between instances is managed by means of security groups, which are virtual firewalls with state. They are a cornerstone of virtual private cloud security because they allow users to set protocol-, port-, and IP address-based rules for regulating access to instances.

Key characteristics of security groups:

1. Instance-level filtering: Individual or collective instances may be assigned to security groups to assess network traffic in accordance with predetermined policies. Traffic is enabled to access certain instances or prevented, providing access control at the instance level.
2. Stateful: Because of their statefulness, security groups allow outgoing response traffic whenever an incoming rule permits it. As a result, security rule administration is streamlined, and only appropriate actions are authorized.
3. Dynamic updates: Modifications to security groups may be made on the fly and take effect instantly. Because of this adaptability, businesses may make rule adjustments to meet changing needs with little to no downtime.

Use cases for security groups:

- Instance-level security: Instances may be further safeguarded by ensuring that only approved traffic is allowed to access them using security groups. By establishing rules, businesses may restrict communication to authorized parties and shut off unused ports and protocols.
- Application security: By defining the parameters for both incoming and outgoing traffic, security groups ensure that apps may be accessed safely. They allow for the definition of granular restrictions, which in turn enables enterprises to compartmentalize their applications and implement access policies tailored to each one.

AWS VPC security relies heavily on network ACLs and security groups. Security groups provide protection at the instance level and stateful traffic management, whereas network ACLs operate at the subnet level and provide stateless traffic filtering. Organizations may safeguard their VPC resources with several layers of security and fine-grained access restrictions by combining ACLs and security groups.

9.6   VPC FLOW LOGS

Customers using AWS may use a feature called VPC Flow Logs to record data about the data transfers occurring inside a VPC. They may use it to better understand the VPC's security status by analyzing incoming and outgoing traffic, as well as by keeping tabs on how the network is behaving and fixing any connection problems that may arise. Key features of VPC Flow Logs include the following:

1. Logging network traffic: Information regarding IP traffic flows in a VPC, subnet, or network interface is recorded in the VPC Flow Logs. Each network connection's metadata comprises its source and destination IP addresses, port numbers, protocol, packet sizes, and timestamps.
2. Customizable log content: The fields and information that are recorded in VPC Flow Logs may be customized. Depending on the business's requirements, it's possible to either choose certain categories of traffic to record or record all traffic for in-depth analysis.
3. Visibility and monitoring: How VPC's network traffic is distributed can be seen when VPC Flow Logs is enabled. For the sake of troubleshooting and performance improvement, users may track throughput, look for patterns, and examine network activity. Subnets, AZs, and the connection between the VPC and external networks may all be better understood with the help of Flow Logs.
4. Security analysis: Improved network security analysis is made possible in large part by VPC Flow Logs. Log analysis may help administrators spot and examine unusual network activity, discover failed login attempts, and spot other dangers to the company VPC's security. Monitoring network security and regulatory compliance is greatly aided by Flow Logs.

5. Integration with other AWS services: VPC Flow Logs may be easily analyzed and automated using other AWS services and tools. For long-term
archiving, real-time monitoring, or running sophisticated analytics with
tools such as Amazon Athena, Amazon Kinesis Data Analytics, or third-
party log analysis solutions, users may export the flow logs to Amazon S3,
Amazon CloudWatch Logs, or Amazon Elasticsearch Service.
6. Troubleshooting and diagnostics: When investigating problems with VPC network connection, the Flow Logs may be quite helpful. Bottlenecks in the network, packet loss, latency issues, and even the cause of connection failures may
all be found by digging into the Flow Logs. This expedites the process of identifying and fixing network problems and decreases the time spent doing so.

Additional expenses for data storage and log processing are incurred when VPC
Flow Logs is enabled. However, it is a vital tool for efficiently monitoring and managing the VPC system owing to the improved network visibility, security analysis,
and troubleshooting capabilities it provides.

9.7 VPC PEERING

VPC peering is a networking setup in AWS that permits secure, one-to-one communication between two VPCs. [120, 121, 125] It's a safe and efficient approach to
link and share resources across various AWS accounts or regions, letting resources
in different VPCs communicate as if they were on the same network. Figure 9.4

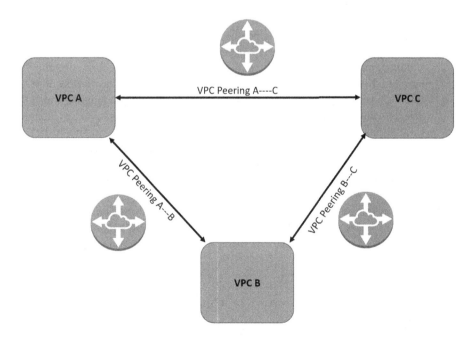

FIGURE 9.4   VPC peering.

explains VPC peering in a diagrammatic way. To better understand VPC peering, consider these factors:

1. Direct private connectivity: Through the use of AWS private backbone architecture, VPC peering allows for a direct network connection to be established between two VPCs. The data shared between the VPCs is private and untampered with since the connection is encrypted and does not go over the public internet.
2. Inter-VPC communication: When two VPCs are "peered," instances inside each VPC may exchange private IP addresses and interact as if they were on the same network. Because of this, resources, applications, and services in the peer VPCs may be accessed without any extra gateways or NAT.
3. Cross-account and Cross-Region connectivity: Connectivity between VPCs in various AWS accounts or Regions is possible via a process called "VPC peering." To preserve network isolation and control, this is especially helpful when resources need to be shared or accessed across multiple organizational units or locations.
4. Transitive peering: Using VPC peering, users may set up a mesh network of interconnected peers. This allows for indirect peering, or transitive peering, between VPCs, allowing resources in one VPC to interact with those in another VPC. As a result, less sophisticated routing configurations are required, which simplifies network design.
5. Security and access control: Peering across VPCs doesn't interfere with the built-in safety and access controls of individual VPCs. To ensure that only the necessary traffic is permitted to pass between the peer VPCs, network ACLs and security groups may be utilized.
6. Scalability and resilience: VPC peering can handle a huge number of simultaneous connections and scales quite well. Since traffic flows directly between VPCs rather than traveling via a centralized gateway, it does not establish a single point of failure. Because of this, scalable and highly available distributed systems are possible.
7. Limitations: There are a few caveats to VPC peering that we should be aware of. There are limitations on the number of Regions where a peering connection may be made, the number of IP addresses that can overlap, and the ability to change or remove an existing VPC peering relationship.

To facilitate resource sharing, cooperation, and faster network connection across VPCs, AWS provides a powerful tool known as VPC peering. It streamlines network design, improves data privacy, and lets dispersed applications run smoothly across several VPCs.

9.8   VPC ENDPOINTS

AWS VPC endpoints provide a safe and encrypted tunnel between the VPC and the AWS services it is authorized to use. VPC endpoints provide direct access to the

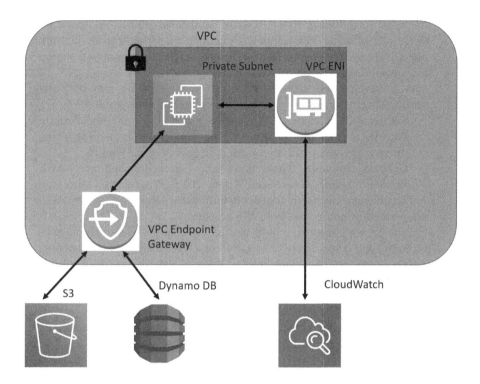

FIGURE 9.5   VPC endpoints.

services from inside the VPC, as opposed to accessing them over the public internet; this improves security and performance and simplifies network setups. Figure 9.5 shows the VPC endpoints. Important features of VPC terminals include:

1. Private access to AWS services: Customers may bypass the requirement for internet gateways, NAT gateways, and virtual private gateways by connecting directly to AWS services such as Amazon S3, DynamoDB, and others via the VPC's endpoints. This increases security by preventing communication with the services from ever leaving the AWS network and going over the public internet.
2. Secure and isolated connectivity: Secure and segregated access to AWS services is made possible using VPC endpoints. There is no requirement for data traveling between the VPC and the service to leave the AWS network backbone. The possibility of data being intercepted or leaked while in transit across the internet is reduced.
3. Simplified network configuration: Network setup, routing, and access control may all be made easier using VPC endpoints. Users may access AWS services without setting up and managing internet gateways, NAT gates, or VPN gateways. This simplicity improves network efficiency by decreasing the amount of time spent on administrative tasks.

4. Improved performance: Reduced latency and enhanced network speed are the results of using VPC endpoints to connect a virtual private network directly to an AWS service. This is especially useful for programs that need to transport large amounts of data quickly to AWS.
5. Service-specific and gateway endpoints: VPC endpoints may be either service-specific or gateway, both of which are available from AWS.
   • Service-specific endpoints: Customers may utilize these nodes within the VPC to connect to various AWS services. An Amazon S3 endpoint, for instance, gives VPC users immediate access to S3 buckets.
   • Gateway endpoints: These nodes allow users to connect to AWS PrivateLink-enabled services. Using AWS PrivateLink, users can securely and discreetly connect to third-party services offered by AWS partners or housed in other AWS accounts.
6. Integration with security groups and access control: Users may manage incoming and outgoing traffic to and from a VPC endpoint by associating it with a security group. They may set fine-grained access control rules to permit or deny traffic to the endpoint using security groups and network ACLs.
7. Cross-Region VPC endpoints: Multiple AWS Regions may be used as VPC endpoints. Connectivity and data transfer across Regions are enhanced by using a VPC endpoint to access supported services in another area.

Accessing AWS services from inside a VPC is now easier than ever with the help of VPC endpoints, which are safe, performant, and streamlined. VPC endpoints allow businesses to simplify network setups, boost network speed, and fortify application security.

9.9 NETWORKING SOLUTIONS IN VPC

Connecting on-premises facilities to AWS cloud resources securely and reliably is made possible by two networking technologies offered by AWS: Site-to-Site VPN and AWS Direct Connect. Figure 9.6 shows the networking solutions in AWS. Let's look at each of these options.

9.9.1 SITE-TO-SITE VPN

Connecting the network located on premises to an AWS VPC requires setting up a secure, encrypted tunnel via the public internet, which is what Site-to-Site VPN does. Customers may use it to safely connect any on-premises data center or office to cloud-based services.

Key aspects of Site-to-Site VPN:

1. Encrypted connectivity: When connecting the on-premises network to the VPC, data is encrypted using IPsec (Internet Protocol Security) to protect its privacy and integrity during transit across the public internet.

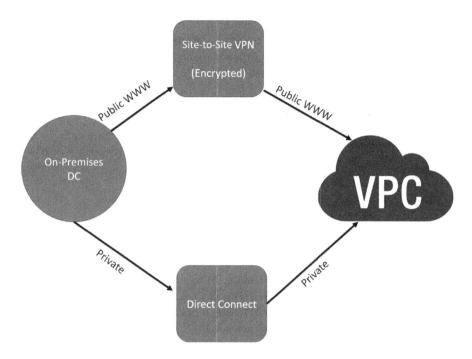

FIGURE 9.6   Networking solutions in VPC.

2. Flexible connectivity options: Site-to-Site VPN works with many different VPN configurations and devices, letting users connect with any VPN appliance that uses an approved VPN protocol.
3. Scalability: Using AWS Transit Gateway, which allows centralized administration and connection for various VPCs and on-premises systems, customers may grow a Site-to-Site VPN solution to handle bigger network installations.
4. Redundancy and high availability: Site-to-Site VPN lets users set up parallel tunnels, allowing for high availability and automatic failover. Connecting the on-premises network to the VPC in a robust fashion requires setting up numerous VPN connections.

Use cases for Site-to-Site VPN:

• Extending an on-premises network: Site-to-Site VPN allows users to extend an on-premises network into AWS, providing safe access to cloud services while retaining connection to on-premises resources.
• Hybrid cloud deployments: Site-to-Site VPN is ideal for hybrid cloud architectures that distribute apps and data across on-premises and cloud environments. It offers seamless connection between on-premises infrastructure and cloud services.

- Disaster recovery and business continuity: Site-to-Site VPN may be used to create a secure connection between a primary on-premises site and a secondary site on AWS, allowing disaster recovery and business continuity plans to be implemented.

9.9.2   AWS DIRECT CONNECT

AWS Direct Connect is a dedicated network connection that connects the on-premises network to AWS through a private, high-bandwidth link. When compared with Site-to-Site VPN, it provides a more constant and stable network experience.

Key aspects of AWS Direct Connect:

1. Dedicated connection: Direct Connect creates a direct physical link between the network and AWS, avoiding the use of the public internet. This connection is made through a Direct Connect site or a partner data center.
2. Higher bandwidth and lower latency: When compared with Site-to-Site VPN's internet-based connection, Direct Connect provides more bandwidth possibilities (from 1 Gbps to 100 Gbps). It offers low-latency connections, which are advantageous for latency-sensitive workloads or data-intensive applications.
3. Private and secure connectivity: Direct Connect establishes a private connection, preventing visitors from using the public internet. This improves security and allows users to comply with industry-specific standards and requirements.
4. Virtual interfaces: Direct Connect enables the creation of several virtual interfaces, allowing access to various VPCs or AWS services via the same physical connection.
5. Redundancy and high availability: One may set up redundant connections to AWS using Direct Connect to achieve high availability and fault tolerance.

Use cases for AWS Direct Connect:

- Hybrid cloud deployments: Direct Connect allows for easy integration and communication between on-premises infrastructure and AWS cloud services. It offers a dedicated and private connection that improves hybrid cloud architectures' performance, security, and dependability. This is especially important when enterprises wish to extend their on-premises networks into AWS or set up a hybrid architecture to make use of the advantages of both environments.
- Data transfer and workload migration: Direct Connect speeds up data flows between on-premises data centers and AWS. It enables large-scale data transfers, such as shifting massive databases or undertaking mass workload migrations, by using high-speed, dedicated connections. This decreases the time necessary to transport data over the public internet, saves network costs, and assures effective cloud migration.

- Latency-sensitive applications: Certain applications, such as real-time data processing, financial services, or gaming, need low-latency networking to function well. By offering a dedicated connection with consistent network performance, Direct Connect reduces network delay. This is advantageous for latency-sensitive applications that need constant, rapid connectivity between on-premises and AWS resources.
- High-volume data access: Direct Connect may help organizations working with massive datasets, such as scientific research, big data analytics, or media processing. It provides high-bandwidth, low-latency connectivity to AWS services such as Amazon S3, Amazon Redshift, and Amazon EC2 instances, allowing for quicker and more efficient data processing and analysis.
- Regulatory compliance and data privacy: Organizations may use Direct Connect to ensure compliance with industry-specific legislation or internal data privacy rules. By creating a private connection to AWS, data is not exposed to possible security threats or compliance breaches on the public internet.
- Disaster recovery and business continuity: Direct Connect is crucial in providing effective disaster recovery solutions. Organizations may set up redundant AWS connections to provide high availability and fault tolerance for important workloads. Organizations may swiftly resume operations in the case of a catastrophe or interruption in their core on-premises environment by duplicating data and apps in the AWS cloud.

9.10   TRANSIT GATEWAY

AWS Transit Gateway is a centralized and highly scalable networking solution that streamlines network connections across various Amazon VPCs, on-premises networks, and AWS Direct Connect. Figure 9.7 shows the architecture of Transit Gateway. It serves as a hub for traffic routing and as a single point of entrance and departure for network communication.

Key aspects of AWS Transit Gateway:

1. Centralized network hub: Transit Gateway serves as a central hub, connecting many VPCs and on-premises networks through a single gateway. This eliminates the difficulty of maintaining separate connections for each VPC and simplifies network design.
2. Simplified routing: With Transit Gateway's streamlined routing paradigm, administrators can easily design and maintain route tables to direct data across networks. Using Border Gateway Protocol (BGP) and other dynamic routing protocols, it is possible to change network routing tables quickly and efficiently.
3. Scalability: Transit Gateway supports a large number of VPCs and private networks because of its horizontal scalability. Up to 5,000 VPCs may be linked, and thousands of AWS Direct Connect and VPN tunnels can be established.

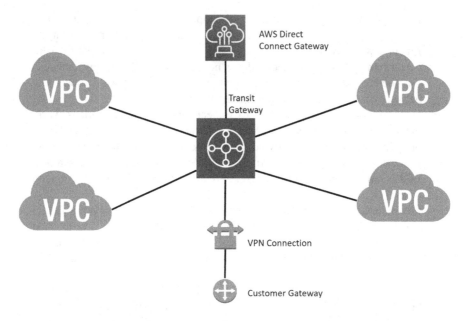

FIGURE 9.7   Transit Gateway.

4. Inter-Region connectivity: Users may link VPCs in various AWS Regions by using Transit Gateway's inter-region peering capabilities. This paves the way for global network topologies and improves the flow of data between geographically dispersed resources.
5. Simplified network security: Because of its compatibility with AWS Network Firewall, traffic passing through the gateway may be subject to a unified set of firewall rules. This aids in enforcing uniform security policies across all interconnected networks.
6. Network insights and monitoring: The network traffic going via Transit Gateway may be monitored and analyzed using a number of different AWS services and tools, consisting of CloudWatch measurements, VPC Flow Logs, and the ability to integrate with other network monitoring systems.

Use cases for AWS Transit Gateway:

- Hub-and-spoke network architecture: Transit Gateway works effectively in hub-and-spoke network architectures, where many VPCs or on-premises networks (spokes) are linked to a central hub. It reduces the number of necessary connections and streamlines administration of the network.
- Multi-VPC communication: Without requiring VPC peering connections between every pair of VPCs, Transit Gateway offers efficient communication between several VPCs. It enables VPCs to securely connect with one another, exchange resources, and administer their network's rules from a single location.

- Hybrid cloud connectivity: By acting as a central entrance and exit point for traffic between AWS and on-premises networks, Transit Gateway streamlines interoperability between the two. It supports hybrid cloud deployments by easing the connection between on-premises resources and AWS services.
- Global network architectures: Transit Gateway's capability for peering across AWS Regions makes it possible to build global network topologies that span several data centers. It's a scalable and unified networking option for companies with a worldwide footprint.

Because of the flexibility and simplicity of AWS Transit Gateway, even the most complicated network infrastructures can be easily managed and scaled. It improves network throughput, streamlines routing, and facilitates smooth interoperability between virtual private clouds and on-premises infrastructure.

9.11 CONCLUSION

When it comes to deploying resources in the cloud, the AWS VPC is the best bet for safety and flexibility. Subnets, internet gateways, NAT gateways, network access control lists, security groups, VPC Flow Logs, VPC peering, and connectivity methods including site-to-site VPN and AWS Direct Connect have all been covered in this chapter. With the help of VPC, businesses may create network infrastructures that are both adaptable and secure.

10 Account Management, Billing, and Support in AWS Cloud

10.1 INTRODUCTION

When it comes to streamlining operations and making the most of cloud services, flawless assistance and careful financial management are crucial. This chapter delves into the fundamentals of AWS's billing, invoicing, and customer service infrastructure. By learning the ins and outs of these structures, organizations can better manage their AWS expenses, allocate their resources, and benefit from AWS's complete support.

To kick off our investigation, we take a look at how AWS Organizations can accommodate a wide variety of account setups and ensure they work well together. This architecture enables businesses to administer and manage many AWS accounts from a single location, which improves security, resource sharing, and cost control. We explore the idea of service control rules, which allow administrators to specify granular access restrictions, and we talk about how AWS Control Tower may help streamline and automate the process of establishing a properly designed, multi-account infrastructure.

We look at the many tools and methods available on AWS for cost optimization, which is at the core of any cloud strategy. We delve into the AWS total cost of ownership (TCO) methodology, which helps companies determine whether it is more cost-effective to operate their workloads using AWS than using on-premises alternatives. Furthermore, we study cost allocation tags, cost and use reports, and the Cost Explorer tool, all of which provide detailed insights and reporting options for monitoring and assessing spending habits.

AWS Budgets is a robust tool for establishing cost and use criteria, generating alerts, and monitoring spending, and we explore its capabilities and advantages in light of the importance of budgeting in financial planning. We also stress the significance of AWS Trusted Advisor, an AI-powered consultant that provides advice on how to save expenses, beef up security, and boost performance.

Finally, we'll discuss AWS support plans, which are available in a variety of tiers to meet the needs of different businesses. We break down the various support levels, response times, and resource availability so that companies can choose the plan that best suits their needs and keeps operations running smoothly.

In this chapter, we'll explore the AWS accounting, billing, and support systems so that customers are prepared to handle the financial challenges of cloud computing. This chapter will serve as a comprehensive guide to making the most of AWS,

DOI: 10.1201/9781003406136-10

whether one is an administrator looking for cost optimization strategies, a financial analyst trying to allocate resources efficiently, or a support professional trying to provide exceptional customer experiences.

10.2 AWS ORGANIZATIONS

AWS Organizations is a robust tool that streamlines the administration of several AWS accounts throughout a company. It serves as a command center from which administrators may manage and oversee account-wide AWS resources, security configurations, and policies.

By creating a hierarchy of accounts in AWS Organizations, businesses are better able to enforce security policies, compartmentalize resources, and control spending. [129] It allows for a centralized management structure while also allowing for individual departments, initiatives, or business units to have their own accounts and, therefore, more autonomy.

The ability to set up Service Control Policies (SCPs) is a major perk of AWS Organizations. SCPs let managers set very specific permissions and access limits for certain groups or users. Organizations may use SCPs to enforce security standards, limit access to certain services or resources, and guarantee compliance with applicable regulations.

Integration with AWS Control Tower is also a crucial part of AWS Organizations. AWS Control Tower streamlines and automates the process of establishing and regulating a properly designed, cross-account infrastructure. To guarantee that accounts and workloads are provisioned in accordance with AWS's security and compliance rules, it provides pre-configured guardrails and best practices. With AWS Control Tower, creating new accounts is easy, and the administrative burden of maintaining many accounts is much reduced.

Organizations may enhance their security and compliance, share and collaborate more efficiently, and have more insight into their AWS infrastructure by using AWS Organizations. By standardizing billing and expense management procedures for all clients, it facilitates cost savings.

AWS Organizations is a cornerstone offering that gives businesses the tools they need to administer and manage their AWS accounts and resources. To fully take advantage of AWS, while still keeping a scalable and well-organized cloud architecture, it offers the required tools and controls to assure security, compliance, and effective resource management. Features of AWS Organizations can be seen in Figure 10.1.

10.2.1 MULTIPLE ACCOUNT CONFIGURATIONS

When discussing AWS Organizations and the ability to establish and manage numerous AWS accounts inside an organization, the term "multiple account configurations" is used. [126, 127] One may create a hierarchical structure of accounts in AWS Organizations, allowing for centralized administration and governance while still maintaining security limits and resource isolation. Here's how AWS Organizations handles numerous account configurations:

FIGURE 10.1   Features of AWS Organizations.

1. Hierarchical structure: With AWS Organizations, businesses may set up a group of accounts with a parent account and several sub-accounts, called members. The root account is the most powerful account in an organization and serves in an administrative capacity. Each member of the company will have their own AWS account.
2. Account isolation: Within AWS Organizations, every member account has its own set of tools and capabilities. Each user's workloads, apps, and data are kept safe and separate because of this separation.
3. Centralized management: All of the business's accounts on AWS can be managed and governed from a single location with AWS Organizations. Policies, permissions, access restrictions, and security measures must be

enforced for all accounts. Service Control Policies enable administrators to set limits on the services and activities that users are permitted to access and perform.

4. Resource sharing: AWS Organizations makes it easy for several accounts to pool their resources. Amazon S3 buckets, AWS Lambda functions, and Amazon RDS databases are just some of the resources that may be shared across accounts in the same company. This facilitates teamwork and allows for the isolation and security of individual accounts to be maintained when working together.

5. Security and compliance: The use of AWS Organizations allows for the uniform application of security and compliance policies to all associated AWS accounts. Organization-wide policies may be put in place to ensure uniformity in security measures and compliance with laws and regulations across all accounts.

6. Cost optimization: Billing and expenses may be managed centrally using AWS Organizations. Billing for all members may be merged into one statement for streamlined budgeting and reporting. By establishing cost controls, allocating funds, and gaining insight into spending habits, AWS organization service facilitates improved cost optimization.

Managing an organization's AWS resources across numerous accounts using AWS Organizations is a scalable and adaptable solution. It streamlines administrative processes, boosts safety and compliance, makes it easier to pool resources, and optimizes money management. This feature allows businesses to more easily manage their AWS infrastructure, streamline their operations, and improve their cloud's management and governance.

10.3   SERVICE CONTROL POLICIES

AWS Organizations' SCPs are a powerful tool for defining granular permissions and access restrictions at the account or organization level. [129] SCPs aid in enforcing security and compliance requirements across an organization's many AWS accounts. A hierarchy in Service Control Policies can be seen in Figure 10.2. Here's a deeper look at how they work:

1. Scope and hierarchy: AWS Organizations is where SCPs are managed and implemented. All accounts, even those belonging to subordinate members, are affected. Organizational units (OUs) serve as containers for accounts, and SCPs may be associated with either the root of the organization or individual OUs.

2. Permissions and access control: Permissions for using AWS services and performing activities may be defined using SCPs. They function by preventing unauthorized access and replacing account-level or IAM (Identity and Access Management) policy-based permissions. The "deny by default" concept used by SCPs means that all activities and services are forbidden until specifically authorized.

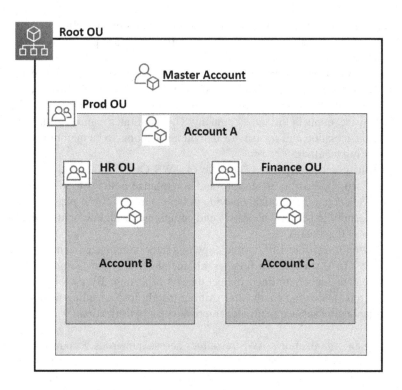

FIGURE 10.2 Hierarchy in Service Control Policies.

3. Granular controls: SCPs let users fine-tune their account's access privileges for certain tasks and services. Policymakers have the option of dictating which users have access to which services behaviors, and even which geographical areas they may visit. This paves the way for businesses to mandate account-wide adherence to security standards and regulatory mandates inside AWS.

4. Compliance and security: SCPs are essential to an organization's ability to remain compliant and secure. By outlining stringent controls and limits, businesses can make sure no services or activities that might compromise security or run foul of regulations are authorized. By enforcing uniform security policies across all accounts, SCPs lessen the possibility of intrusion or misconfiguration.

5. Policy inheritance: In a hierarchical structure, SCPs are passed down to subordinate accounts. All accounts within the scope of an organization or OU will be subject to the SCPs set at that level. Account-specific SCPs, however, may be created and connected to use in place of inherited policies.

6. Evaluation order: There is a precise sequence in which SCPs are considered when numerous ones are applied to a single account. Policies that are assigned to an account directly take priority over those that are inherited

from the organization or OUs. This permits granular policy adjustment and account-specific customization without compromising the organization-wide uniformity of controls.

Strong governance and control over AWS accounts in an organization may be established by using Service Control Policies in AWS Organizations. SCPs provide a potent method for implementing security, compliance, and access restrictions, guaranteeing that a company's AWS infrastructure is consistently governed by the same set of rules.

10.4   CONTROL TOWER

AWS offers a solution called AWS Control Tower that makes it easier to establish and manage a safe multi-account arrangement with good architecture. [127] It provides a standardized, automated method for establishing and administering numerous AWS accounts in a manner that adheres to best practices and security guidelines. The primary advantages and characteristics of AWS Control Tower are as follows:

1. Account provisioning: With AWS Control Tower, users can quickly and reliably set up many AWS accounts with a unified configuration. It implements security best practices recommended by AWS, such as enabling logging and monitoring, assigning IAM roles, and enforcing security policies.
2. Multi-account environment: AWS Organizations' Control Tower facilitates the creation of multi-account structures. It establishes a primary account, known as the "guardrail account," which acts as the nerve center for regulatory compliance and security. This setup permits compartmentalization, pooling of available resources, and account-wide optimization of workload management.
3. Security guardrails: Guardrails are provided by Control Tower and are pre-configured sets of rules and controls that are used to ensure security and compliance. These boundaries assist in avoiding insecure deployments and misconfigurations and make the system more reliable overall.
4. Account baseline: All members' accounts are brought up to the same standard by Control Tower. Networking and VPC setups, as well as security measures, fall under this category. The consistency and safety of user accounts are both improved by the account baseline.
5. Continuous compliance: Control Tower is always keeping watch to make sure everyone is following the rules. Any discovered infractions are immediately fixed, and the compliance status of all accounts is made clear. This preventative method is useful for keeping things safe and legal.
6. Account lifecycle management: Control Tower provides support throughout the account lifespan, from the initial onboarding of a new account, through the management of any updates or adjustments that may occur along the way, to its eventual retirement. It simplifies the process of administering a large number of accounts and speeds up routine administrative processes.

7. AWS Marketplace integration: As a result of its compatibility with AWS Marketplace, Control Tower facilitates the search for, purchase of, and roll-out of, verified third-party services and applications. The process of implementing and administering AWS Marketplace services and applications is streamlined as a result.

AWS Control Tower allows businesses to set up and manage a multi-account environment, which is secure and compliant and has good architecture, in record time. It reduces the operational burden and complexity of managing many AWS accounts by providing automation, standardization, and centralized management. Control Tower allows businesses to manage a safe and reliable AWS infrastructure without diverting attention from essential operations.

10.5   TOTAL COST OF OWNERSHIP

The TCO of an AWS infrastructure or application is the sum of all the money spent on it over a certain time frame. Employee salaries, computer purchases, software licensing, data center upkeep, and other incidental expenditures are all included in the total cost of ownership. Components of total cost of ownership can be seen in Figure 10.3. Consider the following items while determining the AWS TCO:

1. Compute resources: The cost of using computing services, such as EC2 instances, Auto Scaling groups, and Elastic Load Balancers, is included here.
2. Storage: Data preservation and backup storage options, such as Amazon S3, Amazon EBS, and Amazon Glacier, come at a cost.
3. Data transfer: Costs are incurred while sending data to or from an AWS service via the internet. Both incoming and outgoing data transmission fees are included.
4. Networking: This includes VPC expenses, subnet expenses, NAT gateway expenses, VPN connection expenses, and so on.
5. Database services: Amazon RDS (Relational Database Service), Amazon DynamoDB, and Amazon Redshift are examples of managed database services.
6. Management tools: Costs are associated with using Amazon Web Services' management instruments, including CloudTrail, CloudWatch, Config, and Systems Manager.
7. Support plans: There are costs for AWS support plans, which provide varied degrees of technical help and advice.
8. Third-party services: The charges for any AWS Marketplace or other provider-purchased third-party applications or services must be accounted for.
9. Personnel: There are staffing expenses for AWS administration, maintenance, and new-app development. Pay, training, and certification are all factored in.

FIGURE 10.3 Components of total cost of ownership.

10. Data center and infrastructure: While AWS takes care of the core infrastructure, customers may incur extra expenses for things such as networking hardware, electricity, air conditioning, and security.

To effectively calculate AWS TCO, businesses must take into account use patterns, application design, scalability needs, data transfer volumes, and other unique aspects that impact AWS expenditures. AWS offers a TCO calculator tool that may assist the process of estimating the TCO for different scenarios based on the inputs and assumptions.

10.6   COST ALLOCATION TAGS

AWS cost allocation tags are key–value pairs that may be assigned to AWS resources, including EC2 instances, S3 buckets, RDS databases, and many more. [128, 129] These tags enable administrators to identify and monitor resource consumption and expenditures in accordance with the business's demands and organizational structure. Cost allocation tags are generally utilized inside AWS accounts for cost allocation and reporting. Here are some important factors to remember regarding cost allocation tags:

1. Flexible tagging: Tags created in the AWS Management Console, AWS Command Line Interface, or AWS API may be applied to resources. Key–value pairs (such as "Department:Marketing" or "Project:ABC") are the standard for tags.
2. Granularity and hierarchy: Assigning numerous tags to a single resource allows for finer-grained cost monitoring and distribution. Users may even establish nested associations with tags (such as "Environment:Production" or "Environment:Production/Region:US") owing to the hierarchical nature of the tagging system.
3. Cost allocation reporting: For further in-depth reporting and analysis, organizations may use the cost allocation tags available in AWS Cost Explorer and AWS Cost and Usage Reports. Tags allow users to sort and organize expenses according to several categories, including work groups, projects, and settings.
4. Budgeting and forecasting: Users can make more accurate projections and budgets with the help of cost allocation tags. They may specify spending limitations per tag and be alerted when those restrictions are exceeded.
5. Resource grouping: Using tags, users may organize resources into categories, which are logical groupings of resources with similar properties. By offering a centralized view of connected resources, resource groupings ease administration and monitoring duties.
6. AWS Cost allocation tagging API: Users may manage the resources' tags in a programmable manner using AWS's API. This application programming interface may be used to automate and standardize tagging procedures.

Users may optimize expenditure and properly divide expenses across various aspects of the company with the help of cost allocation tags, which allow users to obtain more insight into AWS bills. Using these tags wisely will allow companies to track and control their AWS budget with more precision and accuracy.

10.7   COST AND USAGE REPORTS

The AWS Cost and Usage Reports (CUR) function allows users to see comprehensive data about AWS expenditure and use. Better cost management and optimization are possible with its in-depth analysis and tracking of AWS expenditure. Some highlights of the Usage and Cost Reports are as follows:

1. Report contents: Information about how much businesses used an AWS resource, how much it costs users, and more metadata may be seen in the Cost and Usage Reports. The reports feature itemized information that may be tailored to cover any number of characteristics and kinds of use.
2. Granularity and frequency: The reports may be tailored to demand in terms of both detail and frequency. Users may choose between hourly, daily, and monthly report generation. Hourly, daily, and monthly summaries of consumption and associated expenditures are also available.
3. Data formats: Comma-separated values (CSVs), Parquet, and Apache Arrow are just some of the formats that may be used to create Cost and Usage Reports. Data processing and analysis needs should guide the format selection.
4. Data delivery: Cost and Usage Reports may be sent to customers by whatever method they like. Delivery to an Amazon S3 bucket, direct data input into Amazon Redshift, and email delivery are all possibilities offered by AWS.
5. Customization and filtering: The reports may be modified to include any relevant use categories, tags, or metadata fields in the cost breakdown. This gives businesses the flexibility to modify the reports to reflect the cost factors that are most important to them.
6. Cost and Usage Report with resource IDs: This function enriches the reports by including resource IDs. It improves the accuracy of the expense attribution and analysis by linking consumption and billing information to individual AWS services.
7. Integration with cost management tools: There is no disruption in service between AWS Cost Explorer, AWS Budgets, and third-party cost management tools, and the same is true of the Cost and Usage Reports. Customers may then use this information to plan expenditures and draw out forecasts.
8. Historical and current data: Organizations may use the information in the Cost and Usage Reports to look at trends in expenditure over time and track the current cost of doing business.

Using the information provided by the Cost and Usage Reports, businesses can better understand AWS expenditure, find potential areas for making savings, and distribute those savings fairly across the company. They need these reports so that they can see how much they're spending on AWS, where the cash is going, and how they may reduce expenditures.

10.8 COST EXPLORER

AWS offers a web application called AWS Cost Explorer that does just that: It lets customers see, evaluate, and comprehend AWS expenditures and use. It gives businesses a bird's-eye perspective of the AWS budget, so they can monitor expenditures, pinpoint the sources of those costs, and make educated choices about how to reduce those costs. Some highlights of AWS's Cost Explorer are as follows:

1. Cost visualization: Organizations may get a visual depiction of AWS expenditure over time with the help of Cost Explorer's interactive charts and graphs. They may use it to obtain insight into the costs by investigating cost patterns, outliers, and trends.
2. Customizable time frames: Daily, monthly, or custom date range analyses are all possible for both expenses and consumption. This adaptability allows users to zero in on certain time frames of interest and make cost comparisons across many time frames.
3. Cost breakdowns: AWS expenses may be broken down further by the many dimensions offered by Cost Explorer, including service, associated accounts, tags, geographies, and use kinds. This level of detail allows for more precise cost optimization and spending allocation.
4. Forecasting: Using past data, users can make sound forecasts about future expenses with the help of Cost Explorer's cost forecasting features. Budgets, expenditure goals, and estimated monetary effect of changes to the AWS environment may all be planned for with the aid of these projections.
5. Anomaly detection: Anomaly detection capabilities included in Cost Explorer help keep users apprised of any strange fluctuations in prices or deviations from the norm in purchasing habits. Cost spikes, wasteful resource use, and billing anomalies may then be investigated.
6. Savings opportunities: To assist in making savings, Cost Explorer offers suggestions and insights. It identifies areas where savings might be made, including buying reserved instances, downsizing instances, or maximizing storage capacity.
7. Integration with AWS Cost and Usage Reports: Cost Explorer's integration with AWS CUR makes it easy to see particular line-item data and tailor cost analysis to needs based on characteristics, tags, or metadata.
8. Data export: Cost Explorer lets users export information for analysis or to be used with other programs. Because of this, users may integrate AWS pricing information with their own company's data for a deeper cost study.

AWS Cost Explorer may be viewed by authorized users using the AWS Management Console. It gives businesses the data and analysis necessary to control and reduce overall AWS spending.

10.9   AWS BUDGETS

AWS Budgets is a service that allows users to plan, monitor, and control AWS expenditures. They may set spending limits, be notified when they've hit those limits, and otherwise exert more control over their AWS bill. Budgeting on Amazon Web Services involves, briefly:

1. Budget Creation: Users may tailor AWS Budgets to meet their unique requirements for cost control with the Budget Creation feature. Individual accounts, account groups, or even individual AWS services may all have their own spending limits established.

2. Budget types: AWS Budgets supports various budget types, including cost budgets, usage budgets, and reservation budgets. Cost budgets track actual spending, usage budgets monitor resource usage, and reservation budgets focus on monitoring and optimizing reserved instances.

3. Budget threshold: Users may restrict spending to a certain amount each month or each quarter by establishing a budget threshold. Financial or time-based thresholds may be set, as well as thresholds based on particular aspects of cost and use (such as service, location, or tags).

4. Alerts and notifications: AWS Budgets has monitoring and notification options to keep customers abreast of the spending plan at all times. Email, Amazon's SNS, and the AWS Personal Health Dashboard are all options for getting notifications.

5. Forecast costs: Forecasted costs are predictions of future expenditure based on previous data and patterns and may be included in budgets. The ability to foresee and prepare for future expenditure on AWS is facilitated by accurate cost estimates.

6. Multiple time frames: Users can set budgets for monthly, quarterly, or arbitrary time periods. Because of this adaptability, spending plans may be coordinated with billing periods and other aspects of financial planning.

7. Actuals vs Budgets comparison: AWS Budgets allows users to compare actual expenditures with planned expenditures. The ability to monitor progress and spot discrepancies is a prerequisite for proactive cost management and course correction.

8. Integration with Cost Explorer: AWS Budgets works in tandem with AWS Cost Explorer to provide customers with a unified picture of the economy and financial projections. With this connection, they may examine spending patterns and adjust as needed to reduce expenses.

9. Budget actions: With AWS Budgets, users may set up actions to be taken when a certain amount of money is spent. Sending alerts, running AWS Lambda functions, and automating tasks in AWS Systems Manager are all examples of possible actions.

Organizations can set spending limits, track use, and stay on top of their AWS bill with the aid of AWS Budgets. It assists in keeping an eye on AWS expenditure and ensuring it doesn't exceed limits.

10.10   TRUSTED ADVISOR

If users are looking to save money, beef up security, and streamline operations on AWS, they should go no further than AWS Trusted Advisor. In order to determine where a present AWS setup may be improved, it uses AWS best practices and compares them with the current setup. Some highlights of AWS Trusted Advisor are as follows.

1. Service checks: Cost optimization, performance, security, fault tolerance, and service restrictions are just some of the topics that Trusted Advisor will examine in the AWS architecture. Potential problems and optimization possibilities are uncovered via an examination of the resources, setups, and use patterns.

2. Cost optimization: Trusted Advisor provides advice on how to save money on AWS bills. It suggests ways to reduce costs by right-sizing instances, taking advantage of discounted pricing plans, and doing away with unused assets.

3. Performance: Trusted Advisor analyzes the AWS infrastructure and settings to spot any sluggish spots or wasted effort. It may help businesses improve application speeds and optimize the infrastructure.

4. Security: Trusted Advisor performs a security audit of the AWS infrastructure and offers advice on how to fix any flaws it finds. It provides advice on how to fix problems with IAM permissions, security group setups, and information safety.

5. Fault tolerance: The infrastructure's fault tolerance and availability may be enhanced with the help of Trusted Advisor's analysis. It aids in identifying potential weak spots, recommends doubling up on resources, and details how to organize for emergency situations.

6. Service limits: If users are getting close to or have already reached one of AWS's service restrictions, Trusted Advisor will let them know. They can avoid interruptions in service and ask for higher limits if they need them if they use this.

7. Integration and notifications: Trusted Advisor syncs with the AWS Management Console to provide customers with access to a dynamic dashboard that summarizes the health of the account, along with any relevant advice. Users can also set up alerts to be notified if there are changes or new suggestions.

8. Business and Enterprise Support plans: Customers with Business and Enterprise Support subscriptions get access to extra inspections and suggestions from Trusted Advisor. These policies allow participants to gain entry to broader screenings and better assistance programs.

AWS Trusted Advisor offers proactive advice and suggestions to help businesses optimize existing AWS infrastructure, improve security, and reduce expenses. They may increase the efficiency, performance, and reliability of the AWS resources by following its suggestions while adhering to AWS best practices.

10.11 SUPPORT PLANS

A variety of AWS support plans are available to meet the demands of a wide range of clients. To help users maximize the AWS infrastructure and resolve any difficulties that may develop, AWS offers several support options that provide access to technical assistance, tools, and other perks. Support plans in AWS can be seen in Figure 10.4. The primary AWS support packages are as follows:

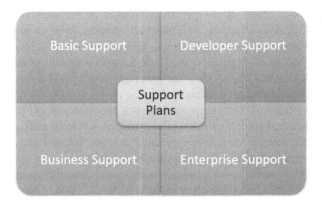

FIGURE 10.4 Support plans in AWS.

1. Basic Support: All AWS clients may make use of the company's free basic support services which include access to customer care for account and billing questions, as well as documentation, white papers, help forums, and more. There is no technical assistance or promised response times with the Basic Support plan. Here are some key features and benefits of the Basic Support plan:

   - Documentation and resources: Access to AWS documentation, white papers, frequently asked questions (FAQs), and the AWS Knowledge Center are all part of the Basic Support package. A variety of technical resources are available to users to help them learn about and make the most of AWS.
   - AWS Community Forums: As AWS clients with Basic Support, users get access to the AWS Community Forums, where they may discuss topics of interest with other AWS customers, learn from their experiences, and provide their own insights. The forums serve as a hub for mutual aid and education.
   - Service Health Dashboard: Customers can access the AWS Service Health Dashboard which displays real-time data on the availability of AWS services and AWS Regions. Customers can know in advance when there may be downtime, problems with performance, or scheduled maintenance.
   - Access to AWS Trusted Advisor (limited checks): AWS Trusted Advisor, which provides automatic reviews and suggestions for cost optimization, security, performance, and fault tolerance, is included in the Basic Support tier. Keep in mind that Basic Support does not include all of the safeguards and functions that come with Trusted Advisor.

   It is essential to keep in mind that the Basic Support plan does not include any technical assistance or guaranteed response times for the purpose of addressing technical difficulties. Customers may need to consider subscribing to one of the premium support plans, such as Developer Support, Business Support, or Enterprise Support, in order to get technical help and quicker response times. These benefits are only available to paying customers. In general, the Basic Support plan will assist in getting started with AWS by providing the necessary core tools and access to basic account and invoicing assistance.

2. Developer Support: Developer Support is a premium support package that offers technical help with AWS infrastructure, services, and applications. It provides general advice, best practice suggestions, and assistance with service-specific queries. Response times are determined by severity, with urgent situations receiving quicker responses. Here are the key features and benefits of the Developer Support plan:

   • Technical support: Access to email-based technical help from AWS specialists is part of the Developer help package. Users may send in questions on the infrastructure, applications, and services offered by AWS. When asked for tips on best practice or general advice, AWS Support typically responds within 12–24 business hours.

   • Service limit increase support: If users are AWS clients with Developer Support, they may go to the AWS Support Center and ask to have the service's limits raised. Help with analyzing and processing these requests will be provided by AWS Support to meet businesses' unique workload needs.

   • AWS Trusted Advisor: AWS Trusted Advisor is a service that helps users optimize the environment for cost, security, performance, and fault tolerance, and it's included in the Developer Support package. Trusted Advisor's information may help businesses optimize the AWS infrastructure.

   • AWS Support Center: The AWS Support Center is a web-based platform for managing and tracking support issues, gaining access to technical documentation and tools, and being updated on the status of services. It's a one-stop shop for handling all of the interactions with customer service.

   • Documentation, white papers, and FAQs: Developer Support provides access to a wealth of technical documentation, white papers, and FAQs. These resources can help users learn about AWS services, implement best practices, and troubleshoot common issues.

   • AWS Community Forums: Customers who pay for Developer Support get access to the AWS Community Forums, where they may talk to other people who use AWS and get answers to their issues or tips and tricks.

   • Service Health Dashboard: Developer Support gives users access to the AWS Service Health Dashboard, which offers real-time status information for AWS services and Regions. Users may be informed about service disruptions, performance concerns, and scheduled maintenance events.

The Developer Support plan provides technical support as well as expanded access to AWS resources, allowing users to obtain help with technical problems, optimize the AWS setup, and get the most out of AWS services. Response times for technical enquiries are normally quicker than with the Basic Support plan, but for even faster response times and extra advantages, higher-tier support plans such as Business Support or Enterprise Support may be considered.

3. Business Support: Business Support is a premium support package that combines all of the advantages of Developer Support as well as extra features. It gives businesses access to AWS Trusted Advisor, which delivers automatic assessments and suggestions to help them optimize their existing AWS setup. In addition, Business Support provides quicker response times for essential situations. The following are the primary features and advantages of the Business Support plan:

- Technical support: Business Support gives access to AWS professionals through email, chat, and phone, 24 hours a day, seven days a week. Customers may contact AWS Support for help with technical questions, troubleshooting, and best practice advice. Response times are determined by the severity of the problem, with severe concerns receiving quicker responses.

- Service limit increase support: Like the Developer Support package, Business Support offers assistance with increasing service limits. Limit increases may be requested via the AWS Support Center, and AWS Support can help customers evaluate and execute these requests.

- AWS Trusted Advisor: Business Support offers complete access to AWS Trusted Advisor, which runs automatic tests on the AWS setup and makes suggestions for cost optimization, security, performance, and fault tolerance. Trusted Advisor can help businesses find areas for improvement and increase the efficiency of AWS resources.

- Architectural reviews: One may request architectural reviews for the AWS workloads as a Business Support client. AWS Support will provide advice and best practices to help user optimize the architecture, assure scalability, and improve performance.

- Well-Architected Reviews: AWS Well-Architected Reviews, which are in-depth examinations of the architecture based on AWS best practices, are available via Business Support. These assessments assist employees in identifying possible hazards, areas for improvement, and chances for workload optimization.

- AWS Support Concierge: The AWS Support Concierge service is offered to Business Support clients. It provides customized and proactive support, including advice, ideas, and help with the AWS setup. Architectural evaluations, best practice advice, and collaboration with other AWS teams may all be handled by the AWS Support Concierge team.

- AWS Trusted Advisor suggestions summary: AWS Trusted Advisor suggestions are summarized weekly for Business Support customers. This summary allows users to keep track of the status of the suggestions, prioritize actions, and measure progress toward improving their AWS setup.
- Service Health Dashboard and personalized notifications: Business Support provides users with access to the AWS Service Health Dashboard, which displays real-time service status updates. Customers may also set up personalized notifications to get proactive warnings about service events such as service outages or maintenance operations.

The Business Support plan provides thorough technical assistance, architectural evaluations, and increased access to AWS resources to assist in optimizing the AWS infrastructure, improving performance, and successfully addressing technical problems. It is intended for clients with high support requirements and critical workloads. Consider the Enterprise Support package for even greater levels of service and extra advantages.

4. Enterprise Support: Enterprise Support is a comprehensive support package for clients that have mission-critical workloads and complicated infrastructures. Features such as a dedicated technical account manager (TAM), round-the-clock access to the AWS Support concierge team, and help with planning and executing complicated installations are all part of the package. Critical problem response times are the quickest of any support plan.

- Technical support: Enterprise Support customers get access to AWS-trained technical support staff via email, live chat, and phone every minute of every day of the year. Technical questions, troubleshooting, and advice on best practices may all be sent to AWS Support. The urgency of the reaction is determined by the perceived severity of the problem, with the most pressing problems receiving the quickest attention.
- Account management: Enterprise Support assigns customers a dedicated TAM who will be the primary point of contact within AWS. The TAM is familiar with unique needs and can advise businesses on architecture, assist with strategic and operational planning and optimization, and serve as a point of contact within AWS.
- Architecture and design reviews: AWS workloads are available upon request for an Enterprise Support client. In-depth evaluations of the architecture will be performed by AWS Support and AWS Solutions Architects, who will then provide suggestions and assist in achieving optimal performance, security, and affordability.
- Well-Architected Framework: With Enterprise Support, businesses get access to the AWS Well-Architected Framework, which is a collection of best practices and recommendations for building and maintaining AWS workloads that are safe, dependable, and efficient. The framework may be used to determine how well the layout adheres to AWS recommendations and how to make any adjustments.

- Operational support: Enterprise Support provides operational support to aid with operational difficulties, risk assessment, and troubleshooting. Businesses can count on AWS Support to help them figure out what went wrong, how to handle incidents, and take corrective measures.
- Service limit increase support: Enterprise Support may assist customers in raising their AWS resource limitations to meet workload needs. Help in assessing and fulfilling these requests will be provided by AWS Support.
- AWS Support Concierge: Customers with Enterprise Support have access to the AWS Support Concierge service. In addition to coordinating with other AWS groups, the Support Concierge offers individualized direction, aid with architectural assessments, suggestions for best practices, and more. They will act as a point of contact inside AWS and guide customers through the support channels.
- Business and technical reviews: Enterprise Support comprises business and technical reviews carried out by AWS Support and AWS Solutions Architects. Companies' AWS consumption may be better understood, optimization possibilities can be found, and the AWS strategy can be better aligned with companies' goals with the aid of these audits.
- Customized reporting: Enterprise Support clients get customized reports that give insight into their AWS consumption, support case history, and suggestions for cost management and performance enhancement.
- Service Health Dashboard and personalized notifications: Enterprise Support offers users access to the AWS Service Health Dashboard, where they may examine real-time service status updates. Proactive alerts concerning service events, including service outages or maintenance operations, may be configured based on preferences.

The Enterprise Support package provides companies with the highest-quality service and individual attention. It helps in every way possible with AWS infrastructure, whether it be technical, architectural, operational, or strategic. Customers with complicated workloads and infrastructures who need proactive help and direction from AWS would benefit from this service.

Each support plan includes varying degrees of assistance, response times, and resource availability. The pricing of the support plans varies depending on consumption, AWS service usage, and the degree of help needed.

To understand the services included, response times, and restrictions, it is essential to check the full information and conditions of each assistance plan. The AWS Management Console allows customers to choose and manage AWS assistance plans, enabling them to pick the amount of assistance that best meets their requirements.

10.12   CONCLUSION

This chapter has looked at AWS accounting, billing, support systems, architecture, and ecosystems. It has discussed AWS Organizations' numerous account setups and how to manage and administer AWS accounts. The chapter has covered service control rules, AWS Control Tower, AWS total cost of ownership, cost allocation tags, cost and use statistics, and Cost Explorer. These tools let users track, allocate, and optimize AWS expenditure. The chapter has also emphasized AWS budgeting and Trusted Advisor's automatic cost optimization, security, and performance assessments. It should help readers understand AWS's accounting, billing, support, and architecture in order to make educated choices and optimize their AWS investments.

11 Data Extraction for Spot Instance Pricing in AWS

11.1 INTRODUCTION

Amazon Elastic Compute Cloud (EC2) is a leader among cloud computing service providers because of the scalability and adaptability of the computing resources it provides to companies and consumers. Since EC2 instances may be spun up on demand, customers can swiftly increase or decrease their available computing resources as needed. EC2's pricing approach is one of its most distinguishing characteristics, as it offers a range of plans to suit a variety of situations and budgets.

The purpose of this chapter is to investigate EC2 Spot Instances' pricing strategy over three months. Using Amazon's spare capacity, Spot Instances provides an inexpensive way to acquire computing resources. Spot Instances are a good option for workloads that are very variable in terms of schedule and can endure interruptions, since their cost varies depending on supply and demand.

We describe a data extraction approach that will allow users to collect historical price data for the preceding 90 days, which will shed light on the dynamics of the Spot Instance pricing structure. This information is useful for observing trends and price changes in Spot Instances. By seeing these trends, organizations and individuals will be better able to decide how and when to use Spot Instances to achieve their financial and performance goals.

Numerous beneficial applications may be found for such information. First, it gives customers a sense of where prices have been in the past for Spot Instances, so they can better plan when and how much to bid. In addition, organizations and individuals may analyze Spot Instance price trends and patterns to better allocate computer resources and control costs.

The purpose of this chapter is to help readers make educated decisions about utilizing Spot Instances as a cost-effective computing resource in their cloud infrastructure by delving into the historical pricing data for EC2 Spot Instances and analyzing its implications.

11.2 PRICING STRATEGY OF INSTANCES

Amazon EC2 provides a variety of price plans to meet the requirements of a wide range of customers and use scenarios. [90] The goal of these pricing models is to provide customers with more leeway in how they spend their money. Figure 11.1 shows the pricing strategy in detail. Key pricing mechanisms in EC2 are as follows:

FIGURE 11.1   Pricing strategy in EC2 instances.

1. On-Demand Instances.
2. Reserved Instances.
3. Spot Instances.
4. Dedicated Hosts.
5. Savings Plans.
6. Capacity Reservations.

Amazon EC2's several price tiers are designed to meet the demands of customers with varying computing requirements and habits, enabling customers to find the best balance between cost and efficiency.

1. On-Demand Instances: Users may get computing power on an as-needed basis with no upfront costs or lengthy contracts when they select Amazon EC2's On-Demand Instances. This pricing model should be used for projects with irregular consumption, fluctuating demand, or short-term needs. On-Demand Instances have the following essential properties and characteristics:

- Pay-as-you-go model: Depending on the instance type, customers of On-Demand Instances pay for computing capability on a per-hour or per-second basis. Users may start and end On-Demand Instances without incurring any fees beyond those associated with real consumption, since there are no setup expenses or minimum commitments.
- No long-term commitment: Customers aren't tied down to a contract for an extended period of time, as they are with Reserved Instances or Savings Plans. This provides the greatest degree of adaptability, allowing users to rapidly increase or decrease the quantity of available computing resources to meet their specific requirements.
- Instance availability: Businesses can always use On-Demand Instances to obtain EC2 resources when they need them. Depending on geography and availability, users may start instances from a wide variety of instance types, operating systems, and Availability Zones.
- Pricing transparency: Amazon's pricing for On-Demand Instances is straightforward and can be easily seen on its website. Instance types, Regions, and use patterns affect price, but the AWS Pricing Calculator and the EC2 pricing page make it easy for customers to get a ballpark figure.
- Cost-efficiency considerations: Though On-Demand Instances provide a great deal of leeway, they may not be the most cost-effective choice for persistent workloads or steady-state applications. Reserved Instances or Savings Plans may be a better option for such uses in terms of cost savings. On-Demand Instances, on the other hand, shine in cases of erratic workloads, bursty applications, or instances needed for brief periods of time.
- Integration with other AWS services: On-Demand Instances are compatible with many other AWS services, so customers may make use of a wider range of features and advantages. By combining On-Demand Instances with Auto Scaling, for instance, customers may have the system dynamically alter the number of instances to meet their needs, resulting in better performance and lower costs.

With EC2's On-Demand Instances, customers can manage fluctuating workloads without having to commit to a certain number of instances for an extended period of time. Since customers only pay for the computing capacity they consume, On-Demand Instances are flexible enough to accommodate a broad variety of applications and use cases.

2. Reserved Instances: With Amazon EC2's Reserved Instances, customers may lock in lower prices than those for On-Demand Instances in return for committing to a fixed instance configuration and instance lifetime. Reserved Instances excel at offering stability and cost optimization over a long period of time, making them ideal for workloads with constant and predictable consumption patterns. Key features and advantages of Reserved Instances include the following:

- Cost savings: Reserved Instances may save clients a lot of money compared with using On-Demand Instances. An instance type, term (one or three years), and payment method commitment enables consumers to lock in a reduced hourly rate for the life of their reservation. A larger rebate is offered for a longer commitment and more immediate payment.
- Instance flexibility: Reserved Instances provide customers options when it comes to the kind of instance, the operating system, and the Region in which it is running. As a result, customers may save money by reserving a configuration that best fits their needs without sacrificing flexibility.
- Instance reservation: When a Reserved Instance is purchased, capacity is reserved within the selected Availability Zone, ensuring that the specified instance type is available whenever needed. Because of this, businesses won't have to worry about the availability of instances, even during times of heavy demand.
- Instance utilization: Users may spread their Capacity Reservations over many instances in the same instance family, provided that the total number of reserved instance hours is equal to consumption.
- Payment options: Reserved Instances offer many payment methods to accommodate individual customer needs. Users have the option of either paying the whole price up front and skipping monthly installments or paying a lesser portion of the total price up front and making smaller monthly payments for the duration of the contract.
- Convertibility and Marketplace: Amazon's Reserved Instances are convertible and may be traded for other Reserved Instances so that users can adapt them to their current and future needs. Existing reservations may be switched to a new instance type, OS, or tenancy choice at any time. Reserved Instances may be bought and sold on the AWS Reserved Instance Marketplace, allowing customers to better manage their resources and expenses.
- Integration with other AWS services: Reserved Instances work well with other AWS offerings, allowing customers to get the most out of their money. They may be used in tandem with AWS Elastic Beanstalk to reserve capacity for applications or with Auto Scaling to automatically scale the number of instances in response to demand.

For workloads with stable and predictable consumption patterns, Reserved Instances may reduce costs and ensure consistency. When users commit to reserved capacity, they have access to significant savings over a long period of time without giving up any control over their instances' specifications. Users may save a lot of money on EC2 installations by taking advantage of this pricing option, which is especially helpful for workloads with stable resource needs.

3. Spot Instances: When compared with the cost of an Amazon EC2 On-Demand Instance, the cost of a Spot Instance is far more reasonable. Workloads that prioritize cost savings over strict adherence to schedule flexibility, non-mission-critical applications, and availability should use Spot Instances. Spot Instance prices change as a result of supply and demand in the EC2 Spot market. Key features and advantages of Spot Instances include the following:

- Cost savings: Spot Instances provide the possibility of considerable cost reductions, with rates that are often much lower than those of On-Demand Instances. Users may take advantage of surplus resources and set their own bidding prices for instances on EC2, since the pricing is determined by the market.

- Bidding and interruption model: Spot Instances feature a bidding mechanism where customers set the highest amount they're prepared to pay for each instance hour and then have their bids interrupted at random intervals. Instances are distributed to the top bidders until all available capacity is used up, and the current Spot price is decided by the highest offer among all users. However, if the Spot price goes over the bidder's maximum bid, Amazon will suspend the Spot Instance.

- Flexible timing: Spot Instances are appropriate for workloads that can withstand interruptions or have variable scheduling because of their third flexibility feature. Spot Instances allow users to take advantage of low-cost resources by completing computational jobs during times of low demand. Workloads that are a good fit include things such as batch processing, big data analytics, continuous integration and continuous delivery (CI/CD) pipelines, and web applications with varying amounts of traffic.

- Instance types and Availability Zones: Spot Instances provide a number of different instance kinds so that customers may pick and choose the optimal setups for their applications. Spot Instances may be launched from anywhere the user chooses and can be launched in one of many Availability Zones that the user specifies.

- Spot market and pricing history: Amazon customers have access to historical Spot price data, which they may use to identify and evaluate patterns in the market. This provides useful data for customers to utilize in determining the best bidding methods and when to deploy Spot Instances. Users may access and analyze the Spot market's price history programmatically through APIs.

- Integration with other AWS services: Spot Instances also work with many other AWS offerings without any hitches. Spot Instances may be used in conjunction with Auto Scaling to allow users to scale up or down their instance count on the go. In addition to being utilized with AWS Batch for low-cost batch processing workloads and Amazon EMR for large data processing and analytics, Spot Instances may also be used with Amazon Elastic MapReduce.

If the workload has a little leeway in terms of scheduling and cost optimization, users may find that using Spot Instances on EC2 is the most cost-effective solution. They may save a lot of money while still making use of all of Amazon EC2's features by taking advantage of its spare capacity at discounted costs. Spot Instances are a cost-effective option, but users should be aware that they must build their applications to tolerate disruptions smoothly and have backup plans in place in case their instances are recovered.

4. Dedicated Hosts: The Amazon EC2 Dedicated Hosts service gives customers their own private server. Workloads that must adhere to rules, have stringent licensing requirements, or satisfy particular hardware or software use constraints are the target for this price tier. When compared with other EC2 instance types, Dedicated Hosts provide superior control, visibility, and isolation. Key features and advantages of Dedicated Hosts include the following:

   • Physical server isolation: Dedicated Hosts provide total isolation from all other EC2 instances and tenants by giving users exclusive access to the underlying physical server. Dedicated Hosts are well suited for workloads that must adhere to strict compliance or regulatory standards, since their isolation offers increased security and privacy.

   • Compliance and licensing: Dedicated Hosts let customers fulfill licensing and compliance requirements that call for isolated hardware. By having their own dedicated servers, customers can ensure that their data is never held on a shared server. Furthermore, software licensing methods necessitating specialized infrastructure are supported by specialized hosts.

   • Instance placement control: Users have complete control over where their instances run on the dedicated hardware using dedicated hosts. Users may choose how many instances will operate on a Dedicated Host, which instance types will be used, and which Availability Zones will house the Dedicated Hosts within a given area.

   • Instance capacity planning: Customers are able to plan and optimize the distribution of their instances thanks to dedicated hosts' transparency about available capacity. In this way, users can better control their workloads and plan accordingly to meet their performance and resource needs.

   • Cost-efficiency: Dedicated Hosts may have higher prices than other EC2 instance types owing to the dedicated infrastructure required, but they may still be cost-effective in certain use cases. Workloads that have stringent hardware or software dependencies may benefit from Dedicated Hosts, since they avoid the need for extra licenses and the performance swings that come with using shared resources.

   • Integration with other AWS services: Dedicated Hosts are easily integrated with other AWS services, giving customers access to a wider range of features. Using Dedicated Hosts and AWS License Manager, for instance, customers may centrally manage software licenses for a fleet of servers. With AWS Elastic Beanstalk and Dedicated Hosts, users can quickly and easily set up dedicated hardware for applications. Amazon EC2 Dedicated Hosts provide consumers with a private, secure, and manageable server. Workloads that have strict licensing restrictions or need access to specialized hardware resources might benefit from this solution. By giving customers fine-grained control over instance placement and improved insight into capacity, Dedicated Hosts allow them to satisfy the specific requirements of their workloads while maintaining compliance and relying on a solid, safe infrastructure.

5. Savings Plan: Users may save a lot of money on their compute needs by signing up for a Savings Plan on Amazon EC2. In return for committing to a certain level of compute utilization, measured in dollars per hour, customers may get a discount on their EC2 and AWS Fargate usage with Savings Plans. Key features and advantages of Savings Plans include the following:

- Cost savings: Customers may save money by using EC2 and AWS Fargate via the discounts provided by the Savings Plans. Users may save money on compute expenses compared with On-Demand pricing since the discount is applied to the consumption they have committed to. For workloads with consistent and predictable resource use, the cost reductions may be considerable.

- Flexible usage commitments: Savings Plans provide wiggle room in terms of how much money must be spent and when. Customers have the option of selecting between a Compute Savings Plan or an EC2 Instance Savings Plan. When it comes to instance families, sizes, operating systems, and Regions, Compute Savings Plans offer users more leeway, whereas EC2 Instance Savings Plans require a more serious commitment but give customers more control.

- Term options: Users may set their Savings Plans for a period of one year or three years. The amount of discount depends on the length of the period, with greater savings available for longer-term agreements. The length of the contract should reflect users' commitment to the service and the value they place on cost savings.

- Usage flexibility: Savings Plans offer customers a lot of leeway in how they put their reduced rates to use, which is a major selling point. As long as the consumption is within the Savings Plan's parameters, it doesn't matter what instance family, size, OS, or location the committed usage is spread across. Because of this leeway, consumers may save money while making the most of their computing capabilities.

- Auto Scaling integration: Savings Plans are fully compatible with Auto Scaling, letting customers automatically scale up or down the number of instances they use at a subsidized cost, depending on their use. Users may flexibly grow their resources without jeopardizing the money they've earned with their money plans owing to this connection.

- Easy management: Users may manage a Savings Plan with the click of a button in the AWS Management Console or via the power of APIs. They may monitor their participation in the Savings Plan, assess their monetary gains, and alter their contributions as appropriate. In addition, participants may track their Savings Plan protection and get advice on how to make the most of their plan.

EC2 and AWS Fargate users may benefit from the savings and adaptability offered by a Savings Plan. Users may save a lot of money on their computing expenditures by committing to a certain quantity of use ahead of time. Users may maximize cost reductions while still preserving scalability and performance thanks to the plan's flexibility in terms of consumption commitments, term lengths, and application scope.

6. Capacity Reservations: Users of Amazon EC2 may reserve resources for their instances in a certain AZ with the help of Capacity Reservations. Even during times of heavy demand or capacity limits, this functionality guarantees that the specified instance type will always be accessible. Capacity Reservations excel when used with programs that need exclusive usage of resources or have stringent location preferences. Key features and advantages of Capacity Reservations include the following:

- Guaranteed capacity: Capacity Reservations ensure that the reserved instance type will be readily accessible at the scheduled time of use. Users may guarantee that mission-critical workloads and applications always have access to the resources they need, regardless of changes in demand, by reserving capacity in advance.

- Instance placement control: Capacity Reservations also provide consumers with fine-grained control over where their instances are deployed. When reserving instances, users may choose the Availability Zone and the number of instances they need to run their applications.

- Placement tenancy options: Capacity Reservations' placement tenancy choices range from "default" to "dedicated" to "host." Dedicated tenancy guarantees that instances operate on hardware that is devoted entirely to the user, whereas the default tenancy permits instances to be put on shared hardware. Users may deploy instances on designated Dedicated Hosts with more access to and knowledge of the underlying infrastructure thanks to host tenancy.

- Instance size flexibility: Capacity Reservations provide for scalability in the size of running instances. At start time, users may pick the instance size that best suits their needs, depending on the requirements of their applications. This scalability guarantees that customers may make the most efficient use of the reserved capacity by adjusting the size and type of their instances.

- Integration with other AWS services: Capacity Reservations work well with other AWS services so that customers may make use of all the features they provide. To guarantee that instances deployed through

Auto Scaling always use the reserved capacity, users may combine Capacity Reservations with Auto Scaling. Capacity Reservations and AWS Elastic Beanstalk work together to provide apps with their own committed resources.

- Cost optimization: When compared with other pricing alternatives, Capacity Reservations don't save money directly, but they may help save money by making sure that instances are always accessible when users need them. Users may avoid possible capacity restrictions or the need to pay higher fees during peak demand by reserving capacity in advance.

When it comes to reserving resources for EC2 instances, customers benefit from the precision, dependability, and adaptability provided by Capacity Reservations. Capacity Reservations are helpful for customers who need to reserve resources for particular purposes, such as running mission-critical applications. Users may secure the availability of their preferred instance types, optimize their instance sizes, and keep their applications running smoothly by reserving capacity in advance.

11.3 SPOT INSTANCES VS ON-DEMAND INSTANCES

Amazon EC2's two price tiers, Spot Instances and On-Demand Instances, serve various purposes and come with their own set of advantages. So, to put that in perspective:

Pricing model:

- Spot Instances are priced according to the fluctuating supply and demand of the Spot market. Instances are given to the highest bidders when users place bids on EC2 capacity that is not being utilized. The Spot Instances price shifts as a result of market forces.
- Pricing for On-Demand Instances is static and on a pay-as-you-go basis. Standard hourly prices are paid by users, and no commitment or contract is required. No matter what happens to demand, the prices won't change.

Cost savings:

- Spot Instances may offer considerable cost reductions compared with On-Demand Instances, which is why they are the focus of this section. Users may get access to available resources and execute their workloads at a lesser cost by purchasing instances on the Spot Instances market.
- Flexibility and no initial outlay are two advantages of On-Demand Instances; however, these instances often cost more than Spot Instances. It's best to use On-Demand Instances for tasks where cost-efficiency is not an issue and constant access to computing resources is needed.

Availability:

- Spot Instances are only available if there is enough unused capacity in the Spot Instances market. Therefore, if the Spot Instances price is higher than the user's bid, there is a chance of disruptions or termination. Users should build their programs to recover gracefully from disruptions or have alternative plans ready.
- With On-Demand Instances, users can always count on having access to a machine. Instances may be started at any time without interruption or cancellation due to price changes.

Workload flexibility:

- Spot Instances are ideal for workloads that may shift their start and end times or that can handle interruptions. They perform well for tasks that benefit from being executed during times of low demand, such as batch processing, large data analytics, CI/CD pipelines, and web applications with variable traffic.
- Cases created instantaneously: Since On-Demand Instances provide continuous, exclusive access to computing resources, they are best suited for applications with regular or constant resource requirements. They are an excellent choice for mission-critical programs that can't afford any downtime.

Instance types and Availability Zones:

- Spot Instances provide a large selection of instance kinds and Availability Zones, which brings us to instance types and Availability Zones. Spot Instances may be started in any of AWS's Availability Zones, and users can choose which ones they wish to use.
- There are many different instance types and Region options with On-Demand Instances. Users may start instances in any of the Available Zones and can choose the instance type they need.

On-Demand Instances provide assured availability but at a higher cost; Spot Instances offer lower prices and more flexibility but are subject to disruptions. The workload's needs, the value placed on optimizing costs, and tolerance for disruption should all be factored into the decision to use Spot Instances or On-Demand Instances. Users often combine the two pricing models to achieve cost savings and guaranteed availability throughout their whole application.

11.4   USE OF CLI IN AWS

AWS has become an industry leader by consistently delivering cloud services that are highly scalable, adaptable, and reliable. While AWS's web-based dashboard for resource management is feature-rich, the Command Line Interface (CLI) offers a robust option for working with AWS services. [131–134] In this section, we'll look at the features and functionalities of the AWS CLI and discuss how organizations can put them to use in a variety of real-world situations.

11.4.1 GETTING STARTED WITH AWS CLI

1. Installation and configuration: There are step-by-step instructions for setting up the AWS CLI on Windows, macOS, and Linux. [130]
2. Authentication and authorization: Setting up AWS credentials (such as access keys and roles) is crucial to have safe and secure interactions with AWS services.

11.4.2 KEY FEATURES AND BENEFITS

- With the AWS CLI, customers may reduce the amount of time spent on repetitive tasks by automating them with scripts and performing bulk operations.
- Adaptability and extensibility: The CLI offers more flexibility and extensibility than the web-based console, allowing users to modify their workflows and integrate AWS CLI commands into existing scripts and other applications.
- AWS resources may be deployed, managed, and orchestrated with more efficiency because of the CLI's tight integration with popular DevOps tools such as Jenkins, Terraform, and Ansible.
- The CLI is appropriate for high-volume or time-sensitive activities because of its speed and performance, which are both enhanced by its lightweight nature.

11.4.3 NAVIGATING AWS SERVICES WITH CLI

- EC2 Instances: The CLI can be used to create, tag, and start instances in Amazon's Elastic Compute Cloud.
- S3 storage: The CLI can be used to manage Amazon S3 buckets, files, permissions, and lifecycle policies.
- Networking and security: CLI commands can be used to manage Amazon VPC, security groups, network access control lists, and more.
- Serverless computing: The CLI can be used to deploy, administer, and monitor serverless applications via the use of serverless services such as AWS Lambda and API Gateway.
- Database and analytics (e.g., Amazon RDS, DynamoDB, Redshift, and Athena): CLI procedures can be used to manage and analyze data stored in these services.

11.4.4 BEST PRACTICES AND TIPS

- Syntax and parameters for commands: There is an introduction to the AWS Command Line Interface and its command structure, options, and common parameters.
- Output formatting: Various output formats (such JSON, YAML, and text) can be tried, and filtering methods can be used to glean useful data.
- Aliases and shell integration: The shell's built-in functionality can be used to automate routine tasks and take advantage of aliases for commonly used AWS CLI commands.
- There are methods for fixing mistakes, tracking the source of problems, and making the most of the logging and debugging tools provided by the AWS CLI.

The AWS CLI provides a powerful, convenient, and extensible way for users to manage their interactions with AWS resources. The CLI is an effective tool for administering AWS settings because it allows for the automation of activities, the incorporation of DevOps processes, and the provision of fine-grained control over cloud resources. Developers, administrators, and DevOps teams can optimize their use of the AWS cloud by becoming expert at using the AWS CLI and putting its power to work for them.

11.5   SPOT INSTANCE DATA EXTRACTION

To extract Spot Instance pricing data for the past 90 days using the AWS CLI, users can follow these steps:

1. Install and configure the AWS CLI: If users haven't already done so, they should install the AWS CLI on the local machine and configure it with AWS credentials. They can refer to the AWS CLI documentation for instructions on how to install and configure it. [130]
2. Retrieve Spot Instance pricing history: Use the "ec2 describe-spot-price-history" command to retrieve the Spot Instance pricing history for the past 90 days. Specify the desired parameters such as the instance type, Availability Zone, start time, and end time.

The output of the implementation can be seen in Figure 11.2. By following these steps, businesses can use the AWS CLI to extract Spot Instance pricing data for the past 90 days and process it for further analysis or usage. They must remember to adjust the command parameters according to their specific requirements, such as instance type, time range, and output format.

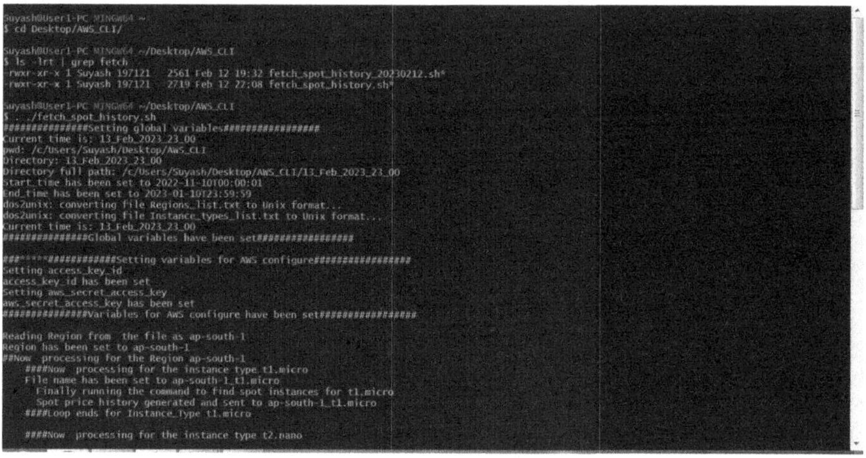

FIGURE 11.2   Extraction of Spot Instance data.

11.6   CONCLUSION

To conclude, this chapter has presented an in-depth examination of pricing schemes in EC2 instances, with an emphasis on the comparison of Spot Instances and On-Demand Instances. Users may make well-informed judgments about which of these two pricing models is best for them by first familiarizing themselves with the important differences between them and concerns. We've looked at the pros and cons of using Spot Instances and found that they're best for workloads that can be scheduled around disruptions and have a high tolerance for downtime. The availability and predictable price of On-Demand Instances, on the other hand, make them a good fit for applications that need both high performance and high availability.

We've also covered how Amazon CLI can be used to manage EC2 instances and get information for Spot Instances. The Command Line Interface allows customers to quickly and easily access AWS resources, automate routine processes, and compile Spot Instance pricing history. By using this information, businesses and people may better understand the factors that influence Spot Instance prices. The cloud computing industry is always changing, and so it's important to keep up with pricing plans and use tools such as the Amazon CLI. Users may maximize the effectiveness and cost savings of their AWS installations by regularly evaluating the appropriateness of Spot Instances and On-Demand Instances based on workload requirements and budget considerations.

References

1. M. D. Ryan, "Cloud computing privacy concerns on our doorstep," *Communications of the ACM*, vol. 54, no. 1, pp. 36–38, Jan. 2011, doi: 10.1145/1866739.1866751.
2. M. Haghighat, S. Zonouz, and M. Abdel-Mottaleb, "CloudID: Trustworthy cloud-based and cross-enterprise biometric identification," *Expert Systems with Applications*, vol. 42, no. 21, pp. 7905–7916, Nov. 2015, doi: 10.1016/j.eswa.2015.06.025.
3. I. Indu, P. M. R. Anand, and V. Bhaskar, "Identity and access management in cloud environment: Mechanisms and challenges," *Engineering Science and Technology, an International Journal*, vol. 21, no. 4, pp. 574–588, Aug. 2018, doi: 10.1016/j.jestch.2018.05.010.
4. "Archives," Los Angeles Times. https://www.latimes.com/archives
5. E. Messmer, "Security of virtualization, cloud computing divides IT and security pros," Network World. https://www.networkworld.com/article/2244954/security-of-virtualization--cloud-computing-divides-it-and-security-pros.html
6. "Cloud computing – Wikipedia," Mar. 01, 2021. https://en.wikipedia.org/wiki/Cloud_computing
7. "What is hybrid cloud? Everything you need to know," Cloud Computing, Sep. 01, 2021. https://www.techtarget.com/searchcloudcomputing/definition/hybrid-cloud
8. J. Fruhlinger, "What is hybrid cloud computing? The benefits of mixing private and public cloud services," Network World. https://www.networkworld.com/article/3233132/what-is-hybrid-cloud-computing.html
9. "Mind the gap: Here comes hybrid cloud – Thomas Bittman," Thomas Bittman, Sep. 24, 2012. https://blogs.gartner.com/thomas_bittman/2012/09/24/mind-the-gap-here-comes-hybrid-cloud/
10. @TechRadar, "Hybrid cloud: Is it right for your business?," TechRadar, Aug. 24, 2014. https://www.techradar.com/news/internet/cloud-services/hybrid-cloud-is-it-right-for-your-business-1261343
11. M. Vizard, "How cloudbursting 'rightsizes' the data center," Dice Insights, Jun. 22, 2012. https://www.dice.com/career-advice/how-cloudbursting-rightsizes-the-data-center
12. Q. Li, Q. Hao, L. Xiao, and Z. Li, "Adaptive management of virtualized resources in cloud computing using feedback control," 2009 First International Conference on Information Science and Engineering, 2009, Published, doi: 10.1109/icise.2009.211.
13. "Cloud computing architecture – Wikipedia," May 27, 2012. https://en.wikipedia.org/wiki/Cloud_computing_architecture
14. "Definition of SaaS," PCMAG. https://www.pcmag.com/encyclopedia/term/saas
15. Y. Sun, J. Zhang, Y. Xiong, and G. Zhu, "Data security and privacy in cloud computing," *International Journal of Distributed Sensor Networks*, vol. 10, no. 7, p. 190903, Jul. 2014, doi: 10.1155/2014/190903.
16. Y. Jiang, K. Zhang, Y. Qian, and R. Q. Hu, "Efficient and privacy-preserving distributed learning in cloud-edge computing systems," Proceedings of the 3rd ACM Workshop on Wireless Security and Machine Learning, Jun. 2021, Published, doi: 10.1145/3468218.3469044.
17. J. Furrier, "Exclusive profile: Andy Jassy of Amazon Web Service (AWS) and his trillion dollar cloud ambition," Forbes, Jan. 28, 2015. https://www.forbes.com/sites/siliconangle/2015/01/28/andy-jassy-aws-trillion-dollar-cloud-ambition/

18. R. Miller, "How AWS came to be," TechCrunch, Jul. 02, 2016. https://techcrunch.com/2016/07/02/andy-jassys-brief-history-of-the-genesis-of-aws/

19. M. Mehra, V. Sahai, P. Chowdhury, and E. Dsouza, "Home security system using IOT and AWS cloud services," 2019 International Conference on Advances in Computing, Communication and Control (ICAC3), Mumbai, India, 2019, pp. 1–6, doi: 10.1109/ICAC347590.2019.9089839.

20. F. Bracci, A. Corradi, and L. Foschini, "Database security management for healthcare SaaS in the Amazon AWS Cloud," 2012 IEEE Symposium on Computers and Communications (ISCC), Cappadocia, Turkey, 2012, pp. 000812–000819, doi: 10.1109/ISCC.2012.6249401.

21. S. Mishra, M. Kumar, N. Singh, and S. Dwivedi, "A survey on AWS cloud computing security challenges & solutions," 2022 6th International Conference on Intelligent Computing and Control Systems (ICICCS), Madurai, India, 2022, pp. 614–617, doi: 10.1109/ICICCS53718.2022.9788254.

22. A. Sarkar and A. Shah, *Learning AWS: Design, Build, and Deploy Responsive Applications Using AWS Cloud Components*, 2015.

23. I. Pelle, J. Czentye, J. Dóka, and B. Sonkoly, "Towards latency sensitive cloud native applications: A performance study on AWS," 2019 IEEE 12th International Conference on Cloud Computing (CLOUD), Milan, Italy, 2019, pp. 272–280, doi: 10.1109/CLOUD.2019.00054.

24. P. Dubey, P. Dubey, and K. K. Sahu, "An investigation on remote teaching approaches and the social impact of distance education," *Redefining Virtual Teaching Learning Pedagogy*, pp. 275–293, Feb. 2023.

25. P. Dubey, K. K. Sahu, and P. Dubey, "Predicting students' intention to use learning technologies via the mediation of their perceived benefits," *Technology-Driven E-Learning Pedagogy Through Emotional Intelligence*, pp. 145–165, May 2023.

26. K. McLaughlin, "Andy Jassy: Amazon's $6 billion man | CRN," CRN, Aug. 04, 2015. https://www.crn.com/news/cloud/300077657/andy-jassy-amazons-6-billion-man.htm

27. "Harvard i-lab | Fireside Chat with Michael Skok and Andy Jassy: The history of Amazon Web Services," YouTube, Oct. 21, 2013. https://www.youtube.com/watch?v=d2dyGDqrXLo

28. D. W. Vogels – https://www.allthingsdistributed.com/, "Amazon DynamoDB – A fast and scalable NoSQL database service designed for internet scale applications," All Things Distributed, Jan. 18, 2012. https://www.allthingsdistributed.com/2012/01/amazon-dynamodb.html

29. D. W. Vogels – https://www.allthingsdistributed.com/, "Modern applications at AWS," All Things Distributed, Aug. 28, 2019. https://www.allthingsdistributed.com/2019/08/modern-applications-at-aws.html

30. "The everything store: Jeff Bezos and the age of Amazon," Google Books. https://books.google.com/books/about/The_Everything_Store_Jeff_Bezos_and_the.html?id=yG3PAK6ZOucC

31. "Velocity in software engineering – ACM Queue," https://queue.acm.org/detail.cfm?id=3352692

32. "Amazon Web Services – Adam Selipsky at USI," YouTube, Sep. 06, 2013. https://www.youtube.com/watch?v=6PiyzyWXiIk

33. S. Cowley, "LinuxWorld: Amazon's two faces present IT challenge," Network World. https://www.networkworld.com/article/2329864/linuxworld--amazon-s-two-faces-present-it-challenge.html

34. "Former Amazon CISO Tom Killalea joins carbon black board – VMware news and stories," VMware News and Stories. https://news.vmware.com/releases/former-amazon-ciso-tom-killalea-joins-carbon-black-board

35. "Amazon.com launches web services; developers can now incorporate Amazon.com Content and features into their own web sites; extends 'Welcome mat' for developers," Press Center, Jul. 16, 2002. https://press.aboutamazon.com/2002/7/amazon-com -launches-web-services-developers-can-now-incorporate-amazon-com-content-and -features-into-their-own-web-sites-extends-welcome-mat-for-developers

36. "IIT News Archive | ComputerWeekly.com," May 28, 2023. https://www.computer-weekly.com/news/2240054229/Amazon-lauds-Linux-infrastructure

37. "Working Backwards," Google Books. https://books.google.com/books/about/Working_ Backwards.html?id=jgn5DwAAQBAJ

38. D. W. Vogels – https://www.allthingsdistributed.com/, "Happy 15th birthday Amazon S3 – the service that started it all," All Things Distributed, Mar. 23, 2021. https://www .allthingsdistributed.com/2021/03/happy-15th-birthday-amazon-s3.html

39. "What I learned from Jeff Bezos: aka–How to bring millions of books to billions of people – MacArthur Foundation," Aug. 01, 2017. https://web.archive.org/web /20170802040741/https://www.macfound.org/press/semifinalist-perspectives/what-i -learned-jeff-bezos-aka-how-bring-millions-books-billions-people/

40. "Benjamin Black & EC2 Origins," Jan. 25, 2009. http://blog.b3k.us/2009/01/25/ec2 -origins.html

41. "Amazon's game-changing cloud was built by some guys in South Africa," Business Insider. https://www.businessinsider.com/amazons-game-changing-cloud-was-built-by -some-guys-in-south-africa-2012-3

42. "Amazon Web Services launches," Press Center, Mar. 14, 2006. https://press .aboutamazon.com/2006/3/amazon-web-services-launches

43. "Amazon EC2 beta | Amazon Web Services," Amazon Web Services, Aug. 25, 2006. https://aws.amazon.com/blogs/aws/amazon_ec2_beta/

44. P. Gralla, "Computing in the cloud," Computerworld. https://www.computerworld.com /article/2549084/computing-in-the-cloud.html

45. S. Gudat, "Amazon business strategy: 2022 goals, objectives & retail marketing take-aways," CCG, Jan. 17, 2022. https://www.customer.com/blog/retail-marketing/amazon -business-strategy/

46. "2011 AWS tour Australia, closing keynote: How Amazon.com migrated to AWS, by Jon Jenkins," https://www.slideshare.net/AmazonWebServices/2011-aws-tour-australia -closing-keynote-how-amazoncom-migrated-to-aws-by-jon-jenkins

47. "Amazon Web Services launches new certification program," PCWorld. https://www .pcworld.com/article/451608/amazon-web-services-launches-new-certification-pro-gram.html

48. J. O'Dell, "'The first one's free, kid.' Amazon launches AWS Activate to get startups hooked," VentureBeat, Oct. 11, 2013. https://venturebeat.com/dev/the-first-ones-free -kid-amazon-launches-aws-activate-to-get-startups-hooked/

49. "Announcing the launch of the AWS Partner Network (APN) Blog | Amazon Web Services," Amazon Web Services, Nov. 21, 2014. https://aws.amazon.com/blogs/apn /apn-blog-launch/

50. "EdgeIQ orchestration for AWS," Amazon Web Services, Inc. https://aws.amazon.com /iot/partner-solutions/edgeiq-orchestration/

51. "Amazon Web Services 'growing fast,'" BBC News. https://www.bbc.com/news /business-32442268

52. C. Nast and @wired, "Get used to Amazon being a profitable company," WIRED, Oct. 22, 2015. https://www.wired.com/2015/10/get-used-to-amazon-being-a-profitable -company/

53. "Amazon's earnings soar as its hardware takes the spotlight," The Verge, Apr. 28, 2016. https://www.theverge.com/2016/4/28/11530336/amazon-q1-first-quarter-2016-earnings

54. "Exclusive with AWS chief Andy Jassy: The wakeup call for cloud adoption – SiliconANGLE," SiliconANGLE, Nov. 30, 2020. https://siliconangle.com/2020/11/30/exclusive-aws-chief-andy-jassy-wakeup-call-cloud-adoption/

55. R. Miller, "Amazon launches autoscaling service on AWS," TechCrunch, Jan. 17, 2018. https://techcrunch.com/2018/01/17/amazon-launches-autoscaling-service-on-aws/

56. "New AWS auto scaling – Unified scaling for your cloud applications I Amazon Web Services," Amazon Web Services, Jan. 17, 2018. https://aws.amazon.com/blogs/aws/aws-auto-scaling-unified-scaling-for-your-cloud-applications/

57. F. Lardinois, "AWS launches Arm-based servers for EC2," TechCrunch, Nov. 27, 2018. https://techcrunch.com/2018/11/27/aws-launches-arm-based-servers-for-ec2/

58. R. Miller, "AWS launches a base station for satellites as a service," TechCrunch, Nov. 27, 2018. https://techcrunch.com/2018/11/27/aws-launches-a-base-station-for-satellites-as-a-service/

59. "Machine learning textbook," http://www.cs.cmu.edu/~tom/mlbook.html

60. D. Sparks, "Amazon's record 2019 in 7 metrics I The Motley Fool," The Motley Fool, Feb. 06, 2020. https://www.fool.com/investing/2020/02/06/amazons-record-2019-in-7-metrics.aspx

61. M. Sag, "The new legal landscape for text mining and machine learning," SSRN Electronic Journal, 2019, Published, doi: 10.2139/ssrn.3331606.

62. J. Hu, H. Niu, J. Carrasco, B. Lennox, and F. Arvin, "Voronoi-based multi-robot autonomous exploration in unknown environments via deep reinforcement learning," *IEEE Transactions on Vehicular Technology*, vol. 69, no. 12, pp. 14413–14423, Dec. 2020, doi: 10.1109/tvt.2020.3034800.

63. C. M. Bishop, *Pattern Recognition and Machine Learning*. Springer, 2011. doi: 10.1007/b9479810.1007/978-0-387-45528-0.

64. "Jerome H. Friedman – Wikipedia," Jan. 04, 2023. https://en.wikipedia.org/wiki/Jerome_H._Friedman

65. "What is machine learning? I IBM," https://www.ibm.com/topics/machine-learning

66. V. Zhou, "Machine learning for beginners: An introduction to neural networks," Medium, Dec. 20, 2019. https://towardsdatascience.com/machine-learning-for-beginners-an-introduction-to-neural-networks-d49f22d238f9

67. R. P. Lindsay, "The impact of automation on public administration," *Western Political Quarterly*, vol. 17, no. 3, pp. 78–81, Sep. 1964, doi: 10.1177/106591296401700364.

68. P. Dubey and A. K. Tiwari, "Solution architecting on remote medical monitoring with AWS cloud and IoT," *Advanced Technologies and Societal Change*, pp. 189–202, 2023, doi: 10.1007/978-981-99-0377-1_12.

69. P. Dubey and P. Dubey, "Expand patient care with AWS cloud for remote medical monitoring," *Next Generation Healthcare Systems Using Soft Computing Techniques*, pp. 137–148, Jul. 2022, doi: 10.1201/9781003217091-10.

70. J. Alzubi, A. Nayyar, and A. Kumar, "Machine learning from theory to algorithms: An overview," *Journal of Physics: Conference Series*, vol. 1142, p. 012012, Nov. 2018, doi: 10.1088/1742-6596/1142/1/012012.

71. M. Paliwal and U. A. Kumar, "Neural networks and statistical techniques: A review of applications," *Expert Systems with Applications*, vol. 36, no. 1, pp. 2–17, Jan. 2009, doi: 10.1016/j.eswa.2007.10.005.

72. N. J. Nilsson, "Artificial intelligence: A modern approach," *Artificial Intelligence*, vol. 82, nos. 1–2, pp. 369–380, Apr. 1996, doi: 10.1016/0004-3702(96)00007-0.

73. P. Langley, "The changing science of machine learning," *Machine Learning*, vol. 82, no. 3, pp. 275–279, Feb. 2011, doi: 10.1007/s10994-011-5242-y.

74. E. Bernard, *Introduction to Machine Learning Statement of Responsibility Etienne Bernard Publisher Wolfram Media*, 2021.

75. L. Breiman, "Statistical modeling: The two cultures (with comments and a rejoinder by the author)," *Statistical Science*, vol. 16, no. 3, Aug. 2001, doi: 10.1214/ss/1009213726.

76. G. James, D. Witten, T. Hastie, and R. Tibshirani, *An Introduction to Statistical Learning: With Applications in R*, vol. 103, 2013. https://hastie.su.domains/ISLR2/ISLRv2_website.pdf

77. M. Mohri, A. Rostamizadeh, A. Talwalkar, and F. Bach, *Foundations of Machine Learning*, 2012. https://cs.nyu.edu/~mohri/mlbook/

78. M. K. Singh, "Analysing machine learning algorithms & their areas of applications," (PDF) Academia.edu. https://www.academia.edu/50071494/Analysing_Machine_Learning_Algorithms_and_their_Areas_of_Applications

79. D. Bzdok, N. Altman, and M. Krzywinski, "Statistics versus machine learning," *Nature Methods*, vol. 15, no. 4, pp. 233–234, Apr. 2018, doi: 10.1038/nmeth.4642.

80. P. M. Sonsare and C. Gunavathi, "Investigation of machine learning techniques on proteomics: A comprehensive survey," *Progress in Biophysics and Molecular Biology*, vol. 149, pp. 54–69, Dec. 2019, doi: 10.1016/j.pbiomolbio.2019.09.004.

81. B. He, K. Shu, and H. Zhang, "Machine learning and data mining in diabetes diagnosis and treatment," *IOP Conference Series: Materials Science and Engineering*, vol. 490, p. 042049, Apr. 2019, doi: 10.1088/1757-899x/490/4/042049.

82. Z. Akbari, "Classification of heart rate time series using machine learning algorithms," *Advances in Machine Learning & Artificial Intelligence*, vol. 2, no. 1, Sep. 2021, doi: 10.33140/amlai.02.01.09.

83. A. B. Tucker, Ed., *Computer Science Handbook*. CRC Press, 2004. doi: 10.1604/978020349445510.1201/9780203494455.

84. "Weak supervision: A new programming paradigm for machine learning," SAIL Blog, Mar. 10, 2019. http://ai.stanford.edu/blog/weak-supervision/

85. M. van Otterlo and M. Wiering, "Reinforcement learning and markov decision processes," *Adaptation, Learning, and Optimization*, pp. 3–42, 2012, doi: 10.1007/978-3-642-27645-3_1.

86. "What is IAM? – AWS identity and access management," https://docs.aws.amazon.com/IAM/latest/UserGuide/introduction.html

87. "IAM Identities (users, user groups, and roles) – AWS identity and access management," https://docs.aws.amazon.com/IAM/latest/UserGuide/id.html

88. "Security in IAM and AWS STS – AWS identity and access management," https://docs.aws.amazon.com/IAM/latest/UserGuide/security.html

89. "AWS IAM tutorial: Working, components, and features explained," [2022 Edition] Simplilearn.com. https://www.simplilearn.com/tutorials/aws-tutorial/aws-iam

90. D. Kubiak and W. Zabierowski, "A comparative analysis of the performance of implementing a Java application based on the microservices architecture, for various AWS EC2 instances," 2021 IEEE XVIIth International Conference on the Perspective Technologies and Methods in MEMS Design (MEMSTECH), Polyana (Zakarpattya), Ukraine, 2021, pp. 1–6, doi: 10.1109/MEMSTECH53091.2021.9467912.

91. R. Bundela, N. Dhanda, and R. Verma, "Load balanced web server on AWS cloud," 2022 International Conference on Computing, Communication, and Intelligent Systems (ICCCIS), Greater Noida, India, 2022, pp. 114–118, doi: 10.1109/ICCCIS56430.2022.10037657.

92. D. García-Zamora, Á. Labella, W. Ding, R. M. Rodríguez, and L. Martínez, "Large-scale group decision making: A systematic review and a critical analysis," *IEEE/CAA Journal of Automatica Sinica*, vol. 9, no. 6, pp. 949–966, June 2022, doi: 10.1109/JAS.2022.105617.

93. M. M. Chanu, "A deep learning approach for object detection and instance segmentation using mask RCNN," *Journal of Advanced Research in Dynamical and Control Systems*, vol. 12, no. SP3, pp. 95–104, Feb. 2020, doi: 10.5373/jardcs/v12sp3/20201242.

94. A. Choudhary, "A walkthrough of Amazon Elastic Compute Cloud (Amazon EC2): A review," *International Journal for Research in Applied Science and Engineering Technology*, vol. 9, no. 11, pp. 93–97, Nov. 2021, doi: 10.22214/ijraset.2021.38764.

95. E. Malta, C. Rodamilans, S. Avila, and E. Borin, "A cost-benefit analysis of GPU-based EC2 instances for a deep learning algorithm," Anais da X Escola Regional de Alto Desempenho de São Paulo (ERAD-SP 2019), Apr. 2019, Published, doi: 10.5753/eradsp.2019.13588.

96. A. Abuhamdah and M. Al-Shabi, "Hybrid load balancing algorithm for fog computing environment," *International Journal of Software Engineering and Computer Systems*, vol. 8, no. 1, pp. 11–21, Jan. 2022, doi: 10.15282/ijsecs.8.1.2022.2.0092.

97. P. Dubey, P. Dubey, and K. K. Sahu, "An investigation on remote teaching approaches and the social impact of distance education," *Redefining Virtual Teaching Learning Pedagogy*, pp. 275–293, Feb. 2023.

98. P. Dubey, P. Dubey, and K. K. Sahu, "A guide to cloud platform with an investigation of different cloud service providers," *Big Data, Cloud Computing and IoT*, pp. 37–51, Feb. 2023.

99. B. Ward, "Data virtualization and object storage," *SQL Server 2022 Revealed*, pp. 317–350, 2022, doi: 10.1007/978-1-4842-8894-8_7.

100. P. Dubey and A. K. Tiwari, "Solution architecting on remote medical monitoring with AWS cloud and IoT," *Advanced Technologies and Societal Change*, pp. 189–202, 2023, doi: 10.1007/978-981-99-0377-1_12.

101. M. A. Omer, A. A. Yazdeen, H. S. Malallah, and L. M. Abdulrahman, "A survey on cloud security: Concepts, types, limitations, and challenges," *Journal of Applied Science and Technology Trends*, vol. 3, no. 2, pp. 47–57, Dec. 2022, doi: 10.38094/jastt301137.

102. Amazon S3. Amazon Web Services, Inc., 2023. https://aws.amazon.com/pm/serv-s3/

103. Free Databases – AWS. Amazon Web Services, Inc., 2023. https://aws.amazon.com/free/database/

104. R. C. Pathak and P. Khandelwal, "A model for hybrid cloud integration: With a case study for IT Service Management (ITSM)," 2017 IEEE International Conference on Cloud Computing in Emerging Markets (CCEM), Bangalore, India, 2017, pp. 113–118, doi: 10.1109/CCEM.2017.26.

105. I. Bermudez, S. Traverso, M. Munafò, and M. Mellia, "A distributed architecture for the monitoring of clouds and CDNs: Applications to amazon AWS," *IEEE Transactions on Network and Service Management*, vol. 11, no. 4, pp. 516–529, Dec. 2014, doi: 10.1109/TNSM.2014.2362357.

106. K. R. Ferreira et al., "Using remote sensing images and cloud services on AWS to improve land use and cover monitoring," 2020 IEEE Latin American GRSS & ISPRS Remote Sensing Conference (LAGIRS), Santiago, Chile, 2020, pp. 558–562, doi: 10.1109/LAGIRS48042.2020.9165649.

107. D. Clinton and B. Piper, "CloudTrail, CloudWatch, and AWS config," *AWS Certified Solutions Architect Study Guide: Associate SAA-C02 Exam*, Wiley, 2021, pp. 183–210.

108. What is Amazon CloudWatch Logs? – Amazon CloudWatch Logs, 2023. https://docs.aws.amazon.com/AmazonCloudWatch/latest/logs/WhatIsCloudWatchLogs.html

109. AWS Health Dashboard. Amazon Web Services, Inc., 2023. https://aws.amazon.com/premiumsupport/technology/aws-health-dashboard/

110. R. A. P. Rajan, "Serverless architecture – A revolution in cloud computing," 2018 Tenth International Conference on Advanced Computing (ICoAC), Chennai, India, 2018, pp. 88–93, doi: 10.1109/ICoAC44903.2018.8939081.

111. G. Adzic and R. Chatley, "Serverless computing: Economic and architectural impact," Proceedings of the 2017 11th Joint Meeting on Foundations of Software Engineering, Aug. 2017, Published, doi: 10.1145/3106237.3117767.

112. A. P. Rajan, "A review on serverless architectures – Function as a service (FaaS) in cloud computing," *TELKOMNIKA (Telecommunication Computing Electronics and Control)*, vol. 18, no. 1, p. 530, Feb. 2020, doi: 10.12928/telkomnika.v18i1.12169.

113. P. Maissen, P. Felber, P. Kropf, and V. Schiavoni, "FaaSdom," Proceedings of the 14th ACM International Conference on Distributed and Event-based Systems, Jul. 2020, Published, doi: 10.1145/3401025.3401738.

114. N. Mahmoudi and H. Khazaei, "Performance modeling of serverless computing platforms," *IEEE Transactions on Cloud Computing*, vol. 10, no. 4, pp. 2834–2847, 1 Oct.-Dec. 2022, doi: 10.1109/TCC.2020.3033373.

115. G. Zheng and Y. Peng, "GlobalFlow: A cross-region orchestration service for serverless computing services," 2019 IEEE 12th International Conference on Cloud Computing (CLOUD), Milan, Italy, 2019, pp. 508–510, doi: 10.1109/CLOUD.2019.00093.

116. "Serverless computing – Amazon Web Services," Amazon Web Services, Inc. https://aws.amazon.com/serverless/

117. "Serverless computing – AWS lambda – Amazon Web Services," Amazon Web Services, Inc. https://aws.amazon.com/lambda/

118. S. Hamadah and D. Aqel, "A proposed virtual private cloud-based disaster recovery strategy," 2019 IEEE Jordan International Joint Conference on Electrical Engineering and Information Technology (JEEIT), Amman, Jordan, 2019, pp. 469–473, doi: 10.1109/JEEIT.2019.8717404.

119. M. F. Hyder, W. Ahmed, and M. Ahmed, "Toward deceiving the intrusion attacks in containerized cloud environment using virtual private cloud-based moving target defense," *Concurrency and Computation: Practice and Experience*, vol. 35, no. 5, Nov. 2022, doi: 10.1002/cpe.7549.

120. A. M. Gupta, L. Daver, and P. Banga, "Implementation of storage in virtual private cloud using simple storage service on AWS," 2020 2nd International Conference on Innovative Mechanisms for Industry Applications (ICIMIA), Bangalore, India, 2020, pp. 213–217, doi: 10.1109/ICIMIA48430.2020.9074899.

121. M. Niranjanamurthy, M. P. Amulya, N. M. Nivedita, and P. Dayananda, "Creating a custom virtual private cloud and launch an Elastic Compute Cloud (EC2) instance in your virtual private cloud," *Journal of Computational and Theoretical Nanoscience*, vol. 17, no. 9, pp. 4509–4514, Jul. 2020, doi: 10.1166/jctn.2020.9106.

122. A. S. Mane and B. S. Ainapure, "Private cloud configuration using Amazon Web Services," Information and Communication Technology for Competitive Strategies (ICTCS 2020), pp. 839–847, 2021, doi: 10.1007/978-981-16-0882-7_75.

123. D. Clinton and B. Piper, "Amazon virtual private cloud," *AWS Certified Solutions Architect Study Guide: Associate SAA-C02 Exam*, Wiley, 2021, pp. 83–132.

124. B. Beach, S. Armentrout, R. Bozo, and E. Tsouris, "Virtual private cloud," *Pro PowerShell for Amazon Web Services*, pp. 85–115, 2019, doi: 10.1007/978-1-4842-4850-8_5.

125. "Virtual Private Network (VPN) – AWS VPN – Amazon Web Services," Amazon Web Services, Inc. https://aws.amazon.com/vpn/

126. P. Mishra, "AWS security and management services," *Cloud Computing with AWS*, pp. 279–298, 2023, doi: 10.1007/978-1-4842-9172-6_10.

127. P. Mishra, "AWS billing and pricing," *Cloud Computing with AWS*, pp. 299–311, 2023, doi: 10.1007/978-1-4842-9172-6_11.

128. "HEIDI: Pandey, Prashant: AWS Certified Cloud Practitioner CLF-C01," https://katalog.ub.uni-heidelberg.de/cgi-bin/titel.cgi?katkey=68876232

129. "https://docs.aws.amazon.com/account-billing/index.html." https://docs.aws.amazon.com/account-billing/index.html

130. "Step 2.1: Set Up the AWS CLI – Amazon Polly," https://docs.aws.amazon.com/polly /latest/dg/setup-aws-cli.html

131. J. N. P., *AWS Command Line Interface: Easy Guide on AWS CLI*, 2016.

132. S. Alla and S. K. Adari, "Deploying in AWS," *Beginning MLOps with MLFlow*, pp. 229–252, Dec. 2020, doi: 10.1007/978-1-4842-6549-9_5.

133. S. Gulabani, "Getting started with AWS," *Practical Amazon EC2, SQS, Kinesis, and S3*, pp. 1–22, 2017, doi: 10.1007/978-1-4842-2841-8_1.

134. S. Ifrah, "Getting started with containers on Amazon AWS," *Deploy Containers on AWS*, pp. 1–40, 2019, doi: 10.1007/978-1-4842-5101-0_1.

Index

Printed in the United States
by Baker & Taylor Publisher Services